JOYCE AND THE TWO IRELANDS

Literary Modernism Series

THOMAS F. STALEY, EDITOR

Joyce

AND THE

Two Irelands

Willard Potts

UNIVERSITY OF TEXAS PRESS
AUSTIN

Excerpt from "Stephen Dedalus and 'Irrland's Split Little Pea'" by Willard Potts previously appeared in *James Joyce Quarterly* (Spring 1990): 559–575. Excerpt from "The Catholic Revival and 'The Dead'" previously appeared in *Joyce Studies Annual* 1991: 3–26.

Printed in the United States of America

First edition, 2000

♾ The paper used in this book meets the minimum requirements of ANSI/NISO Z39.48-1992 (R1997) (Permanence of Paper).

LIBRARY OF CONGRESS CATALOGING-IN-PUBLICATION DATA

Potts, Willard, 1929–
Joyce and the two Irelands / by Willard Potts — 1st ed.
p. cm. — (Literary modernism series)
Includes bibliographical references (p.) and index.
ISBN 0-292-76591-6 (cl. : alk. paper)
1. Joyce, James, 1882–1941—Knowledge—Ireland.
2. Christianity and literature—Ireland—History—20th century. 3. Joyce, James, 1882–1941—Characters—Catholics. 4. Joyce, James, 1882–1941—Characters—Protestants. 5. Modernism (Literature)—Ireland.
6. Nationalism in literature. 7. Protestants in literature.
8. Ireland—In literature. 9. Catholics in literature.
I. Title. II. Series.
PR6019.09 Z78236 2000
823'.912—dc21 00-025962

For PCP

Contents

Acknowledgments

I owe a well-seasoned debt to my old teacher, the late Malcolm Brown, who was responsible for my first undertaking the subject of this volume. I owe a fresh but equally great debt to Robert Tracy for his generous and helpful reading of the book in its manuscript form. I am obligated to a number of other colleagues for reading various parts of the manuscript, among them Peter Copek, Kerry Ahearn, and Cliona Murphy. Neil Davison not only read parts of the manuscript but also helped through showing me the large importance of Bloom's Jewishness. William J. Feeney, whose knowledge of D. P. Moran is perhaps unmatched, was helpful on that subject as well as others. I would like to thank the late Russell Dickson and his wife Joan whose generous loan of their London flat allowed me important periods of research in the British Library. This work was further supported by an Oregon State University Library Research Travel Grant, for which I am grateful. Also I would like to thank Robert Schwartz for making available to me an office and the help of the Oregon State University English Department staff. Of that staff, Wendy Novak has been miraculously helpful. I want to express my gratitude to members of ACIS-West who have patiently listened to various parts of this volume at annual meetings. I thank Noreen Lyday for searching old periodicals in the vain hopes of finding suitable illustrations. Special thanks to Zjaleh Hajibashi, whose editorial genius has enhanced page after page of this book.

Abbreviations Used

CW	Joyce, James. *The Critical Writings of James Joyce,* eds. Ellsworth Mason and Richard Ellmann. New York: Viking Compass, 1964.
D	Joyce, James. *Dubliners*. New York: Penguin Books, 1976.
E	Joyce, James. *Exiles*. New York: Viking Compass, 1961.
JJI	Ellmann, Richard. *James Joyce*. New York: Oxford Univ. Press, 1959.
JJII	Ellmann, Richard. *James Joyce*. New York: Oxford Univ. Press, 1982.
Letters I II III	Joyce, James. Vol. I, ed. Stuart Gilbert. New York: Viking Press, 1957. Vols. II and III, ed. Richard Ellmann. New York: Viking Press, 1966.
P	Joyce, James. *A Portrait of the Artist as a Young Man*. New York: Penguin Books, 1976.
SH	Joyce, James. *Stephen Hero,* eds. Theodore Spencer, John J. Slocum and Herbert Cahoon. New York: New Directions, 1944–1963.
SL	Joyce, James. *Selected Letters,* ed. Richard Ellmann. New York: Viking Press, 1975.
U	Joyce, James. *Ulysses,* ed. Hans Walter Gabler, et al. New York: Random House, 1986.

CHAPTER ONE

Sectarianism and the Irish Revival

In a diary entry for 1930, W. B. Yeats recalls a day early in the Irish Revival when he and Douglas Hyde were out walking and heard people at work in a field singing words that Hyde recognized as his own. Yeats says he begged Hyde to "give up all coarse oratory" and to write more such songs as a way to "help the two Irelands, Gaelic Ireland and Anglo-Ireland so unite that neither shall shed its pride."[1] The two Irelands Yeats speaks of go by many names in addition to the ones he uses, among them "native and settler," "people and Ascendancy," and "green and orange." The most common, however, are "Catholic and Protestant," hence friction between the groups regularly is called "sectarian," even when religion is not the cause. As F. S. L. Lyons explains, Irish Catholics and Protestants historically have clashed because they represent two different "cultures" rather than two different religions.[2]

As was the case with the United Irishmen in the late eighteenth century and with Young Ireland in the mid-nineteenth, uniting the two Irelands was a central idea in that phase of Irish nationalism called "the Irish Revival." Both Yeats and Hyde played major roles in the founding of this Revival, sometimes dated from the latter's famous speech on "The Necessity for De-Anglicizing Ireland." Hyde delivered this speech in November of 1892, slightly over a year following the death of Charles Stewart Parnell and a few months prior to James Joyce's eleventh birthday. Hyde's speech helped launch a movement that went on to become the most vital force in Ireland during the rest of Joyce's years there. Joyce came into close contact with that force while a student at University College Dublin, then a center of Revival fervor. He also wrote about the Revival in book reviews and essays as well as in his fiction, thus making it a major subject of his work.

In 1905, his older contemporary and a leading figure of the Revival, John Eglinton (W. K. Magee), noted that the Revival had not succeeded in creating the sectarian harmony at which many of its leaders aimed; but that instead, there had been a "recrudescence among us of religious bigotry." Eglinton blamed the problem largely on Revival writers' failure to discuss relations between Irish Catholics and Protestants. He complained that a main canon of the writers forming what is now called the "literary Revival" seemed to be that they "must not give offence by any too direct utterance on the central problem of Irish life, the religious situation."[3] The religious situation, by which Eglinton meant relations between Irish Protestants and Catholics, also was a central problem of the Revival and had been almost from its start.

Hyde and Yeats, along with John Synge, Lady Gregory, A. E. (George Russell), and other leading figures of the literary Revival, including Eglinton, were all Protestants. Whether for fear of giving offense or for other reasons, except for Eglinton, they all avoided the subject of sectarian relations. This is especially apparent in the Abbey Theatre plays, which repeatedly focus on Ireland's legendary past, the Catholic peasants from the West of Ireland, or other subjects safely removed from any discussion of encounters between Catholics and Protestants. It is not until 1925, with the appearance of the Protestant Adolphus Grigson in Sean O'Casey's *The Shadow of a Gunman,* that a major Abbey play even acknowledges the presence of two cultures in Ireland.

Among the major writers of the Revival, Joyce alone was Catholic, and he alone wrote explicitly about the relationship between the two Irelands. This relationship becomes an obvious issue when Protestants, whether fictional or historical, appear among the crowd of Catholics in his work or when they are alluded to. Parnell is the most ubiquitous of the historical Protestants in Joyce's works. Other Protestants figure prominently in the Library episode of *Ulysses,* where A. E., Joseph Lyster, Richard Best, and John Eglinton appear, while Yeats, Synge, and Lady Gregory are alluded to. Of Joyce's fictional characters, Crofton in "Ivy Day in the Committee Room" and "Grace"; Mr. Browne in "The Dead"; Eileen in *A Portrait of the Artist;* Robert and Beatrice in *Exiles;* and Mr. Deasy, the Reverend Hugh C. Love, and Reggie Wylie in *Ulysses* are clearly identified as Protestant. Others, such as the old man in "An Encounter," the stall attendant and her two male friends in "Araby," and the dwarf captain in *A Portrait of the Artist* appear to be Protestant because of their English, "good" or "genteel" accent. Irish Catholics who spoke with an English accent could be found in Joyce's time (as before and since), but the classical minded Joyce dealt with general truths, and the general truth for Ireland was that such an accent meant Protestant, as it does in the case of Reverend Love. The principle of general truths also makes it likely that the combination of Northern accent, position as employer, and English sounding name indicates Protestant ancestry for Alleyne in "Counterparts." Even more English sounding names indicate the same for Mrs. Bellingham, Mrs. Yelverton Barry, and The Honorable Mrs. Mervyn Talboys in *Ulysses*. But issues pertaining to the Catholic/Protestant split arise without any specific mention or appearance of Protestants, as when Stephen Dedalus meditates on that Protestant institution, Trinity College Dublin, in Chapter Five of *A Portrait of the Artist*.

Most readers of Joyce probably recognize that he was not as "indifferent" to the literary achievements of Revival writers as he claims to be in "The Holy Office." If Joyce really were indifferent, would he have taken the trouble to write a piece proclaiming his indifference, paid to have the piece printed, then arranged to have it distributed to relevant parties? What was Joyce's attitude not only toward the literary Revival but also toward the whole range of nationalist movements that comprised the Irish Revival? Likewise what was his attitude toward the relationship between Irish Catholics and Protestants? Did he share the Revival hope that the two Irelands would become united? Does his work offer any insights into the reasons they were not and still are not? Joyce's work is rightfully noted for its freedom from the anti-Semitism found in Pound, Eliot, and other modernist writers. His choice of a Jew as the hero of *Ulysses* demonstrates this freedom from prejudice. Did Joyce also manage to remain free of the sectarian feelings that have marked generations of Irish, including other leading writers of the Irish Revival? More generally, how does his work portray the relationship between the two great cultures that have given Ireland its special character? The present study aims at providing some answers to these questions.[4]

The answers will necessarily take into account the hold that Joyce's Catholic heritage had over him. His many attacks on Catholic culture, particularly in his early work, make it easy to conclude that he felt no strong ties to it. Many years ago in one of the earliest critical pieces about Joyce, fellow Catholic Padraic Colum noted the virulence of these attacks in *A Portrait of the Artist* but then went on to say,

> James Joyce's book is profoundly Catholic. I do not mean that it carries any doctrine or thesis: I mean that, more than any other modern book written in English, it comes out of Catholic culture and tradition—even that culture and that tradition may turn against itself.[5]

As far back as William T. Noon's *Joyce and Aquinas* (1957), attention to Joyce's Catholic heritage has meant examining how doctrines, rituals, and other features of the Catholic Church are reflected in his work. If not an equally important part, then at least a very important part of Irish Catholic culture is its relationship to Irish Protestant culture. As someone pointed out, to call people "Irish Catholics" is to imply a contrast with Irish Protestants, otherwise one would call them simply "Irish."

Another defining feature of Irish Catholic culture is what Stephen Dedalus calls the "nightmare" of its history (*U* 2.377). Initially the nightmare began with the Norman invasion in 1169, which led to the increasing presence in Ireland of the English people from whom most Irish Protestants have been descended. Technically it began in 1536, when the Reformation was introduced into Ireland through an Irish Parliament act that declared Henry VIII "the only Supreme Head on Earth of the whole Church of Ireland." Effectively, however, the nightmare began with the series of plantations and settlements in the sixteenth and seventeenth centuries, when Irish lands were expropriated from Catholics and settled by English—or in Ulster by Scottish—Protestants. The last and most notorious such displacement occurred in the mid-seventeenth century when Oliver Cromwell confiscated vast tracts of Irish land to pay off his soldiers and cover various other debts. Historian Aidan Clarke says of this event, "The Cromwellian settlement was not so much a plantation, as a transference of the sources of wealth and power from catholics to protestants. What it created was not a protestant community, but a protestant upper class."[6] The disparity in wealth and power between the two groups was amplified in the later seventeenth and early eighteenth centuries due to a series of anti-Catholic acts passed by the exclusively Protestant Irish Parliament. These acts, collectively known as the "penal laws," required members of Parliament, the legal profession, and the military to take an oath rejecting the chief tenets of Catholicism. These laws also virtually outlawed the Catholic Church as well as Catholic education and prohibited Catholics from owning any significant property. As the historian Maureen Wall puts it, the penal laws had the aim of "buttressing protestant Ascendancy in all walks of life" and "keep[ing] catholics in a state of permanent subjection."[7]

The Protestant Orange Lodges, founded in 1795, had the same aim and pursued it more militantly than did the Irish Parliament or its forces. One consequence of the penury to which Catholics were reduced is that they became the chief victims of the famine of 1845–1848. Gradually, however, Catholics regained political rights, most significantly as a result of the passage of the Catholic emancipation bill of 1829, which Daniel O'Connell forced the English to approve and which opened virtually all offices in Ireland as well as Parliament in Westminster to Catholics. Catholics also began to prosper, thanks to land reform bills and other measures, such as the one requiring civil service positions be filled by competitive examination rather than appointment. Nevertheless, the division between Catholics and Protestants remained pronounced.

Arthur Clery's description of their relations at the beginning of the twentieth century is of special interest since he was a contemporary of Joyce as well as a fellow Dubliner and schoolmate at University College Dublin. Writing in 1915, Clery noted that a gulf between Catholic and Protestant "exists quite as much in Dublin as in the North." As evidence, he reported that although he had lived in the city for over thirty years, he had dined in a Protestant house only once and had never been invited to a party at one. As further evidence of this cultural separation, Clery cited the great rarity of intermarriage between Catholics and Protestants in Ireland. "A Protestant girl who dances with a Catholic," he said, "knows that she is wasting her time." He went on to remark that the social gulf between the two cultures was accompanied by an equally sharp economic disparity. As an example, Clery pointed out that, "apart from drink, which Protestants make and Catholics sell," all other Irish industries were "in Protestant hands." Moreover, he said, all "the best things in the patronage of the central government" also were in Protestant hands. He admitted that there were occasional friendships and business collaborations between Catholics and Protestants but likened these instances to "the 'fraternisation' of soldiers in opposing trenches." "A single shot," he said, ". . . and they rush to take their places in the opposing firing lines."[8] Another of Joyce's fellow Dubliners and college classmates, Constantine Curran, gives a sanitized version of Clery's account when he says that Catholics and Protestants in Joyce's Dublin occupied "self-sufficing circles rotating on independent axes."[9] Protestant Elizabeth Bowen felt a similar division between the two cultures. Of Catholics, she says, "they were, simply, 'the others', whose world lay alongside ours but never touched."[10]

The episode between Mr. Deasy and Stephen in Chapter Two of *Ulysses* is laden with details dramatizing the sectarian gulf that Clery describes. In what at times sounds like a parody of Hyde's claims about the Irishness of Protestants, Mr. Deasy tries to persuade Stephen of a kinship between Protestants and Catholics. After citing supposed instances of Protestants aiding Catholic causes, he tells Stephen, "We are all Irish. . . ." Stephen answers by silently recalling an occasion from the nightmare of his culture's history when Protestants in Armagh slaughtered Catholics (*U* 2.270–280). Throughout their meeting, the conflicting views of Protestant Deasy and Catholic Stephen undermine Deasy's claims about their kinship. The contrast between the vocal Deasy and the generally silent Stephen also is a significant comment on relations between the two cultures: their lopsided dialogue reminds us that historically, the views of Irish Protestants are the ones that have been voiced and heard, while Catholic views have been unspoken or unheard. In large part, this distinction remained largely true during the Revival, when W. B. Yeats, Lady Gregory, John Synge, Douglas Hyde, A. E., and other Protestant leaders of the Revival were the voices most often heard. Moreover, when it comes to current views of the Revival, these writers' voices still appear to be the ones most often remembered.

The division between the two Irelands, which Clery and Curran describe and which the encounter between Stephen and Mr. Deasy dramatizes, helps explain why we don't see more Protestants in the world of Catholic Dublin, the setting for Joyce's work. But since Protestants made up roughly a quarter of the population in Dublin and environs, Catholics inevitably had some contact with them. For Joyce, who as a child used to play with the little Protestant girl, Eileen Vance, the contact came early. It resulted in Joyce's painful introduction to the religious bigotry that is perhaps the best-known feature of relations between Irish Catholics and Protestants. In an incident that would provide material for *A Portrait of the Artist,* his courtesy aunt, Mrs. Reardon, warned Joyce that he would go to

Hell if he continued to play with Eileen (*JJI* 25). Later, he heard a more oblique warning from his Jesuit teachers, who perceived a threat in the social differences between the two Irelands as well as in the religious differences. According to Stanislaus Joyce, his brother's teachers at Belvedere "used to dwell rather heavily on the danger of 'human respect,'" which meant "doing something or leaving it undone against one's conscience for fear of what people might say or think." The students, he adds, understood perfectly well that the purpose of this warning was to put them "on guard against a certain inferiority complex that might invade them when, in the small world of Dublin, they came in contact with a dominant Protestant class."[11]

Though meant to identify a possible source of his brother's indifference to the opinions of others, Stanislaus' account of the Jesuit warning reveals not only that Joyce's teachers considered the social differences between Catholic and Protestant to be a threat, but also that in Dublin, even school children could be counted on to be aware of such differences. This awareness is confirmed by Enid Starkie. Although her Catholic family had more or less the same social standing as Protestants, she says that she and her brothers and sisters "grew up thinking that Protestants were classier than Catholics."[12]

To whatever extent that relations between Irish Catholics and Protestants impinged on private life in Dublin, they were a key feature of political life. In his youth, Joyce may not have been aware of the often passionate conflict between Catholic Home Rulers and Protestant Unionists that arose during Parnell's Home Rule campaign and that is dimly reflected in "Ivy Day in the Committee Room." By the time Joyce entered UCD and found himself surrounded by eager Revivalists, however, he was old enough and alert enough to recognize the major role that sectarian differences played in the movement.

To associate sectarian friction with the Revival goes against a traditional view that credits the movement with actually bringing the two Irelands together, as Yeats, Hyde, and others hoped it would. It is true that a strong ecumenical spirit marked the movement's early years. An often cited example from this period is the founding of the Gaelic League in 1893 by the Catholic Eoin MacNeill and the Protestant Douglas Hyde. The theatre movement, which evolved into the Revival's most famous institution, the Abbey Theatre, had a similarly ecumenical origin, having been founded by the Protestants W. B. Yeats and Lady Gregory, and the Catholic Edward Martyn. Even the supposed bigot, Michael Cusack, included both Catholics and Protestants in the organizational meetings of the Revival's third major organization, the Gaelic Athletic Association.[13]

Organizers striving for the success of any public undertaking in Ireland would have included both Catholics and Protestants in the planning and execution of their endeavor; but, as was mentioned earlier, bringing the two cultures together was often an end, as well as the means to an end, for Revival leaders. Yeats called this goal "unity of culture," a condition illustrated by the incident recalled in his diary entry about the farm workers who were singing Hyde's words. The incident reflected Yeats' wish to have his poems occupy a place in the popular imagination of the Irish. In helping found the theatre movement, he opened another avenue to "unity of culture" by providing a place where Catholic audiences could attend plays written and produced by the Protestant leaders of the movement. For his part, Hyde hoped the unity would come about through Catholics and Protestants working together to revive Irish culture, particularly the Irish language. His interest in founding the Gaelic League, he said, was prompted by a "dream of using the language as a unifying bond to join all Irishmen together."[14]

Of all the Revival organizations, the Gaelic League was most successful in realizing this dream. In an eloquent assertion of its success, the Irish historian P. S. O'Hegarty describes the League as "all-embracing in the matter of its appeal and its membership." "Into it," he says, "went gentle and simple, old and young, Catholic and Protestant, Fenian and Home Ruler and Unionist."[15] But this account resembles Hyde's dream more than the actual story of the League.

The division between Catholic Home Rulers and Protestant Unionists during the Parnell era strengthened an ingrained assumption among Protestants that politics was the chief cause of sectarian conflict. It seemed to Yeats that Parnell's fall and his death took the force out of Home Rule agitation, leaving Ireland "like soft wax," thereby making it possible for changes in the relationship of the two cultures to occur.[16] He and Hyde reasoned that whereas political nationalism caused sectarian strife, the cultural nationalism of the Revival could bring sectarian harmony. This view explains the "no politics" rule that Hyde insisted on for the League.

If the cultural nationalism of the Revival lessened the problem of political differences between Catholic and Protestant, its emphasis on things Irish gave added weight to an old charge that the English ancestry of most Protestants made them un-Irish or less authentically Irish than Catholics, who generally were descendants of the native Gaelic population. Lennox Robinson alludes to this charge in the novel, *A Young Man from the South,* where his Protestant nationalist hero, Willie Powell, confesses to a friend, "I sometimes wish I were a Catholic. An Irish Protestant! The words, somehow, don't blend, do they?"[17] If historical Irish Protestants shared Willie Powell's doubts about the blending of "Protestant" and "Irish," they did not confess them. On the contrary, like Mr. Deasy, they tended to proclaim that they were Irish. Even such an eccentric as George Bernard Shaw was typical on this matter, asserting in a 1912 pamphlet, "I am an Irishman: my father was an Irishman, and my mother was an Irishwoman; and my father and my mother were Protestants."[18] Yeats made a similar proclamation when he identified himself with the "indomitable Irishry."[19] Of course, the Protestants' claim of being Irish points to underlying questions about their national identity. Irish Catholics would hardly need to make such claims.

Rather than ignore the problem of English ancestry, as Shaw and Yeats did, Hyde addressed this issue directly in his speech on "The Necessity for De-Anglicizing Ireland," which became "a canonical text of Irish cultural nationalism."[20] In this speech, Hyde tried to dispel the notion that Protestants' descent from English immigrants made them less Irish than Catholics. He reminded his audience of the commonplace of Irish history: that the early English settlers became "fully Irished and more Hibernian than the Hibernians themselves." Hyde went on to assert that even the descendants of Cromwell's soldiers, stock examples of the unassimilated and anti-Catholic Protestant, often learned Irish, took Irish wives, and "turned into good Irishmen." As this last insistence on the unity of Catholic and Protestant illustrates, at times, Hyde sounds quite like Mr. Deasy.

While Hyde's portrait of Irish Protestants' English forebears responded to the problem of their ancestry, it also aimed at encouraging his largely Protestant audience to follow in their ancestors' steps. A striking phenomenon of the Revival is the extent to which Protestants did follow those steps, striving to become more Irish. Going beyond what the Unionist Hyde would have approved, Lady Gregory recanted her own early Unionist views and joined the Catholics in favoring Home Rule. Going still further,

Yeats associated himself with the radically separatist and almost exclusively Catholic, Irish Republican Brotherhood. But Lady Gregory and Yeats, as well as other Protestants, also tried to become more Irish in the ways that Hyde meant. Lady Gregory and Synge learned Irish. She and Yeats collected and wrote about Irish myths, legends, and folk tales. Most notably, all three authors wrote plays about Irish subjects. Though they give no hint of sharing Willie Powell's doubts about the words "Protestant" and "Irish" blending, their commitment to plays about Irish subjects typically meant not only writing plays about Catholics but also incorporating Catholic accents and diction. Thus, in their writings, they appeared to accept and confirm the very identification of Catholics and Irish that they publicly rejected.

Synge's extraordinary effort to make himself more Irish is mocked in *Ulysses* when, alluding to the peculiarly Irish shoe worn by Aran Islanders, Buck Mulligan claims that Synge is "out in pampooties" (*U* 9.570). Mulligan also speaks in a parody of the language used in Synge's plays, saying, "It's what I'm after telling you, mister honey, it's queer and sick we were, Haines and myself, the time himself brought it [Stephen's telegram] in" (*U* 9.558–566). Though Mulligan's mockery calls into question the authenticity of Synge's efforts at becoming more Irish, those and similar efforts by other Protestants of the period remain well-known features of the Revival and contribute to its tradition as a time of rapprochement between the two cultures.

This tradition has become so sacrosanct that contradicting even part of it gives a veteran of Irish strife like Connor Cruise O'Brien stylistic fits when he writes, "The story of the Irish literary revival in one of its aspects is one of Protestant and Catholic consciousness in intermittent contact, often leading to increasing mutual distrust."[21] The most famous instances of the "contact" that O'Brien gingerly alludes to were the often violent Catholic protests against the theatre movement, protests in which Joyce's fellow students took a prominent part. Similar sectarian clashes occurred in the Gaelic League and the Gaelic Athletic Association.

Neither the spread of Irish sports by the GAA nor the promotion of the Irish language by the Gaelic League nor the production of Irish plays by the theatre movement altered in any way the inequity described by Arthur Clery. Most Irish industries as well as "the best things in the patronage of the central government" remained in Protestant hands. Though fully committed to the ecumenical ideals of the Gaelic League, Eoin MacNeill angrily remembered his encounter with this inequity. In a letter written in 1907, twenty years after the experience, he said,

> I entered the Accountant-General's Office [in Dublin] in 1887. I was then the only Catholic on the permanent staff of the office. The Accountant-General, the Chief Clerk, the senior clerks and all the junior clerks but myself were appointed before the competition law came into effect. They were all patronage men and they were all Episcopalian Protestants and garrison men.

MacNeill went on to point out that, as a result of the law requiring competitive examinations for civil service appointments, a majority of the employees currently working in the Accountant-General's Office were Catholic but that "the places in the courts still filled by patronage have exactly the same sort of staff that they had in the days of the Ascendancy."[22] Though MacNeill shared Hyde's belief in the importance of the Irish language and collaborated with him in founding the Gaelic League, he hardly could have accepted Hyde's rosy vision of Protestant assimilation into Irish culture.

MacNeill's experience, along with Clery's description of turn-of-the-century Dublin, helps explain why sectarian issues remained very much alive during the Revival, particularly among Catholics. It became clear almost from the start that the Revival's emphasis on cultural nationalism was not going to erase those issues and unite Catholic and Protestant in an effort to restore the country's native heritage. However strong the Gaelic League's ecumenical spirit at first, O'Hegarty's glowing description exaggerates the degree to which its membership reflected that spirit. Protestants never made up a large proportion of the membership and that proportion decreased as Catholics flooded in. By 1902, less than ten years after its founding, one knowledgeable observer claimed that the League was ninety percent Catholic, while another said that it was closer to ninety-nine percent.[23] Hyde's resignation as president in 1915 removed the League's last significant claim to being an ecumenical organization.

The ecumenical spirit with which the Gaelic Athletic Association began didn't even survive the planning stage. Protestant members of the planning committee, who advocated using English rules for sporting events, were repeatedly voted down by Catholic members and quickly dropped out, leaving the GAA essentially an all Catholic organization.[24] In the theatre movement, sectarian differences were more prolonged and complex as well as more openly expressed than they were in either the GAA or the Gaelic League. Trouble erupted at the start of the movement in the spring of 1899, when UCD students protested against the Irish Literary Theatre's performance of Yeats' play *The Countess Cathleen*. In an episode that Joyce observed and that Stephen Dedalus recalls in *A Portrait of the Artist* (*P* 226), the students objected vocally during the play. Later they stated their objections in a letter to the press that Joyce ostentatiously refused to sign. Catholic attacks on subsequent plays by the theatre movement's Protestant playwrights culminated in the weeklong riots that greeted the opening of Synge's *Playboy of the Western World* in 1907.

The theatre organization itself developed along sectarian lines. Three years after its initial season, as a result of differences with Lady Gregory and Yeats over the direction of the theatre movement, Edward Martyn withdrew from the organization. John Synge replaced him, leaving an exclusively Protestant executive committee that remained in control until the founding of the Abbey Theatre and for some years thereafter. The Abbey actors, on the other hand, were largely, and at times exclusively, Catholic. Almost immediately, the problems that typically exist in a theatre organization took a sectarian form. Early in the Abbey's first year, Synge wrote to Lady Gregory, reporting that Frank Fay was "dead against" performing Synge's play *The Well of the Saints* and Yeats' *On Baille's Strand*. He went on:

> I do not know whether all this is [Fay's] own feeling only—in which case it is of no consequence—or whether there is a Neopatriotic-Catholic clique growing which might be serious. [Padraic] Colum finds my play unsatisfactory because the Saint is really a Protestant! Miss [Helen S.] Laird has been frozen out [of the acting company] because she is a Protestant.[25]

Just as the Abbey Theatre company objected to work by Synge and Yeats, so Yeats objected to *The Eloquent Dempsey,* by the Catholic playwright William Boyle. Convinced that Boyle's play needed major revisions, Yeats tried to damp a Catholic reaction by enlisting the aid of Padraic Colum. He explained to Synge that Colum would be "a useful ally against the 'Catholic Laymen' " and added, "I don't want good taste to be suspected of a theological origin."[26] In fact, Yeats along with Synge, Lady Gregory, and doubtless other Protestants believed that "taste" was the sole province of their culture. Though Yeats' diplomacy effectively resolved the problem in the case of Boyle's play, it did not work on other occasions, with the result that there were frequent defections of Catholics from the company to an alternate, Catholic-run company, the Irish Theatre, founded by Edward Martyn.

Not surprisingly, the Protestant leaders of the theatre movement attempted to discount the significance of Catholic objections to it. For one thing, acknowledging any sort of legitimacy to the objections would undercut their own claims to being Irish, which meant having some sort of kinship with Catholics. Yeats always depicted Martyn's problems with the movement as being due to an eccentric obsession with religious scruples, forgetting his own preoccupation with the significance of astrological signs. In a typical passage, he says that Martyn momentarily withdrew his support from the theatre because "some monk" had claimed there was heresy in *The Countess Cathleen*.[27] He was harshly dismissive of the UCD students and other Catholic protesters, portraying them as an ignorant crowd dominated by feelings of piety and patriotism and totally lacking in taste and culture. In a more colorful version of Synge's "Neopatriotic Catholic clique," Yeats called them "tower and wolf-dog, harp and shamrock, verdigris-green sectaries."[28] Because it suited his purposes, Yeats dwelt particularly on the attacks by the irascible and perhaps deranged F. Hugh O'Donnell, whose pamphlet *Souls for Gold* is a hysterical denunciation of *The Countess Cathleen*. He claimed that the UCD students who protested against the play had been influenced by O'Donnell's attacks.[29] His assessment of the protesters simply reflected his view of the theatre movement's Catholic audience. In a letter describing problems he experienced when preparing *Diarmuid and Grania* for performance, Yeats writes that he found himself thinking, "Here are we a lot of intelligent people who might have been doing some sort of work that leads to some fun. Yet here we are going through all sorts of trouble and annoyance for a mob that knows neither literature nor art."[30] Perhaps echoing Yeats, Lady Gregory referred to the protesters simply, and repeatedly, as a "mob."[31] Joyce's description of the Catholic protesters as a "rabblement" (*CW* 68) has lent persuasive, if unintended, support to their depiction by Yeats, Lady Gregory, and Synge.

The present-day view of the theatre protesters is an egregious instance of Protestant rather than Catholic voices being heard. Apparently questioning neither the judgment of Yeats, Synge, and Lady Gregory nor that of the eighteen-year-old who wrote "The Day of the Rabblement," scholars long have accepted their view of the protesters as suffering from various intellectual or esthetic limitations. For example, Hugh Kenner stigmatizes the UCD student protesters against *The Countess Cathleen* as "the orthodox."[32]

There are problems with Yeats' and Lady Gregory's depiction of the protesters as an ignorant mob of narrowly pious and excessively patriotic Catholics. Students from UCD, who were among the more prominent of those protesting against not only *The Countess Cathleen* but also subsequent plays from the theatre movement, would have been some of the brightest and best-educated Catholics in the country. Of the thirty-three students who signed the letter denouncing *The Countess Cathleen,* nearly half belonged to the UCD Literary and Historical Society, whose members were the intellectual elite of the College. A number of the students were friends of Joyce, whom one would not expect to find gladly associating with thoughtless followers of the mob. They included Thomas Kettle, Frank Skeffington, Richard Sheehy, J. F. Byrne, and George Clancy.[33] Clancy, the model for Davin in *A Portrait of the Artist,* may have been pious, patriotic, orthodox, and ignorant, if we can trust at all Stephen's assessment of Davin. But Kettle, who apparently wrote the letter, was famous for his brilliance (some even regarded him as Joyce's superior in intellect). He later became a professor at UCD and a member of Parliament, which might suggest that he had conventional traits, but he was so far from being a typical Irish patriot that he joined the British Army during World War One and was killed at the front. It is hard to find anything "orthodox" in the vegetarian, feminist, pacifist, agnostic Skeffington. Constantine Curran scoffs at Yeats' claim that these young men would have been influenced by the ravings of O'Donnell.[34]

As with other matters, Catholic explanations for the theatre protests differ from Protestant accounts. The Abbey coach and actor Willie Fay blames a simple-minded sectarianism. After noting that Synge's *In the Shadow of the Glen* was attacked while Padraic Colum's lesser play, *Broken Soil,* was praised, Fay explains that Synge was "a Protestant and a member of the 'Ascendancy' class, whereas Colum was a Catholic and of the people." "It was a patriotic duty to howl down the one," he says, "and cheer the other."[35] Seeing a more complex version of sectarian differences behind the protests, Daniel Corkery says that the emotions expressed in the *Playboy* riots derived from "ancestral" memories of "an alien Ascendancy [which], for two centuries or more, have been casting ridicule on everything native." "Wherever there is an alien Ascendancy," he adds, "there is such an attendant protest, perennial, and on occasions quickening into noise and violence."[36] According to Corkery then, the theatre protests were an early manifestation of feelings that were expressed more violently during the Troubles and the Civil War, when Catholics torched the big houses of Ireland's Protestant Ascendancy.

In their letter protesting *The Countess Cathleen,* the students objected to the play for portraying "the Irish peasant as a crooning barbarian, crazed with morbid superstition." This was a serious charge since it was an article of faith among Catholic Revivalists that, having had the least contact with English culture, the Irish peasant was the purest embodiment of everything Irish. As a result, the students claimed that Yeats' peasants were "ludicrous travesties . . . of the Irish Catholic Celt" generally, not simply of the Irish peasant.

The students perhaps overstated their case but it doesn't take much imagination to understand why this group of intelligent and moderately sophisticated Catholics would object to a play in which the characters came close to the stereotype of Irish Catholics as ignorant, superstitious peasants. Neither does it take much imagination to understand why Catholics became increasingly angry when they found that the plays of Synge and other Abbey playwrights continued to depict Catholics as ignorant, comic peasants. In *Playboy,* Synge endows Christy Mahon with wonderful language but also emphasizes his ignorance, using it to comic effect, as when Christy doesn't understand the meaning of "homicide." According to Yeats, one aim of the theatre movement was to eliminate the stage Irishman, but the difference between that stock figure and his comic peasants in *The Countess Cathleen* or those in the plays of Lady Gregory and Synge is hardly great enough to have cheered many Catholics.[37] Referring to Synge's plays in general but particularly *The Well of the Saints,* one observer commented in the Catholic journal *New Ireland Review,* "We have seen a comedy . . . belonging to that earlier tradition of Irish comedy which, we had supposed, the Abbey Theatre came to abolish."[38]

Edward Martyn also objected to the Abbey's emphasis on plays about Irish peasants. In an essay elaborating the rationale for a change of focus, he wrote with heavy irony, "I feel that . . . we have still some inhabitants left in

Ireland besides peasants." He proposed a theatre that would treat "the lives and problems of people more complex" than those featured in the peasant plays.[39] Martyn may have had some eccentricities about him, but his objection to the emphasis on peasant plays seems a perfectly sane reaction to the direction the theatre movement had taken. Presumably he was calling for more complex Catholic characters, thus allowing that not all Catholics in Ireland were ignorant peasants. The "problems" Martyn had in mind probably would have included relations between Catholics and Protestants, an issue that he himself treated in *The Place Hunters,* discussed below. Rather than suggesting the response of a religious fanatic, Martyn's proposal resembles the young Joyce's call for plays, such as those being written on the continent, which dealt with complex people and complex problems.

Joyce happened to be writing "The Dead" when the *Playboy* riots occurred and was so intrigued by them that they interfered with his work on the story (*Letters II* 212). Even if the scene in "The Dead" between the Protestant Mr. Browne and the three young ladies was not inspired directly by the riots, it nonetheless offers a shrewd and succinct parallel to their apparent genesis. Apropos his taste for whisky, Browne assumes "a very low Dublin accent" and tells the young ladies, "Well, you see, I'm like the famous Mrs Cassidy, who is reported to have said: 'Now, Mary Grimes, if I don't take it, make me take it for I feel I want it.'" Offended by Browne's allusion to the stereotypical Catholic fondness for drink, and by his accent, the ladies, "with one instinct," freeze into silence (*D* 183). This episode presents a fictionalized version of the encounters between Synge, Yeats, and Lady Gregory and their Catholic audience, who, like the three young ladies, would have come mainly from the emerging middle class. Like Browne, these three playwrights used a "low" Catholic accent to tell comic stories that typically featured fondness for drink, ignorance, and other elements of the Catholic stereotype; like the three young ladies, Catholic audiences were offended. The episode with Browne and the young ladies reflects differences in what O'Brien calls Catholic and Protestant "consciousness," the very differences that gave rise to the theatre protests. The joke that Browne believes will amuse the young ladies has the opposite effect. Similarly, the plays that Yeats, Lady Gregory, and Synge thought were sympathetic to Catholics, in fact offended them. Browne does not understand why the young ladies react to his joke as they do. It is not clear whether Yeats, Lady

Gregory, and Synge understood why Catholics reacted as they did to their plays.

Now it seems easily understandable why the ecumenism with which the Revival began did not last. Catholic and Protestant Revivalists alike shared a belief in the twin themes of Hyde's de-Anglicizing speech: that English influences in Ireland needed to be curbed or eliminated, and that Irish culture needed to be revived. They also shared a nearly euphoric belief that the country could be changed. The most famous formulation of this optimistic view comes from Yeats, who had a "sudden certainty" that, because of the "lull in politics" caused by Parnell's death, "Ireland was to be like soft wax for years to come."[40] He clung to one or another version of this idea for the rest of his life and to the related idea that he could help mold the soft wax of Ireland. Though most memorably expressed by Yeats, the conviction that Ireland could be molded, even by a single person, was a central premise of the Revival. This conviction was shared not only by other Protestants but also by Catholics, including Joyce. However, the two cultures were at such cross-purposes on how the country should be molded or changed that cooperation between the two populaces was out of the question.

For many Catholic Revivalists, ridding the country of English influence meant establishing Home Rule or some more extreme form of separation from England, whereas Protestants typically insisted that the movement must be kept free of "politics," their code word for agitation to alter the relations with England. The "lull in politics" that Yeats associated with Parnell's death was a lull in agitation for changed relations between England and Ireland through the establishment of Home Rule. Two generations before Parnell's efforts at gaining Home Rule, Daniel O'Connell's successful campaign for Catholic emancipation raised the specter of the Catholic majority wresting political power from the country's Protestants. This threat led to a propensity among Protestants to regard "politics" as a tainted activity pursued by Catholics, and virtually synonymous with "sectarianism."[41] Synge's angry suggestion that problems in the Abbey might be due to a "Neopatriotic-Catholic clique" and Yeats' reference to Catholics as "the political class" reflect a similar distrust of politics.[42] Though they wrote several plays sympathetic to nationalist politics, Yeats and Lady Gregory established a "no politics" policy for the Abbey Theatre similar to the one Hyde insisted on for the Gaelic League. Worried about the largely innocuous political allusions in *Bending of the Bough,* Lady Gregory made a diary entry sternly reminding herself, "We must try & keep politics out of plays in future."[43] She felt that in one of his speeches even Douglas Hyde came "a little too near what may be taken for politics."[44] The Irish historian Willa Murphy shrewdly observes that a large portion of Yeats' efforts during the Revival were aimed at providing "a kind of spiritual substitute for political action—action from which he and the rest of the Protestant Ascendancy had everything to lose."[45] Catholics, on the other hand, had much to gain, which seems a reasonable explanation for their preoccupation with politics.

Joyce reflects this preoccupation in a scene between Stephen and his schoolmate Athy in *A Portrait of the Artist*. Athy, who likes to follow the newspapers, tells Stephen, "Now it is all about politics in the papers." He asks Stephen, "Do your people talk about that too?" Stephen says, "Yes," and Athy adds, "Mine too" (*P* 25). The political issue at the time would have been Parnell, as it is at the Christmas dinner in *A Portrait of the Artist*. But Catholic interest in politics remained strong in spite of Parnell's death and led to objections over the League's "no politics" policy, which among other things caused the League to refuse participation in the ceremonies celebrating the centenary of the 1798 United Irishmen rising. In a piece titled, "The Limitations of the Language Movement," William Rooney denounced this refusal, charging that it placed the League in "a position occupied by every anti-Irish and West-British individual in the country." His main point, however, was that efforts to revive the language needed to be united with efforts to free the country. He claimed that in banning politics, which he explained meant "anything bearing on the relations between us and Britain," the League turned itself simply into an academic exercise.[46]

Other Catholics agreed with Rooney. As their membership in the League increased, so did the League's emphasis on politics. In his speech resigning as President of the League, Hyde explained that this political stance made it impossible for the League to achieve the end he had hoped for. "The moment [the League] became political," he said, "all the significance of the movement as one to build up a nation from all classes and creeds came to an end."[47] One wonders to what extent, if at all, Hyde was aware of the inequities experienced by the co-founder of the League, Eoin MacNeill, and by other Catholics, that helped explain their interest in politics?

While Catholic and Protestant Revivalists were more or less equally concerned about the depressed state of Irish culture, many Catholics also were concerned about their depressed economic state. Attributing their poverty partly to the loss of Irish industry, about which the Citizen complains in *Ulysses* (*U* 12.1240–1257), Catholics campaigned for the manufacture and purchase of Irish-made goods. They also agitated against the sorts of inequities that Clery and MacNeill speak of. This agitation included the demand for a Catholic university, the equivalent of Trinity College Dublin, which led to the so-called "University Question" discussed by Gabriel and Miss Ivors in "The Dead" (*D* 188).

The call for greater equity and for the development of Irish industries and trade was a logical extension of the Revival since it aimed to improve Catholics' economic situation, as the Revival aimed to elevate their language and culture. However, with the exception of A. E., Protestant Revivalists show little concern over, or even awareness of, the inferior position occupied by Catholics. By the simple technique of populating their plays only with Catholics, Yeats, Synge, and Lady Gregory avoided the whole question of the relationship between the two cultures. Protestants writing plays in which no Protestants appear resulted in a theatre movement beset by sectarian friction to which it makes no reference. It is indicative of his Catholic "consciousness" that, in contrast with the plays of Yeats, Synge, and Gregory, Joyce's play *Exiles* pits two Catholics against two Protestants. His depiction of the two pairs as opposites gives the play an effective form, but it also reflects a truth about the two cultures that the Protestant playwrights preferred to leave unspoken, which may help explain why *Exiles* was rejected by the Abbey.

Drawing attention to a quite different problem from the inequities that bothered Catholics, Hyde observed at the outset of his speech on de-Anglicizing Ireland,

> If we take a bird's-eye view of our island to-day and compare it with what it used to be, we must be struck by the extraordinary fact that the nation which was once . . . one of the most classically learned and cultured nations in Europe, is now one of the least so; how one of the most reading and literary peoples has become one of the *least* studious and most *un*-literary, and how the present art products of one of the quickest, most sensitive and most artistic races on earth are now only distinguished for their hideousness.[48]

For Hyde, the main problem in Ireland was not the poverty of Catholics nor the inequities they suffered but their lack of cultivation and taste.

Yeats agreed with Hyde about the parlous state of culture and taste in Ireland and the importance of rectifying the problem. In a letter quoted earlier, Yeats said that he didn't "want good taste to be suspected of a theological origin," but he clearly believed that he had a special duty to defend his esthetics. In a 1901 letter to Lady Gregory, he proclaimed, "I have always felt that my mission in Ireland is to serve taste rather than any definite propaganda."[49] She encouraged him in that mission, reminding him, "Taste, like every other attribute of aristocracy, requires daring."[50] Still in the service of taste some years later, he wrote, "Four-fifths of our energy is spent in the quarrel with bad taste."[51]

Hyde blamed the influx of popular English publications for much of the damage done to Irish taste, and Yeats blamed the importation of popular English plays in particular. By de-Anglicizing Ireland, both writers meant de-vulgarizing it, but they meant more as well. Hyde argued in his de-Anglicizing speech that a revival of the Irish language would return the country to the high level of culture that he claimed existed when Irish was widely used. In those days, he said, wherever Irish was spoken "the ancient MSS. continued to be read, there the epics of Cuchullain, Conor MacNessa, Deirdre, Finn, Oscar, and Ossian continued to be told, and there poetry and music held sway." He added that in those days, even "the Irish peasantry . . . were all to some extent cultured men, and many of the better off ones were scholars and poets."[52] If Hyde saw the language movement as a means for "join[ing] all Irishmen together," he also saw it as a way of returning Ireland to that fabulous time of peasant poets and scholars before taste had been corrupted by English influences. Yeats apparently thought that attending the Abbey plays would have a similar effect.

Because of Synge's extensive contact with and sympathy toward the poverty stricken West of Ireland's peasants, one might expect him to be disturbed by their destitution. However, what upset him to an extraordinary degree was the difference he observed between the Catholic peasants and the Catholic middle class. In a 1905 letter to his friend Stephen MacKenna, he wrote,

> There are sides of all that western life, the groggy-patriot-publican-general shop-man who is married to the priest's half sister and is sec-

> ond cousin once-removed from the dispensing doctor, that are horrible and awful. . . . In a way it is all heartrending, in one place the people are starving but wonderfully attractive and charming and in another place where things are going well one has a rampant double-chinned vulgarity I haven't seen the like of.[53]

Synge's extensive experience with "that western life" probably should be taken into account before one questions the accuracy of his observations. On the other hand, the black and white contrast he draws between middle-class and peasant Catholics seems more like melodrama than reality.

This contrast became something of an obsession with Synge, who made the same comparison between poor Catholics of Innisheer and those on Inishmor who were better off.[54] He referred to class difference yet again in speaking of the attacks on his plays, which he rightly perceived as coming from the Catholic middle class. In language that begins to suggest the pathological, he told MacKenna,

> The scurrility, and ignorance and treachery of some of the attacks upon me have rather disgusted me with the middle class Irish Catholic. As you know I have the wildest admiration for the Irish peasant and for Irishmen of known or unknown genius . . . but between the two there's an ungodly ruck of fat-faced, sweaty-headed swine.[55]

There's something incongruous about Synge's reputation as the Protestant playwright who most closely identified with Catholic Ireland and his near hysterical tirades against middle-class Catholics.

This schizophrenic reaction to Catholics is visible elsewhere in Synge's life. On the one hand, he became engaged to the Abbey actress Molly Allgood, who was Catholic. On the other hand, he kept trying to transform her into a proper, cultivated Protestant lady, badgering her to learn about "literature and the arts" and warning her to avoid "low" contacts, by which he meant her Catholic fellow actors and actresses. Angered to learn that during an Abbey tour Molly had begun rooming with members of the troupe, Synge wrote to her, "I don't want my [underlined] wife [underlined twice] to be mixing with Music Hall artists."[56] One wonders why this director of the Abbey should refer to its actors as "Music Hall artists" and why he should have such scorn for them? There's an interesting contrast here with

Joyce, who delighted in the Music Hall and who wanted his wife to put on weight in the right places, but never attempted to make her a cultivated lady or worried about her contact with "low" people.

One could hardly expect Synge to sympathize with the Catholic cry for improvement in Irish trade and industry since the resulting prosperity would risk transforming "wonderfully attractive and charming" peasants into "fat-faced, sweaty-headed swine." Moreover, when Synge considered the decline of large Protestant estates, what struck him was "the tragedy of the landlord class." "These owners of the land," he said, "are not much pitied at the present day, or much deserving of pity; and yet one cannot quite forget that they are the descendants of what was at one time, in the eighteenth century, a high-spirited and highly-cultivated aristocracy." [57] He apparently could forget the poverty stricken Catholic peasants whose labor had supported that "highly-cultivated aristocracy" and who probably suffered most from the decline of its estates.

Yeats shared Synge's assessment of middle-class Catholics, charging that they did little "But fumble in a greasy till/ And add the halfpence to the pence/ And prayer to shivering prayer." [58] He was even more concerned than Synge about the fate of landlords and their estates. "Upon a House Shaken by the Land Agitation" tells us that the land reform measures called for by Catholics threaten to destroy "all/ That comes of the best knit to the best," along with "the gifts that govern men" and "a written speech/ Wrought of high laughter, loveliness and ease." This poem also tells us that though they gain land, it is not likely that Catholics will gain the ability to govern men or any other "gifts" of the Ascendancy.[59] Yeats' belief in the inferiority of Catholics extended to the Abbey actors. Abbey actress Kathleen Nesbit says that both Yeats and Lady Gregory cultivated the notion that the players were peasants, "pretending they caught us all wild off the trees like monkeys." [60] It is quite possible that one reason for the Abbey's emphasis on peasant drama was a conviction among the directors that peasant roles were the only ones the players could perform.[61]

In spite of what appear to be strong feelings of identification with Catholics, Lady Gregory also shared the Protestant sense of their inferiority. When asked by an American if she were Catholic, she quickly replied, "All who do anything are Protestants." [62] Another version of her belief that Catholics couldn't do anything turns up in a letter to Yeats, where she accuses her friend Edward Martyn of that failing. Speaking of Martyn's reluctance to support the Abbey directors in a quarrel with the actors, she told Yeats, "These RC's haven't the courage of a mouse, and then wonder how it is we go ahead."[63] The preceding examples of Lady Gregory's, Yeats', and Synge's prejudice toward Catholics need to be kept in mind later on when Catholic resentment against Protestants is discussed.

Increasingly angered by various manifestations of that resentment, Yeats shifted from his early attempt at allying himself with Catholic culture to identifying with Swift, Burke, Berkeley, and other distinguished Protestants of the eighteenth century, the same period that Synge looked back to longingly. Also, Yeats became increasingly committed to reviving what he took to be the spirit of eighteenth-century Protestants rather than the culture of the native Irish.[64] This shift was apparent even to the press. Yeats reported to Joseph Hone that a recent newspaper article identified both of them as part of a group of "Anglo-Irish leaders" who were trying to "bring back the Irish Eighteenth Century." He added that the article went on to develop "the usual sort of thing—only the Gael or the Catholic is Irish."[65] For Yeats as for Synge, attempts at a rapprochement with Catholics had not succeeded nor had those attempts dispelled the notion that Protestants were less Irish than Catholics.

While Yeats' identification with the eighteenth-century Protestant Irish marked a shift from his earlier identification with the Irish generally, it continued his habit of locating the Irish ideal somewhere in the past. Hyde had a similar habit, looking on the Revival as a way of returning to the glorious time when Protestants knew Irish and Catholic peasants were poets. Protestant Revivalists in general saw their movement as a way of returning to some finer life in the past. Since they remained relatively untouched by English or modern influences, the peasants admired by Synge and Lady Gregory often represented that past.

Catholic Revivalists, on the other hand, saw a past that often was not at all attractive. For them, as for Stephen Dedalus, history frequently is "a nightmare." During the eighteenth century that Yeats and Synge found so admirable, most Catholics had been reduced to what Giovanni Costigan calls "the status of helots."[66] And things were hardly better for them in either the preceding century or the one that followed. Catholic Revivalists typically looked forward to a "New Ireland." This concept, popular among UCD students, is alluded to in the title of the UCD journal, *The New Ireland Review*.[67] Joyce also refers to "the New Ireland" in *Exiles* and *Ulysses*.

The question remained, how should the country be made new? An answer echoed several places in Joyce's writing is that Ireland should be Europeanized. That is what Robert advocates in *Exiles* (*E* 43). We hear a modified version of this idea in *Ulysses* when Buck Mulligan proposes that he and Stephen "Hellenize" Ireland (*U* 1.158). Joyce himself maintained that Irish writers needed to become more European by learning from continental writers (*CW* 70). His fellow student at UCD, Tom Kettle, agreed. Both he and Joyce battled the popular Revival notion that Irish writers must take their inspiration from Irish literature. Kettle argued, "A national literature that seeks to found itself in isolation from the general life of humanity can only produce the pale and waxen growths of a plant isolated from the sunlight." He claimed further that "in order to become deeply Irish, [Ireland] must become European."[68] Most Catholic Revivalists, however, insisted that the only valid way to make Ireland new was to focus more intensely on Irish culture. For these hard-core Revivalists, "cosmopolitanism" was nearly as great a threat as English influence, and was sometimes even identified with it. In "The Dead," these two positions are reflected in the clash between Miss Ivors, who thinks people should become more Irish, and Gabriel Conroy, whose trips to the continent are meant to make him more cosmopolitan.

CATHOLIC MILITANCY, IRISH IRELAND, AND D. P. MORAN

As much as anything else, it was the militancy of Catholic Revivalists that distinguished them from their Protestant counterparts. Fueled by anger at the inferior position they occupied in what they thought of as their own country, this militancy led to Catholic demands for equity in government and industry as well as in university education. It contributed to the formation of the GAA and to Catholic domination of the Gaelic League. It existed in the country as well as in the city and covered a wide range of Catholics, including even Edward Martyn, one of the well-off landholders known as "Cawstle Cawtholics" because they tended to speak with an English accent and to frequent events at Dublin Castle.

Martyn, in fact, was a leading example of Catholic militancy. He was outspoken in urging Irish opposition to any manifestation of English rule, as in a public speech where he proclaimed that "the Irishman who enters the Army or Navy of England deserves to be flogged," or in a letter to the press urging the Irish to protest the visit of Edward VII, a position too extreme for the "nationalists" in "Ivy Day in the Committee Room." Martyn also attacked the inequities between Catholic and Protestant, which appear to have angered him even more than they did Clery and O'Neill. He called the Protestant Ascendancy "this grotesque minority," which he said dominated the country only because nationalists lacked sufficient purpose to wrest power from them.[69] His one-act play, *The Place Hunters,* which treats Protestant privilege and prejudice in the legal profession, not only exemplifies his Catholic militancy, but also focuses on the sort of "problem" he criticized Yeats and the theatre movement for avoiding.

The play opens with a group of Protestants expressing their consternation at the appointment of a Catholic to a high position in the courts. As one of them puts it, "One of the best salaries in Ireland [going] to a Nationalist, and a Papist into the bargain." A Catholic named Daly enters and has a telling exchange with a member of the Protestant group named Fisher.

> DALY: Oh, I see, all appointments are to be kept for the fashionable religion.
>
> FISHER: And why not? We are alone fitted for them by our standing, by our education.
>
> DALY: Your Government should give us an education we can accept. . . . You had better make up your minds that Ascendancy minorities have seen their best days. The majority in Ireland now must have the Ascendancy and its right proportion of appointments.
>
> FISHER: Oh, what bigotry, what intolerance, when I tell you that want of education unfits your people for appointments.
>
> DALY: My friend you are not thinking about education. You only fear for the minority's monopoly of appointments.[70]

As will be seen later, D. P. Moran, who published Martyn's play in *The Leader,* objected to Protestants controlling all the prized positions not just because they were a minority but also because they were "aliens."

Martyn's inflammatory pronouncements outraged the ultraconservative and largely Protestant Kildare Street Club, to which he belonged. The members, probably all of whom, except for Martyn, believed in loyalty to England and the British military, voted to expel him. In one of the many famous Dublin trials, Martyn fought expulsion from the Club, though he was completely at odds with its members. Denis Gwynn suggests that Martyn sought to remain in the Club partly to show "his contempt for those who looked down upon him as a Catholic."[71]

An even more prominent and influential figure of the period imbued with the spirit of Catholic militancy was Father Tom Finlay. Owen Dudley Edwards reports that while serving as Rector of Belvedere Finlay "was concerned with turning people out for jobs which would have to be eased away from the grasp of the Protestant elite," whom he viewed as "an effete aristocracy [and] an alien caste." Edwards adds that Finlay also was intent on preparing Catholic students to become the country's "ruling class" and "campaigned very hard against the Freemasons," believing the society's "economic exclusiveness and favouritism" helped perpetuate Protestant control of the country.[72] Finlay carried these ideas to UCD, where he gained such influence during Joyce's time that "his position [as Professor of Economics] . . . was hardly less important than that of the President himself."[73]

While at UCD, Finlay founded and edited *The New Ireland Review,* which became a platform for Catholic militancy, as well as a UCD house organ. An *NIR* essay titled "A Question of Self-Respect" opens with a quote regarding Protestant control of Ireland from one Father O'Donovan of Loughrea, who said:

> Personally I do not blame Protestants very much. Catholics were themselves very much to blame. If they had grit and self-respect and cohesion they could have very soon . . . forced any minority, no matter how powerful, to regard their rights. . . . The Irish Catholic wants some stiffening put into him. He is too limp and invertebrate.

The author goes on to describe the Ascendancy "solely as a sort of English colony in the country." Its members, he says, are "subsidised by official position, social honours and patronage to hold themselves prepared at all times to further the spread of English influence . . . in opposition to the furtherance of native ideals."[74] An additional inequity was pointed out in another *NIR* article, where a Maurice Joy noted that "the Irish Literary Revival . . . connotes the work of A. E., Mr. Yeats, Lady Gregory, and Mr. Synge chiefly." "Not one of them," he added, "has been raised in the Catholic tradition."[75] In 1905, when Joy's article appeared, James Joyce already had begun to change that.

As should be clear by this point, the Irish Revival, like much else in the country, developed a Protestant side and a Catholic side. Whereas the former focused on the literary Revival and emphasized literary principles, the latter dominated the Gaelic League and the GAA and tended to follow a rigorous form of cultural nationalism known as "Irish Irelandism," which called for an Ireland where everything possible, from the language to manufactured goods, was Irish. Catholic Revivalists such as Miss Ivors or the student nationalists whom Joyce encountered at UCD typically were Irish Irelanders. Referring to UCD during Joyce's time there, a fellow student said, "We had all gone Irish Ireland."[76] In *Stephen Hero,* we hear the battle cry of these nationalists when Madden tells Stephen, "We want an Irish Ireland" (*SH* 54). Their voice also can be heard in the school paper, *St. Stephen's,* the inaugural issue of which carried the editorial proclamation, "However broad be the basis of an University or College ideal, it should not embrace cosmopolitanism. . . . The ideal at which we shall aim will be a distinctively Irish one."[77] Irish Irelanders thought "cosmopolitanism" as bad as, and often indistinguishable from, "West Britonism."

While Yeats was the leading spokesman for the Protestant side of the Revival, Arthur Griffith, and D. P. Moran were the main champions of Catholic Irish Irelandism. Though Griffith and Moran both flew the Irish Ireland flag, there were major differences in what it meant to each of them. Like his friend Douglas Hyde, Griffith was a tireless promoter of ecumenism, but he parted company with Hyde and joined the ranks of Catholic Revivalists by being militantly political. In the *United Irishman,* he regularly celebrated Grattan, Tone, Davis, and other Protestant heroes of political nationalism. Griffith considered Davis, in particular, to be his guiding master.[78] Following the tradition of Protestant nationalists, he urged Catholics and Protestants to unite in throwing off English rule. If he did not openly advocate physical force, he tacitly encouraged it. Early issues of his paper carried a series of articles on Fenianism by a pseudonymous "Raparee," who wrote approvingly, "Fenianism is patriotism militant, patriotism voiced by the ring of steel rather than by a chord of harp."[79] In a piece that reveals Griffith's interest in both physical force and cooperation between Catholic and Protestant, he noted the existence of a Protestant "Boys' Brigade" and a Catholic "Boys' Brigade," which he praised for providing Irish boys military training. But he protested that "the matter ought not be allowed to narrow down to sectarianism" and went on to call for "a National Boys' Brigade" that would include both Protestants and Catholics.[80]

In his famous account of the supposed Hungarian parallel to Ireland, Griffith argued that Hungarian independence had been achieved by just the sort of cooperation between Catholic and Protestant that he envisaged in the National Boys' Brigade. As was mentioned earlier, he blamed England for the strife between Catholics and Protestants in Ireland, maintaining that, "all foreign tyrannies encourage religious dissension and sectarian animosity amongst the people of the nation over which they tyrannise."[81] Drawing on the parallel with Hungary, he claimed that once Ireland became independent, Catholics and Protestants would live in perfect harmony.[82] His Sinn Fein program, which grew out of his early ideas and which he saw as a reincarnation of the principles embodied in Grattan's Parliament of 1782, reflected his continued allegiance to the old Protestant nationalists. Likewise, his paper *Sinn Fein* continued to promote the old nationalist ideal of cooperation between Protestant and Catholic. In a *Sinn Fein* article James Stephens said,

> Almost always the leaders of a purely patriotic movement in this country have been members of the Protestant religion, and I believe that when the units as well as the leaders of any Irish movement are Protestant that day will see the freedom of this country a fact, stable, triumphant and impregnable.[83]

Stephens, of course, was wrong; Irish independence came about largely as a result of Catholic efforts, first in the Easter Rising of 1916 and then in the following "Troubles."

Though Moran agreed with Griffith about the importance of having an Irish Ireland, he disagreed with him on virtually every other issue. Moran believed that Ireland's main problem was not its relationship with England, as traditional Irish nationalism and Griffith maintained, but the relationship between Irish Protestants and Catholics. Consequently, Moran discussed the latter relationship more openly and in more detail than probably anyone else before or since. Rather than being the disinterested observer that Eglinton hoped for, however, Moran was boldly pro-Catholic and anti-

Protestant. This stance justifies the claim that the appearance of Moran's writing "marked an epoch in modern Irish political thought."[84]

Moran's pronounced sectarianism appears to have put off scholars. In spite of his importance, little has been written about him; finding even simple biographical details is difficult. One mystery is why Moran left his position as a journalist in England in the late 1890s and returned to Ireland where he commenced his campaign of Irish Ireland propaganda. A common explanation is that he was recruited by militant Catholics within the Gaelic League, who supposedly wanted him to take over the League's official publication *An Claidheamh Soluis*.[85] Stanislaus Joyce, however, reports hearing that Father Finlay engineered the return, with the intention of having Moran run a paper that was sympathetic to the Catholic clergy to counter Griffith's sometimes anti-clerical *United Irishman*.[86] If Finlay had a hand in the return, the reason is just as likely that he recognized in Moran an effective person to advance his own long-term campaign of preparing Catholics to take over the country's leadership. In any event, Moran's Irish Ireland campaign was launched in the pages of Finlay's *New Ireland Review* with a series of six essays, later published as *The Philosophy of Irish Ireland* (1905). The first essay appeared in 1898, the year Joyce matriculated at UCD. The others followed rapidly, often as lead pieces, the last appearing in 1900. That year, six months following the publication of Griffith's *United Irishman,* Moran founded his weekly paper *The Leader,* which became the main platform for his campaign and which he continued to edit until his death in 1936. He also published a baldly propagandistic novel, *Tom O'Kelly* (1905), a copy of which Joyce owned.[87]

Writer after writer testifies to the immediate and widespread popularity of Moran's work. Joyce's contemporary William G. Fallon says that Moran's "flair for ridiculing the assumed superiority of the ruling classes [i.e. Protestants] quickly caught the public imagination."[88] Though sympathetic to Griffith's ecumenical politics, P. S. O'Hegarty confesses that the *United Irishman* "never had the popular appeal, nor the circulation, of *The Leader*."[89] More recently, F. S. L. Lyons has said that it became "one of the most widely read papers of the time."[90] By 1901, Moran had gained such prominence that Lady Gregory included his essay "The Battle of Two Civilizations" in her volume *Ideals in Ireland,* where his writing appears alongside that of the chief figures of the Revival—Standish O'Grady, Douglas Hyde, A. E., W. B. Yeats, and George Moore.[91] For understandable reasons,

Moran was not a favorite among Protestants despite his appearance in Lady Gregory's book. Concerned about Moran's militancy, A. E. wrote to Yeats, "I am afraid there is a warlike spirit let loose over Ireland. I suppose Moran's paper will be its organ." [92] In fact, Moran always argued against the folly of taking up arms against England, but A. E. was right in recognizing him as the chief voice of Catholic militancy in Ireland. In an article celebrating the paper's first anniversary, Moran scarcely exaggerated when he wrote, "Today the *Leader* is the most powerful organ of public opinion in Ireland." [93]

Moran addressed his paper explicitly to Irish Catholics, for some of whom reading *The Leader* became a symbol of authentic cultural nationalism, almost in the same category as speaking Irish. Thanks in part to Father Finlay's guidance, Moran paid special attention to UCD, whose students were thought of as "the future leaders of the Irish people." [94] Any time faculty or students strayed from the straight and narrow of Irish Irelandism—by failing to focus an economics course on Irish economics, by organizing a club for the non-Irish sport of hockey, or, worse yet, by playing football with students from Trinity College—Moran carefully noted their transgressions in *The Leader*.[95] A classmate of Joyce reports that Moran's "original and fiery writing soon began to make a deep impression . . . upon the College students." [96] Sarsfield Kerrigan, another student from the period, says that while Griffith's *United Irishman* had an influence on the nationalist movement at UCD, it was *The Leader* that "gave the movement the popular and active shape it took in the college." [97] Whether or not Moran directly inspired the Irish Ireland editorial policy of *St. Stephen's,* the students recognized him as a kindred spirit and sent him copies of their paper. He gave *St. Stephen's* sympathetic mention in *The Leader,* reporting with special pleasure a jocular note in the paper announcing that at UCD, "cigarettes and copies of the *Leader* are . . . to be allowed as extra-canonical indulgences." [98]

While Moran was popular among UCD students generally, he had his greatest impact on the Literary and Historical Society, with which Joyce was closely associated during his college years. Following the suggestion of Father Finlay, who was an important supporter of the L & H, Moran appeared at several meetings of the Society, both as visitor and speaker. He also shrewdly invited its members to contribute to his paper.[99] Before long, the L & H had become a center of his influence. His converts there included Joyce's contemporaries Louis J. Walsh, the "boy orator" of the Society, along with the more talented Arthur Clery, who was co-organizer of the Society and its Auditor for the year 1898–1899, and was also, under his pseudonym "Chanel," the humorist of *St. Stephen's.* Years later, Walsh still remembered how he and other students eagerly awaited Thursday mornings "to see what the young *Leader* had to say that week."[100] Recalling the same period, another L & H convert, William Dawson, said, "*The Leader,* then in its pristine splendour, was our Gospel."[101] Both Dawson and Clery were so won over by Moran that they became writers for *The Leader,* as did Conor Cruise O'Brien's father from the next generation of L & H students. The gentle and humane Constantine Curran names Arthur Griffith as the guiding spirit of UCD nationalists,[102] but according to the student and faculty memoirs compiled for the histories of UCD and the L & H, neither Griffith nor Padraic Pearse nor any other Catholic nationalist had the following attained by Moran.

In an editorial several years ago, Conor Cruise O'Brien described recent instances of sectarian politics as examples of "Moranism."[103] Such allusions have encouraged the popular perception of Moran as a simple-minded sectarian not worthy of further attention. In another context, however, O'Brien says of Moran, "He spoke for a people—the Irish Catholics."[104] If any figure from the Revival could be said to speak for Irish Catholics it was Moran, and that makes him worthy of considerable attention. His extraordinary popularity among Joyce's generation of Catholics, however, makes Moran particularly important to this study.

Moran fully agreed with the premise of the Irish Revival that English influences had almost completely destroyed Irish culture and that this process must be reversed; but departing from other Irish Revivalists as well as from the tradition of Irish nationalism, he denied that Protestants could contribute to its solution. On the contrary, he insisted that Protestants were the source of the problem and could never be otherwise because their English ancestry made them racially and hence indelibly English. He rejected the notion that they had ever become even minimally Irish, let alone "fully Irished," as Hyde claimed. Protestants in Ireland, he said, have remained "more or less alien in blood and almost exclusively alien in feeling."[105] Putting it more bluntly, Moran informed readers of *Tom O'Kelly,* "The term 'Protestants' is used throughout this book to designate generally the foreign racial element in Ireland."[106] According to Moran, because they lived within the country, this foreign element had done far more to spread the contamination of English culture and to destroy Irish culture than had the English across the sea. Being the chief source of the problem, they hardly could be expected to help solve it.

Shifting the blame for Ireland's troubles from England to Protestants in Ireland required a major revision of Irish nationalist history with its array of Protestant heroes. Moran provided this revision most notably in his 1899 essay, "The Pale and the Gael," which announces nearly all the premises of his Irish Ireland program.[107] The essay sets out to explain why, until the eighteenth century, "the line of demarcation between the races of [Catholic Gael and Pale Protestant] was scarcely blurred," whereas "now it is very much to seek." The turning point, according to Moran, came in 1782, when Henry Grattan won the Irish Parliament.

That hitherto celebrated event of nationalist history was a disaster for Irish culture, Moran said, because it "placed the Pale at the head of Ireland for the first time in history and ever since the Pale has retained that place." Looking back to Grattan's announcement of his success, Moran imagined the victory shouts in College Green being drowned out "by the mournful peals of the death knell rising on all sides outside the Pale," since, by planting "the spirit of English civilization . . . in our midst," Grattan's victory meant "the inevitable corruption of Ireland." As to the motives for the Parliament, Moran explained,

> In an evil hour the Pale got into the grumps, and after awhile adorned this temper, which had sprung largely from sordid motives, with the title of patriotism. But there was little patriotism in it. There was some spirit, some nobility, a little genius, greatly exaggerated, in the movement commenced by [William] Molyneux and carried to success by Grattan, but beyond a few traces of local color, the whole thing was English, where it was not inspired by the American and later on by the French, Revolution.[108]

For Moran, American and especially French influences were only slightly less insidious than English.

Having pulverized three Protestant icons of Irish nationalism—Molyneux, Grattan and the Irish Parliament—Moran moved on to others: Jonathan Swift, "who had not a drop of Irish blood in his veins, no Irish characteristics and an utter contempt for the pack of us;" Henry Flood, who was "a bigoted opponent of Catholic emancipation;" and Wolfe Tone, who was "a Frenchman born in Ireland of English parents." He was a bit less harsh on Thomas Davis and the other "second rate '48 men," those "large hearted, well intentioned fools whom we magnify into our great heroes." Still, there's barely concealed scorn in his reference to "Davis' comprehensive idea of the Irish people as a composite race drawn from various sources, and professing any creed they like." Though he carefully avoided assessing Parnell, Moran included "Parnellite agitation" among the "Pale movements," not just because it had been led by a Protestant, but also because it ignored "the great canker . . . of English ideas, ideals, and manners" that was sapping the country's strength.[109]

Ignoring that canker was only one of many faults that Moran identified in the Pale movements. He also faulted them for not being revolutionary enough, by which he meant that they were merely political, rather than cultural. Instead of being concerned with some "academic republic," he said, they should have been devoted to "the re-conquest of the land, the re-establishment of old ways and manners, and the sweeping away not only of the English connection but, I fear, of the Paleman as well." (That final clause is one of several places where Moran hints at a "Protestants out" policy.) Another fault of Pale movements, according to Moran, was that their leaders were indifferent to, and the movements themselves irrelevant to, the Catholic peasantry, "the leaderless, powerless millions, the real historic Irish race," who formed a majority of the population. In a series of pointed rhetorical questions alluding to Grattan's Parliament and Tone's United Irishmen, Moran asked, "What did the peasants know of republics? What did they understand about English-speaking independent states? What did they care about the glorious Pale victory of 1782?" The implied answer, of course, is "nothing": the "crushed and ignorant" peasants remained crushed and ignorant.[110]

At the conclusion of his essay, Moran proclaimed, "The next few years will decide for all time whether the Gael is to lift up the Irish race once more, or whether the Pale is to complete its effacement." This has the note of urgency typical of Revival rhetoric, but Moran is unique among nationalist leaders in asserting that the survival of Irish culture depends on Catholics and on Catholics alone.

In "The Pale and the Gael," Moran's treatment of Protestant nationalists is couched in the New Testament form of "You have heard it said . . . , but I say unto you. . . ." His tone, however, is that of an Old Testament prophet, exhorting the chosen—that is the Catholics—to throw off the alien and false gods of Grattan, Tone, Davis, and other Protestants mistakenly revered by Catholics as national heroes. Though Moran thought contemporary Protestants had a less damaging influence on Catholic thinking, he nonetheless kept up a running attack on them, referring to them as "the Queen's men," "England's Faithful Garrison," "the Saved," or more often, simply as "Sourfaces." He heaped special scorn on those Protestants such as Robert Martin, the composer of "Gilhooly" and other supposedly Irish songs, who capitalized on their Irish connection. With a pungency that characterizes much of his writing, Moran referred to Martin's talent as "that microbe from the unwholesome carcase of Trinity College."[111] Moran's favorite targets, however, were W. B. Yeats and "his school," that is Lady Gregory, the "Hairy Fairy" A. E., and other Protestant writers who formed the core of the literary Revival.

A major preoccupation of Revival writers was to determine what literature could do for the country. They debated the question not only in private but also in the newspapers and in books such as *Literary Ideals in Ireland*. On this subject as on others, Moran had pronounced ideas, which he outlined in an early essay. "The Irish," he said,

> have never been analysed, as all other civilised people have been, by their own literary men. If an Englishman is curious to understand his own countrymen, he goes to some of his novelists, and he is put at once on the track where he can see things which, unaided, he probably would never have seen for himself. Our case is different. We practically have no literature of national self-criticism. No brilliant Irish minds have ever turned themselves with sincerity on to their own countrymen.[112]

The "literature of national self-criticism" Moran called for is precisely the kind Joyce would produce a decade later when he wrote *Dubliners*. This type of literature might be called a characteristically Catholic form of self-criticism in that it was meant to prepare for the new Ireland by identifying problems in the old.

Whatever else they might be called, Hyde's popular *Love Songs of Connaught,* Lady Gregory's and Synge's plays about Irish peasants, and Yeats' plays and poetry about the legendary figures of the Celtic Twilight could not be called a "literature of national self-criticism." Moran claimed that most of the work done by these and other Protestant writers of the literary Revival was not even particularly Irish. Their supposed "Celtic note," he said, was "one of the most glaring frauds that the credulous Irish people ever swallowed."[113] Recognizing Yeats as the leader of the literary movement, Moran focused his attacks on him, charging not only that Yeats "lack[ed] every attribute of genius except perseverance" but also that he was so "dreamy," mystical and obscure "practically no one in Ireland" could understand him.[114]

As for the Abbey Theatre, Moran attacked it for being a coterie institution, catering to a Protestant audience and dominated by Protestant writers. Reporting on a recent outing to see a Yeats play at the Abbey, Moran commented that he felt as though he had "strayed by mistake into some prayer meeting of the foreign element of Ireland."[115] He suggested that the directors catered to this audience by writing and producing plays that reflected Protestant tastes and prejudices. He cited *Playboy* as an example, commenting that the play's "references to 'Fa-ather Reilly' and 'The Holy Fa-ather,' no doubt tickled the Sourfaces present immensely."[116] He also observed that while "the mere Irish" (i.e., Catholics), denounced Synge's play, "England's Faithful Garrison have tended instinctively" to favor it. He went on to wonder how the garrison Sourfaces would react to a similar play about them.[117]

The Leader joined its voice to the chorus of Catholic protest against the Abbey's emphasis on peasant plays. A review titled "The Shabby Theatre" described the Abbey as "that metamorphosed morgue wherein the National Theatre Company hold intermittent inquests on the Irish peasant."[118] In his own review of Lady Gregory's *Spreading the News,* Moran made it clear that one chief offense of the peasant plays was their repeated depiction of Catholics as comic figures. "We would like to witness a rollicking farce that would provide us with a good laugh at the expense of the Sourfaces," he said, "but that might come under the head of sectarianism; even in laughter you must be strongly non-sectarian—all being free, of course, to laugh at Papist goms."[119] In a later piece, he posed the obvious questions:

> Why does not Lady Gregory (nee Persse) write funny plays about the proselytising Persses of Galway? Why does not Yeats write blank

> verse about his kinsfolk, the Pollexfens of Sligo? . . . Papist Paddy is operated upon, but the Pollexfens . . . and the Persses . . . are not to be "lawfed" at. It is a much too one-sided argument for our taste.[120]

These are questions worth meditating on.

Moran's call for comedies about Protestants was only part serious. A *Leader* article titled "A National Theatre" announced what he really wanted: "a few comedies in English satirising Shoneen Ireland and West Briton Ireland, comedies dealing with transient problems rather than what Mr. Yeats would call eternal conflicts."[121] In other words, Moran wanted "comedies in English satirising Ireland as it is," which comes close to describing Joyce's achievement in *Dubliners*. The same issue of the *Leader* underscores a similarity in the perspectives of the two men when Moran describes a key theme of "After the Race" observing that "the mere Irish are at the moment largely composed of mean-souled people who cringe and fawn upon people of foreign extraction."[122]

While admitting that Catholic reaction to the Abbey plays was perfectly justified, Moran argued that it was way out of proportion. Speaking of the *Playboy* performance, he said that he found it "difficult to get hot over this affair."[123] Apart from generally maintaining that the affairs of contemporary Protestants had little bearing on the country's future, Moran also thought the audiences too small for *Playboy* or the Abbey to have any real widespread importance. What counted were Catholics' beliefs and their behavior, and he had no trouble getting hot over that. Moran found example after example of Catholics failing to live up to their high calling as the saviors of the country's culture.

Stating what was to remain the central premise of his form of Irish Irelandism, Moran said, "We have been fighting England as our only enemy, looking to her as the sole source of all our evils. . . . All the while, like Pendennis, we ourselves were our greatest enemy."[124] By "we ourselves" he meant Catholics, and though notorious for his attacks on Protestants, like Joyce, it was upon Catholics that he focused his wrath. He attacked them for their drunkenness, which he argued was a major cause of Catholic poverty and demoralization, in addition to being a good example of a problem that could not be blamed on England. "The English government does not make us drink too much," he said.[125] But he placed part of the blame on the drink trade, which he referred to as "Bung." Though Bung included pub owners, who often were Catholic, its most powerful figures were the producers of drink, most, if not all, of whom were Protestants. The best known of these Protestant drink producers were the owners of the Guinness Brewery, Lord Ardilaun and Lord Iveagh, who compounded their sins by owning the pro-English *Daily Express,* for which Gabriel Conroy wrote his review. Moran acknowledged their ownership of the paper by referring to it as the *Bung Express*.[126] Joyce echoes Moran's terminology in *Ulysses,* where he refers to "Bungiveagh and Bungardilaun" (*U* 12.282–283).

Another failing for which Moran attacked Catholics was their obsession with politics, by which he meant their preoccupation with gaining political independence from England. The real need, he argued, was cultural independence not political independence, which he said would be meaningless if the country ended up as an imitation England. He accused the political nationalists of passively accepting the relentless erosion of Irish culture while ministering to the Catholic fondness for patriotic rhetoric that praised Ireland, condemned England, and threatened rebellion. He repeatedly dismissed such talk, particularly the threats of rebellion, as "rameis," a Gaelic term meaning something like "hot air." The militant Irish patriot's favorite weapon, he said, was the "fearless speech" and the "pulverizing resolution."[127] Always on the lookout for instances of the hypocrisy that he believed riddled political nationalism, Moran gave regular reports on the quantity of non-Irish matter in supposedly nationalist papers like the *Irish Independent* and the *Freeman's Journal*. More pointedly, he called attention to the preoccupation of these papers with social affairs in England, as Joyce has the Citizen do in *Ulysses* (*U* 12.218–237).[128]

Moran's attack on politics is in tune with an important strain of the Revival, particularly among Protestants. This is also the most obvious reason he failed to be the spokesman for Irish Catholics that O'Brien said he was. Their prominent role in the Easter Rising and the Troubles makes clear that Irish Catholics remained profoundly interested in politics. It also makes clear that their patriotic speeches were considerably more than "rameis."

The fundamental failing of Irish Catholics, according to Moran, was that they did not take pride in their own culture. A *Leader* piece by the pseudonymous "Thomond" summed up this failure and its consequences:

> We are proud of being Catholics, but we look up to Protestants as a superior kind of people. They are the freemen, we are the helots.

> They are meant to be at the top of the social ladder, we are content if we are allowed to cling to its lowest round. . . . They are born to wealth, we to poverty. . . . They are to lead, we to follow. They are to teach us how we are to think on politics, on literature, on art, on manners, we are to receive the dictum with becoming meekness and submission. If you, a mere Catholic, want to be somebody in your own land, you must behave after the manner of the foreign section of the community. . . . If you get married, tell it only in the columns of the *Express*. If you want a prayer for a deceased friend advertise for it in the *Irish Times*—Protestant, therefore respectable journals.[129]

Moran believed that besides being a fault in itself this lack of pride in their own culture was the root cause of West Britonism among Catholics.

Long a term of abuse for Irish Protestants, "West Briton" alluded to their support for pro-English political measures such as the Act of Union. Moran did not invent the term, as one scholar claims,[130] but he did make it very much his own. In the first place, he extended it to include Catholics. Secondly, employing a bit of rhetorical jujitsu, he applied it to conventional Irish nationalists, accusing them of "sulky West Britonism," because they spent their time denouncing England while remaining indifferent to the way English culture was swamping everything Irish. Sulky West Britons included "the great majority of 'Nationalists,'" he said.[131] Thirdly, he expanded the term to include cultural as well as political matters. Moran made one of his main targets Catholic West Britons, who, in imitation of Protestants, affected English ways and scorned anything Irish. As typical examples of these "West British Snobs," he cited "the civil servant or commercial clerk who gives champagne suppers" and "the highly dressed grocer's son who lounges at the Dalkey band and lifts his hat to the English national anthem in the hope that he may be mistaken for an officer."[132] He singled out Clongowes College as a center of gravity for "Papist West Britain." Apparently alluding to its well-off students, he described the school as "one of the most valuable of the Imperial West British un-free possessions," adding that "its geographical position with regard to Irish Ireland is somewhere on the 180th degree of east longitude."[133] We learn in *A Portrait of the Artist* that the names for the competing teams in Stephen's class at Clongowes are drawn from English history and that the students play English games, such as cricket, all of which Moran would have viewed as evidence of the school's West British infection. As proof of the school's cozy relationship with the British army, Moran noted that, besides employing ex-military men as athletic instructors and often featuring military bands, it had scheduled a cricket match with an English army unit. He called Clongowes "quite a Tommy Atkins college" and suggested that the school's prospectus "should state that besides receiving a 'sound English education,' students may have an opportunity of drinking wine with Private Tommy Atkins."[134] He also noted a Tommy Atkins flavor in Belvedere, which employed a Sergeant Major Wright as instructor of gymnastics and hosted a performance by the Sixteenth Lancers band.[135]

In general, students at Clongowes came from that small group of prospering Catholics referred to earlier. According to Moran, the most extreme instances of cultural West Britonism occurred in this group, particularly among the males. They nearly always wanted to be "a gentleman of some kind," he said, "to be socially 'superior,' " and "what," he asked, "is a gentleman from the point of view of an English-speaking Irishman?" The answer was, "Manifestly the same thing as a gentleman in England."[136] In *A Portrait of the Artist,* Stephen recalls answering, "A gentleman," when Nasty Roche asked him at Clongowes, "What is your father?" (*P* 9). Moran's analysis of what it means to be a "gentleman" gives a special edge to this episode. He would have seen it as altogether logical that a boy who valued being a gentleman should be at the Anglicized Clongowes.

Prosperous West British Catholics are targets not only in *The Leader* but also in *Tom O'Kelly,* which was Moran's attempt at writing "the literature of national self-criticism," thereby filling the gap left by Protestant writers of the literary Revival. The novel treats the O'Kelly family, who live in the Anglicized village of Ballytown. In an authorial aside addressed to an imagined group of Yeats clones, Moran implies a contrast between his attempt at a realistic treatment of contemporary Irish life and Yeats' work:

> My parting word is reserved to the young gentlemen in the cloaks, with long hair and solemn, pale faces, who hear "lake water lapping" even when they are stirring their punch. Lifting up their voices they will mournfully chant, "Where, oh where, is the Celtic Note?" I have only to answer frankly, I don't know. I never met it in Ballytown.[137]

What Moran does find in Ballytown especially in the O'Kelly family, is both political and cultural West Britonism.

The O'Kelly father, a successful merchant, and his son Tom are enthusiastic Home Rulers, whom Moran shows wasting their time at political rallies and meetings. In the sort of crude satire that characterizes the novel, Moran calls the Home Rule Catholics "Twaddleites" and the Protestant unionists "Tweedleites"; his point being that both political groups are equally indifferent to the plight of the peasant and of Irish culture. Apparently having read "The Pale and the Gael," Mrs. O'Kelly recognizes that from the start, nationalist political movements have been Protestant affairs. "When there was a Parliament here," she says, ". . . 'twas all Protestants were in it, and . . . the real poor Irish were trodden down as bad as they are now, an' worse."[138] Unlike her husband and her son Tom, who become disillusioned nationalists, Mrs. O'Kelly never expects Home Rule agitation to have any bearing on "the real Irish." Tom's brother, a medical doctor, might be considered an extreme sulky West Briton since he affects the violent language of Fenianism, denouncing Protestants in private as descendants of "unscrupulous adventurers." Moran explains that in public, however, the brother "will cringe to the Cromwellians."[139]

While the male O'Kellys are "sulky West Britons," Tom's feather-witted sister is a "West British snob," who works at transforming herself into the model of an Ascendancy lady by taking "private lessons in French" and cultivating an English accent. She also pleads with her father to dress the family stable boy in "chocolate colored livery" such as she has seen the servants wearing at the local Protestant big house. Though the less well-off Catholics in the town don't think of aspiring to Ascendancy style, they nonetheless look up to the Protestant owners of a local drapery store "as people of a superior mould."[140] As for the owners, Moran explains that "they made their money on the shillings and pounds of their Catholic neighbors, but lost no opportunity of parading their assumed contempt for the 'ignorant papists.' "[141]

Writing *Tom O'Kelly* apparently convinced Moran that his talents were not suited to fiction; the book contains a well-justified authorial disclaimer regarding its literary merits. Thereafter he stuck to writing the journalism of "national self-criticism," where he continued his attacks on West Britonism. Moran found only one group free from Protestant influences. The Irish peasantry, he said, "could not be rooted out of its traditions by any

Pale-steeped emissary." Their resistance to Pale culture meant that Irish peasants retained "the marks of the Gaelic race" untouched by West British contamination. "An impassable gulf," Moran said, "separates them from any type to be met with in England."[142]

While he celebrated Irish peasants as embodiments of all that was authentically Irish, Moran did not idealize them, as Yeats and Lady Gregory did. On the contrary, Moran emphasized that the peasants were ignorant and poor and led generally miserable lives; however, he maintained that they provided "the unspoiled raw material for the making of a vigorous and a real Irish character." He saw the peasant fulfilling two functions in the development of this vigorous Irish character: one was to serve as a model of stern, unbending resistance to Protestant influences; the other was to provide a source of "national pride," the lack of which he believed to be a major cause for the slide into West Britonism. Moran argued that the "ancestral line of grim, hard-suffering Irish peasants who sacrificed everything at one time to their principles and traditions" provided far greater cause for pride than the vaunted ancestral lines of the English and of Irish Protestants. As for the refined virtues typically associated with the Ascendancy, he claimed, "you will find as good [a] natural capacity and native courtesy in a western cabin as in the families that send their children to Trinity College." But Moran cited things other than the peasantry that Catholics could be proud of—chief among these things was their religious faith, which he said had "the nature of a polar star, and [would] not be moved so as to ease their path down the line of least resistance," whereas the Protestant God was "a portable deity, easily shifted."[143]

Moran's assessment of Protestantism was enough of a commonplace among Catholics to be echoed in *Stephen Hero,* where Stephen says that "Protestant Orthodoxy is like Lanty McHale's dog: it goes a bit of the road with everyone" (*SH* 112). It also was a point of pride among Catholics that the peasantry had resisted the "Pale steeped emissaries" of Protestantism. But Moran insisted that Catholics needed to go beyond simply resisting Protestant influences and start taking aggressive action against them.

Mocking the sort of sabre rattling against England that was characteristic of patriotic speeches, Moran said,

> We do not advise young men to buy revolvers in order to beat the British army, but we do advise the people to be no longer fooled by

> the Sourfaces who love Britain and hate Ireland. We do advise them not to be frightened to be men, because someone may say that they are 'bigots.' If Irish Ireland is to be realised, the mere Irish [that is the Catholics] must be predominant.[144]

Moran repeatedly chided Catholics for cringing to Protestants. "The Irish Catholic," he said, "being still a slave, is afraid to say boo to his master the Protestant for fear he might be called intolerant." "And so long as we cringe," he added, "we deserve all the kicks we get every day from the Ascendancy."[145] A good deal of what Moran wrote about Protestants was aimed at reversing this condition.

In issue after issue of *The Leader,* Moran reiterated the message that the fear of being called intolerant or bigoted was a crippling one for Catholics because Protestant power rested on bigotry, and as long as Catholics sought to be tolerant, they would lose out. "We hate bigotry," he said, "but while the mere Irish have been playing 'tolerance' the Sourfaces have been fighting and marching in a solid square. We are all for tolerance but not at all for being walked upon and befooled."[146] Putting this message more forcefully several years later, he warned,

> Catholics may go along . . . 'proving their tolerance,' demonstrating their sweet reasonableness, but so long as . . . the Protestants have drums and beat them whilst the Catholics keep on 'proving their tolerance' and are afraid to bite, so long the Catholics may look for justice and keep looking for it, we promise they won't get it.[147]

He made it clear that Catholics should focus their energies on attacking the "solid square" of Ascendancy domination, not individual Protestants.

As a matter of policy, Moran treated individual Protestants as irrelevant to the country's future. That policy, along with his scorn for rhetorical displays, led him to ridicule the Gaelic League Executive Committee for calling it "an outrageous scandal" that the anti-Irish Trinity professor John Pentland Mahaffy had been appointed to the commission on using Irish in the schools. Moran commented,

> Why, as the Executive Committee were about it, not a 'vile, foul, dastardly and nefarious scandal in the face of a civilized and uncivilized

> world'? Really this sort of childishness has gone too far. Dr. Mahaffy may have been put on the commission to do the bigots' work. If so, then stand up to the bigots, and don't make fools of yourselves by throwing unexplosive adjectives at the bigots' pawn.[148]

Moran usually followed this policy of focusing his attacks on the Protestant population in general, though he abandoned it when writing about the Protestant leaders of the literary Revival.

One of Moran's major campaigns in *The Leader* was aimed at emboldening Catholics by exposing examples of Protestant bigotry in Irish institutions and in private life. Having done a bit of research, he reported in an early *Leader* article titled "The Eldest Bigot of Them All," that the entire Royal Dublin Society, down to the office boys, was staffed by Protestants.[149] Another early article, pointedly titled "Door-mat Toleration," observed that although at least three-fourths of Ireland's population were Catholic, Protestants held the great majority of government positions at every level, from the Lord Lieutenant down to county inspectors and stipendiary magistrates (Moran gave the exact figures for every position).[150] Other articles recounted similar inequities on all the railroads (hence the Great Southern and Western Railway is regularly referred to in *The Leader* as "The Great Sourface Railway"), in all the banks, in the post office service, and in various other private and public institutions.[151] An article about the Great Sourface Railway reported that of eighty-five total employees, sixty-two were Protestant and twenty-three Catholic. It also noted that the total salary for the Protestants was £36,062, while that for the Catholics was £4,180. So while Catholics made up one-third of the workforce, they received only one-ninth of the salary.[152]

Irish Times "help wanted" ads, specifying that applicants must be Protestant, provided Moran with abundant examples of Protestant bigotry in private life. He regularly reported the number of these ads in the week's papers, often picking out one or two worthy of special note. One such ad came from Lady Gregory's daughter-in-law, who was seeking a Protestant woman as nanny for her child. Another advertised for Protestant applicants for the job of under-housemaid at the Viceregal Lodge. Moran commented caustically that he knew the Lord Lieutenant had to be Protestant but was surprised to learn that the same rule applied to the under-housemaid. As a long-time critic of the damage done to Catholics by the drink trade, Moran was especially interested to discover that the anonymous advertiser for a Protestant estate carpenter turned out to be John Jameson, owner of the famous distillery. "Now John does not stipulate that none but [the] 'saved' should get drunk on his whisky—" Moran observed, "all are free to drink that." "All" of course, meant mostly Catholics, the principal victims of Bung.[153]

If Moran's initial aim had been to revive Irish culture, it soon expanded to include lighting the fire of militancy among Catholics and doing everything possible to advance their position in Ireland. "Part of our work," he said, "is to induce the Catholics to stand up boldly for themselves and to make Protestants accustomed to that strange phenomenon."[154] To Protestants who accused him of aiming at Catholic supremacy in Ireland, he answered,

> Now, if upwards of three millions of Catholics in this land do not aim at supremacy, what are they to aim at? Logically if they do not aim at their own supremacy they must aim, passively, if not actively, at the supremacy of 'the saved' minority.[155]

Whether or not Moran was right that Catholics must dominate or be dominated, the constitution they drew up makes it clear that Free Staters shared the conviction of the writer who proclaimed in an early *Leader,* "Irish Ireland is Catholic Ireland. Catholic Ireland is Irish Ireland."[156]

This account of Moran's ideas has focused on those that were most directly sectarian. He also had other interests: the advancement of Irish industry was an especially prominent concern. According to Donal McCartney, "Contemporaries regarded Moran as the father of what was called the Irish Industrial Revival." McCartney adds, "He was certainly its chief promoter."[157] Along with urging the importance of a successful local industry, Moran insisted that industry must succeed by producing items that were "as good and as cheap" as those from England or elsewhere, not by protective tariffs. Griffith, too, was an ardent supporter of Irish industry but insisted that it had to be protected. Ultimately, even the issue of Irish industry took on a sectarian cast. Though Yeats celebrated "grey Connemara clothes,"[158] neither he nor the other prominent Protestant Revivalists stressed the importance of Irish industry, as did Moran and Griffith. On the contrary, Protestant Revivalists persistently contrasted a corrupt industrial England with an innocent, rural, non-industrial Ireland. Joyce was sufficiently sympathetic to the cause of Irish industry that he procured an agency for selling Irish tweeds in Trieste. It is very difficult to imagine Yeats or Synge or other Protestant Revivalists doing anything similar.

Moran correctly anticipated that his radical departure from the nationalist tradition of locating all evil in England and praising everything Irish would lead to accusations that he was unpatriotic or worse. The most violent attack did not come from Protestants, as one might have expected, but from Arthur Griffith.

Initially, Griffith saw Moran as an ally in the nationalist cause. Having reviewed the first number of *The Leader,* which Moran sent him, Griffith welcomed the new publication as one that "comes to aid us in squelching the Anglicizing methods and systems which foreign schools and fashions have imposed on us."[159] But Griffith hardly would have been comfortable with Moran's attack on Irish Protestants. Aside from admiring the old Protestant nationalists, Grattan, Tone, and Davis, Griffith also had close personal ties to Protestants. His grandfather had been a Protestant, and a stoutly Unionist Protestant family were among his closest friends in Ireland.[160] Six months before *The Leader* began appearing, a pseudonymous article in the *United Irishman* denounced Moran's essay the "Pale and the Gael" for its racism and sectarianism. Reciting once again the story of Catholics and Protestants joining in the fight against England, the article said, "The Gael voluntarily accepted the Palesman as his countryman 250 years ago, and the Pale has led him . . . against the Power [i.e. England] which cares no rap about whether an Irishman be of the Pale or of the Gael so long as he is rob-able."[161]

Griffith also began to feel the sting of frequent barbs from Moran, who found *The Resurrection of Hungary,* with its "Austrian scoundrels," to be just another version of the old denunciations of perfidious England. The melodramatic nature of the pamphlet, Moran said, suggested that it had been written "mostly for boys." He also denied the whole premise of Griffith's so-called "Hungarian plan." "There is no parallel between Hungary and Ireland," he said. He poked fun at Griffith and his followers, calling them "the green Hungarian band." He also mocked Griffith's appeals to physical force as the "tin pike policy."[162] In 1903, Griffith responded with a long and incandescently abusive editorial about Moran. For reasons that would be intriguing to explore, Griffith said nothing whatsoever about Moran's campaign against Protestants. Instead, Griffith denounced Moran for criticizing *Cuman na nGaedheal* and the Gaelic League, and charged him with sabotaging Irish industry by advocating an "as good and as cheap" policy rather than the protectionism that Griffith called for. Using odd language for a supposed enemy of the English, Griffith accused Moran of being not only a liar but also "a dastard and a cad." Turning to a more serious charge, he accused Moran of being a British fifth columnist or "felon setter." "Sailing under the flag of Irish Ireland," Griffith said, "the *Leader* has sought on all occasions to stab at every individual, organisation or movement inimical to the British government in Ireland." In fact, according to Griffith, Moran's paper had been founded with the aim of putting the *United Irishman* and the Gaelic League's *An Claidheamh Soluis* out of commission. Rather than succeeding in this aim, he said, the *Leader* had lost circulation and had become "bankrupt in prestige and influence," while the *United Irishman* had grown stronger.[163] Three years later, however, Griffith's paper was defunct, while Moran's continued for another fifty years. Griffith's biographer notes that even at the time, "*The Leader* [had] more of a circulation than *The United Irishman* and [was] more effective in ridiculing West Britonism."[164]

While it may not be demonstrable that Moran spoke for Irish Catholics generally, there is plenty of evidence that he spoke for, or reflected the "consciousness" of, those militant Catholics who were becoming the most prominent Irish nationalists of the period. These nationalists believed that the new Ireland should be fundamentally Catholic, not only because that was the native culture, but also because it was superior to the culture of Ireland's Protestants.

The pull of Catholic militancy was strong enough to sway even Griffith's political and publishing partner, William Rooney. In a *United Irishman* article that often reads like something out of the *Leader,* Rooney asked, "Is not every position of importance [in Irish government] in the hands of the Ascendancy, except for an occasional one thrown as a sop to a renegade from the popular side? Is there a fair proportion of the important posts in commercial life in the hands of the Catholics? . . ." "We may be told," he said, "that a Catholic can gain, if his abilities entitle him to it, almost the highest offices in the government of Ireland," but Rooney pointed out that this clearly was not true. In another piece, he referred to the "alien sympathies" of Protestants. Sounding still more like Moran, he condemned Grattan's Parliament as "never truly Irish or National." "All the members," he said, "were descendants of the enriched and ennobled followers of Cromwell and William, with a slight sprinkling of Old Norman and one or two perverted Celtic families: the electors were, in the main, exactly similar." Rooney denounced the popular idea, largely shared by Griffith, that "the salvation of the land depends upon the restoration of this foreign-conceived and foreign-influenced body."[165]

The question is not whether Joyce was influenced by Moran (there is no evidence that he was) but whether he, too, in any way shared the militant Catholic consciousness that Moran articulated more explicitly than anyone else of the time.

CHAPTER TWO

The Critical Writings

Along with a few biographical details, the essays, book reviews, and other items collected in *The Critical Writings* give a preliminary answer to the question asked at the end of Chapter 1: to what extent did Joyce embrace a militant Catholicism? The collection contains pieces that Joyce wrote before leaving Ireland in 1904, including book reviews written during his 1902–1903 sojourn in Paris, as well as his later work, written in Italy between 1907 and 1912. The first group of writings deals primarily with literature from a point of view bluntly antagonistic to Irish nationalism. Appearing to demonstrate the truism that nothing turns people into patriots more quickly than living in a foreign country, the second group focuses on Irish history and politics and is full of nationalist sympathies. The one piece to mention relations between Irish Catholics and Protestants, the 1907 lecture, "Ireland, Island of Saints and Sages," condemns sectarian feelings; nevertheless, the nationalist sympathies expressed in the articles and essays Joyce wrote in Italy become progressively more Catholic.

Commenting on Joyce's UCD years, Padraic Colum writes that during this period, "For the new nationalist movement, the Gaelic League, he had no regard. 'I distrust all enthusiasms,' he said." Colum adds that Joyce's lack of regard was not limited to the Gaelic League but extended to the whole range of "post-Parnell Irish nationalism."[1] By thoroughly distancing himself from the Revival, Joyce was following the principle that he announced in the opening sentence of "The Day of the Rabblement" (1901): "No man, said the Nolan, can be a lover of the true or the good unless he abhors the multitude; and the artist, though he may employ the crowd, is very careful to isolate himself" (*CW* 69). The idea, here identified with Giordano Bruno, that writers must isolate themselves from the multitude is one that Joyce emphasizes repeatedly in his early essays. The particular multitude he usually had in mind were Catholic Revivalists or nationalists. For example, in "The Day of the Rabblement," he writes about the sub-group of Catholics who protested against *The Countess Cathleen* and other productions of the Irish Literary Theatre. At the opening performance of the play, he had demonstrated his isolation from this group by clapping in approval while his fellow students noisily protested. In a similarly isolating if less histrionic gesture, he later refused to sign the student letter criticizing the play.

His early essays show Joyce isolating himself not just from the UCD Revivalists but from the whole literary side of the Revival. He accomplishes this by praising Ibsen and other European playwrights, citing their works rather than anything Irish as the models for Irish writers to follow. Joyce also preserved this distance initially by maintaining a complete silence about the literary issues of the Revival. This silence, as well as key features of Joyce's esthetics, was inspired in part by Ibsen's example. In his 1901 review of *When We Dead Awaken,* he expresses unqualified admiration not only for the play but also for Ibsen himself. Joyce singles out the playwright's "reticence" for special praise,

> Seldom, if at all, has [Ibsen] condescended to join battle with his enemies. It would appear as if the storm of fierce debate rarely broke in upon his wonderful calm. The conflicting voices have not influenced his work in the very smallest degree (*CW* 48).

The essays "Drama and Life" and "James Clarence Mangan," which Joyce delivered at meetings of the L & H, show him following the example of Ibsen's "reticence," another form of isolation. In them he almost completely ignores the often fierce debates that were part of the Revival.

Joyce's reticence is especially marked in "Drama and Life." Constantine Curran notes that like all L & H contributions, "Drama and Life" was an invited paper. Curran adds that, coming in the term following Joyce's refusal to join the protest against *The Countess Cathleen,* the invitation "was a clear and friendly recognition of his minority stand and of the general desire to hear him on a subject he had made peculiarly his own." [2] Following Ibsen's example, however, Joyce doesn't say anything at all in his paper about *The Countess Cathleen*. Instead he presents an esthetic of drama, which, like the one that Stephen posits for literature generally in *A Portrait of the Artist,* is based on universal principles and ignores the literary demands of Revivalists. Joyce doesn't even mention the Revivalists' demands, the main one being that Irish literature be "national." Instead, he contrasts his esthetic with the much older belief that literature "should instruct, elevate, and amuse." He rejects this old notion, along with its corollary that literature has "special ethical claims," on the grounds that it is outdated. Again following Ibsen's lead, Joyce says that the one requirement of drama is "to portray truth" as it is manifested in contemporary life. Acknowledging that contemporary life has "no clank of mail, no halo about gallantry, no hat-sweeping, no roystering," all of which had been a staple of drama, Joyce proclaims his belief that "out of the dreary sameness of existence, a measure of dramatic life may be drawn." "Even the most commonplace, the deadest among the living," he says, "may play a part in a great drama." Predictably, he finds his conception of drama most fully realized by contemporary European writers and above all, by Ibsen (*CW* 39–46).

Though "Drama and Life" does not specifically allude to the Revival, Joyce's arguments in this essay constantly conflict with the dominant literary beliefs and practices of the movement. In a passage that seems aimed specifically at Yeats, Joyce says that audiences and dramatists alike must accept life "as we see it before our eyes, men and women as we meet them in the real world, not as we apprehend them in the world of faery" (*CW* 45). His celebration of continental models clashed with the beliefs held not only by Yeats and other leaders of the literary Revival but also with the ideas of the UCD Revivalists, who would have recognized in Joyce an example of the "cosmopolitanism" that they deplored. His rejection of the notion that literature has moral or ethical obligations might not have bothered the Protestant leaders of the literary Revival, but it went against a fundamental assumption of Catholics. In "Drama and Life," Joyce attributes this assumption that literature has moral or ethical requirements to "the compact majority," a version of the phrase he uses in *Stephen Hero* to describe the pious and patriotic Revivalists at UCD (*CW* 44, *SH* 38–39). But this view of literature was shared by the college President and doubtless by the faculty as well, and it likely led the President to prohibit Joyce from giving his paper at the L & H. When he did finally present it, Joyce's view of literature provoked "strong opposition" from the student audience.[3]

The Revivalists in the L & H must have looked forward to Joyce's paper on James Clarence Mangan with special anticipation. The leading poet of the nationalist Young Ireland movement, Mangan's work had appeared in the movement's paper *The Nation* and included patriotic poems that were well known. If the students expected Joyce's paper to confirm their nationalist feelings, they were disappointed. Ignoring all the current issues of the Revival, Joyce begins his paper with a discussion of the old conflict between classicism and romanticism. Moreover, instead of agreeing with the Revivalist belief that an Irish heritage is a literary advantage, Joyce presents Mangan's Irishness as his chief literary liability. He calls Mangan "a type of his race" whose imagination has become trapped by Ireland's sorrowful history, resulting in a "narrow and hysterical nationality" expressed through the worship of "an abject queen" and through melancholy protests "against the injustice of despoilers." Joyce objects not only to the tiresomeness of Mangan's complaints but also to their superficiality. "All his poetry," Joyce says, "remembers wrong and suffering . . . ," but "never laments a deeper loss than the loss of plaids and ornaments." He suggests that Ireland's sad lot has sapped the country's vitality, resulting in a tradition marked by "love of sorrow for the sake of sorrow and despair and fearful menaces." He finds this lack of vitality even in Mangan's most famous Irish poem, "Dark Rosaleen," the music of which, he says, "does not attain the quality of Whitman." The central question that Revivalists asked of Irish writers was, to what degree did their work support the aims of the Revival? The question that Joyce asks of Mangan is, to what extent is he a great lyric poet, and the answer he provides is, only occasionally (*CW* 73–83).

Joyce's remarks about Mangan often seem designed to provoke antagonism from nationalists, as when he says that Mangan "was little of a patriot" (*CW* 76). His reticencies, such as his failure even to mention Mangan's connection with Young Ireland and *The Nation,* also seem deliberately provocative and aimed at underscoring Joyce's isolation from the "compact majority" of nationalists. The one hint of any nationalist sympathy in the essay comes when Joyce says, ". . . Mangan can tell of the beauty of hate; and pure hate is as excellent as pure love" (*CW* 82). Here Joyce is probably referring to the hatred of tyrannical forces, especially as exemplified by Parnell's implacable hatred of the English. A fault that Joyce repeatedly associates with Irish nationalists is that their hatred of English rule is only a pretense. He appears to have felt that Mangan's poetry might solve this problem.

Joyce attributes the weakness in Mangan's work not only to an Irish habit of dwelling on the country's sorrows but also to his having written for "a public which cared for matters of the day, and for poetry only so far as it might illustrate these" (*CW* 78). With their concern over the decline of Irish culture and their call for literature that would help reverse this decline, Revivalists formed a similar public, which threatened literature's universality by requiring it to focus on current Irish problems. This threat and the consequent necessity for artists to isolate themselves from the people is a repeated theme of Joyce's early essays. The discussion of romanticism and classicism at the start of the Mangan essay may have been a device to isolate the essay from current literary debates. The opening discussion has no clear relevance to Mangan; it is not referred to after the first paragraph, and Joyce dropped the section entirely from the version of the Mangan paper that he later delivered in Italy (*CW* 175–186). But Joyce's argument that romanticism and classicism are "constant states of mind" reflects his determination to deal with universal issues rather than "the matters of the day." A similar determination is evident in "Drama and Life," where he situates his discussion of drama in a context that reaches back to ancient Greece.

Constantine Curran says that though the paper on Mangan, like the one on "Drama and Life," contained "deliberate and obvious" challenges to their beliefs, the members of the L & H generally admired both papers. As one sign of this admiration, Curran notes that *St. Stephen's* published the paper on Mangan.[4] But on those occasions when Joyce clashed with L & H members, his chief antagonists often were Moran's followers, Walsh and Clery. "Outraged by Joyce's assault on our nationality and traditions," Curran says Walsh attacked the paper on Mangan with what someone called "the untamable squadrons of his irrelevant eloquence."[5] In *Stephen Hero,* where Walsh appears as "Hughes," Joyce returned the favor by making him the most unsympathetic character in the book. Joyce criticized a paper Clery gave titled "The Theatre, Its Educational Value" that emphasized the moral or didactic side of literature and accused Ibsen of having an "evil" effect on readers. In turn Clery joined other L & H members in attacking "Drama and Life" (*JJI* 72–75).[6]

Besides giving him an opportunity to dramatize his isolation from the "compact majority," Joyce's presence at the opening performance of *The Countess Cathleen* reflected his strong interest in drama, a taste that he shared with the leading writers of the literary Revival. There are many other signs of this interest. In addition to writing a play and translating two others, Joyce devoted three of his earliest essays to the subject of drama: "Drama and Life"; his review of *When We Dead Awaken,* where he heaps lavish praise on Ibsen; and "The Day of the Rabblement" (1901). In this third essay, a short but intense reaction to the clash between the Irish Literary Theatre and its Catholic audience, Joyce makes clear his high hopes for the Theatre project as a force "against the sterility and falsehood of the modern stage" as well as "against commercialism and vulgarity." He also makes clear his mistaken anticipation that it would lead to the production of plays by Ibsen, Hauptmann, and the other European playwrights whose work he admired. (Edward Martyn made the same mistake.)

Joyce's anger at finding that the Literary Theatre intended to produce nothing but plays on Irish subjects by Irish writers was so great that in "The Day of the Rabblement" he abandons Ibsen's policy of "reticence" and enters the "storm of fierce debate" over the Theatre. Joyce attacks its directors for failing to present European drama, claiming that this failure is crippling the development of drama in Ireland. In a frequently quoted passage, he proclaims, "A nation which never advanced so far as a miracle-play affords no literary model to the artist, and he must look abroad (*CW* 70)." He blames the Theatre's failure to present examples of plays from abroad on a more fundamental failure to maintain the isolation commanded by Giordano Bruno. He also accuses the theatre of a cowardly capitulation to the mass of "intensely moral" Catholics whom he calls the "rabblement." "[T]he directors," he says, "are shy of presenting Ibsen, Tolstoy or Hauptmann, where even *Countess Cathleen* is pronounced vicious and damnable." For Joyce, this fear of presenting "such improper writers" is the primary evidence that "the Irish Literary Theatre must now be considered the property of the rabblement." He implies that the rabblement also have come close to owning Yeats, whose "floating will" and "treacherous instinct for adaptability" make him particularly subject to its demands (*CW* 69–72).

"The Day of the Rabblement" occasioned Joyce's second encounter with censorship. The advisor to *St. Stephen's,* where Joyce had hoped to publish his piece, rejected it. Joyce appealed to the college president, as he had with his paper on "Drama and Life," but the president refused to intervene. The enterprising Joyce then joined with Frank Skeffington, whose essay proposing equal status for women in the college also had been refused publication in *St. Stephen's,* and the two shared expenses in publishing both essays together (*JJII* 88). Following its publication "The Day of the Rabblement" was discussed in *St. Stephen's,* which reminded Joyce that the people he attacked as the rabblement were Catholics (*JJII* 90). The reminder hardly was necessary, but its import—that Catholics should not attack Catholics—points to a significant sectarian current among UCD students. This negative press is an example of the coercive pressure that the UCD nationalists were prone to exercise and that Joyce accused Yeats of giving in to. His own encounter with that pressure helps explain his muted warning in "The Day of the Rabblement" that if an artist "joins in a popular movement he does so at his own risk" (*CW* 71). It also may explain his exaggerated sense of Catholic influence over the Literary Theatre. The Theatre did not focus on Irish subjects and writers because of Catholic pressure: that had been Yeats' intention from the start. As increasingly violent protests made clear, no phase of the theatre movement was Catholic "property." From the beginning, the movement's direction was firmly controlled by Yeats, who had an iron will, not a "floating" one as Joyce imagined. It was Yeats' decision to emphasize Irish works, and it was his determination that prevented any wavering from that course.

"The Day of the Rabblement" is a paradoxical essay. On the one hand, it is Joyce's first explicit assertion of isolation or alienation from both Catholic and Protestant Revivalists. On the other hand, it reveals his profound interest in the theatre movement. Joyce may have been indifferent to the sides of the Revival having to do with language, sports, music, and so on, but "The Day of the Rabblement" shows that he was far from indifferent to its literary side. Moreover, this essay shows that he shared a key aim with Yeats, A. E., John Eglinton, and other leaders of the literary Revival: they wanted to raise the level of literature in Ireland and so did he. They debated how to achieve this aim in a series of essays collected in the volume *Literary Ideals in Ireland*. Written just two years after the volume's publication in 1899, "The Day of the Rabblement" can be seen as Joyce's contribution to the debate it featured. Having in hand a play of his own and his translations of two plays by Hauptmann, Joyce had a special stake in the outcome of this debate. If the Literary Theatre maintained its current policy, where would these works have a chance for production? This problem would seem a powerful motive for Joyce to relinquish his reticence and enter the debate.

As book reviewer for the *Daily Express* during parts of 1902 and 1903, Joyce found both Protestant and Catholic examples to illustrate the point he made in "The Day of the Rabblement" about the dangers facing the writer who "joins in a popular movement." The Protestant example was Lady Gregory's volume, *Poets and Dreamers*. Joining the effort to become more Irish, which Hyde had promoted and which later became an important feature of the Protestant side of the Revival, Lady Gregory collected and published Irish folktales, presumably as a contribution to the revival of Irish culture. These folktales, which have much in common with the "world of faery" that Joyce speaks against in "Drama and Life," form a major part of *Poets and Dreamers*. In his review, Joyce describes them as reflecting "a land almost fabulous in its sorrow and senility." Treating the tales as unworthy of serious critical attention, he simply mocks them. Joyce is almost as harsh on the four one-act plays by Douglas Hyde that Lady Gregory translated for the volume. Originally written in Irish, the plays were part of Hyde's efforts at promoting the language, but Joyce ignores their didactic purpose. He judges them strictly as works of art and says that as such they fail, being instances of an "improper and ineffectual" literary form, "the dwarf-drama" (*CW* 103–105).

The Catholic example Joyce uses to illustrate the unfortunate consequences that result when writers join movements is William Rooney's *Poems and Ballads*. The book was edited by Arthur Griffith, Rooney having died the previous year, after exhausting himself, it is said, traveling around Ireland giving speeches in behalf of the Irish language. Though less well known than the review of Lady Gregory's book, Joyce's review of the Rooney volume is particularly important for the insight it provides into Joyce's knowledge of, and attitude toward, the Catholic side of the Revival. When he says in the review that Rooney is a person "whom many consider the Davis of the latest national movement," Joyce means the movement led by Griffith, later called Sinn Fein; and when he says that the verses "are issued from headquarters," he means Griffith's paper, the *United Irishman,* where the verses originally appeared. Joyce allows that Rooney's "consistently national" poetry may fulfill the author's apparent aim of "enkindl[ing] the young men of Ireland to hope and activity," but he says "good intentions" cannot excuse bad poetry and goes on to maintain that these poems are very bad indeed. "There is no piece in the book," he says, "which has even the first quality of beauty, the quality of integrity, the quality of being separate and whole." He adds, "But one must not look for these things when patriotism has laid hold of the writer" (*CW* 86–87).

In a version of a comment Stephen makes in *Ulysses,* Joyce remarks that Rooney "might have written well if he had not suffered from one of those big words which make us so unhappy" (*CW* 87). Angered by the review, Griffith quoted this passage in an advertisement for Rooney's book, adding a bracketed "patriotism" as the "big word" that was being alluded to (*JJII* 112). It is just as likely, however, that "religion" was the word Joyce had in mind. Summing up his assessment of Rooney's book with a rhetorical flourish, Joyce wrote, "Religion and all that is allied thereto can manifestly persuade men to great evil, and by writing these verses . . . Mr. Rooney has been persuaded to great evil" (*CW* 86). Whatever word Joyce may have meant, the review posits that for Catholic Revivalists such as Rooney, nationalist fervor and religious faith were identical and equally responsible for the kind of verse that Joyce refers to in *Finnegans Wake* as "Paltryattic Puetry" (*FW* 178.17).

In his review of Lady Gregory's *Poets and Dreamers,* Joyce says nothing about the Protestant movement to become more Irish, perhaps because as a Catholic, he wasn't clearly aware of it or did not see it as impinging on him in any way. The Rooney review, however, immediately identifies the author as a member of "the latest national movement." It is this movement Joyce has in mind when he later writes that in contemporary Ireland "literature is assailed . . . fiercely by the enthusiast and the doctrinaire" (*CW* 85). This charge echoes a central point in "The Day of the Rabblement," only now Joyce has added to the "intensely moral" assaulters of literature, the intensely nationalistic. He begins to sound like Synge on the "Neopatriotic" Catholics.

In Chapter Five of *A Portrait of the Artist,* as Stephen stands on the steps of the library observing the birds and thinking for the first time about leaving Ireland, he recalls the protests of the UCD students against *The Countess Cathleen* (*P* 225–226). This episode plants the idea that the nationalists' attitude toward art helps precipitate Stephen's decision to leave Ireland. However in his farewell broadside, "The Holy Office," Joyce attacks Revival writers rather than Catholic protesters. These writers, among them Padraic Colum, George Moore, W. B. Yeats, John Synge and George Russell, include Catholics and Protestants, as well as representatives from the

North and South of Ireland and from the city and the country. He dismisses them all as cowardly "mummers," who in various ways have shrunk from the stern demands of their art. In a melodramatic expression of his old principle of isolation, he distinguishes himself from all these writers, proclaiming,

> Where they have crouched and crawled and prayed
> I stand the self-doomed, unafraid,
> Unfellowed, friendless and alone,
> Indifferent as the herring-bone,
> Firm as the mountain-ridges where
> I flash my antlers on the air (*CW* 152).

If someone were as indifferent to the Revival writers as Joyce claimed to be, would he have taken such pains to assert it?

By the time he had been on the continent for several years and was more or less settled in Trieste, Joyce seems to have forgotten the Revival writers' faults: he launched a campaign to promote the works of both Yeats and Synge. He began by persuading a Triestine acquaintance to help him do an Italian translation of *Riders to the Sea* and later collaborated on a translation of *The Countess Cathleen*. Although reports of the *Playboy* riots in 1907 made him worry that Synge was outstripping him, he nevertheless tried to get *Riders to the Sea* produced in Italy. Joyce wrote the Synge family requesting performance rights and when he returned to Dublin in 1909, he began preparation for a performance by visiting the Abbey to see its costumes for the play. He told people "he hoped to make the Italians interested in the Irish theatrical movement" (*JJII* 290fn). He failed when Synge's family refused permission to have the play performed (*SL* 162). Likewise, Yeats refused permission for an Italian publication of *The Countess Cathleen*. But Joyce persisted and during the war, he arranged a production of *Riders to the Sea* in Zurich as part of a triple bill by the English Players. (It is significant that though he did not join the outcry of Catholics against Synge's portrayal of them as comic figures, the non-comic *Riders to the Sea* is the Synge play that Joyce most favored.)

Eventually both *The Countess Cathleen* and *Playboy of the Western World* were translated into Italian by Carlo Linati. Joyce saw the translations in a Zurich bookstore in 1918, and wrote to Linati, probably with an eye to having him translate *A Portrait of the Artist,* a copy of which Joyce sent along. In his letter to Linati, Joyce referred to Yeats and Synge as "two friends of mine" and congratulated him on choosing to translate their work "rather than the dull novels which the English public devours" (*Letters I* 121). Linati ultimately decided to translate *Exiles,* believing it to be part of the theatre movement. Joyce agreed. "[A]s you observe," he told Linati, "my work enters in the infamy of the movement founded and conducted by [Yeats and Synge]." He also explained, "I am a personal friend of Yeats and knew Synge in Paris" (*Letters I* 133). By the time of this second letter's writing, in December of 1919, Joyce has completely reversed the portrait of himself he painted in "The Holy Office" as the heroically indifferent figure, "unfellowed, friendless and alone." Now he sees himself as not only a friend of Yeats and Synge but also a member of the theatre movement.

This identification with the theatre movement was not a passing whim. In a list of "biographical items" that he prepared for a publisher three years earlier, he included the heading "Irish Literary Theatre," under which he wrote, "[Yeats] invited me to write a play for his theatre and I promised to do so in ten years" (*Letters I* 98–99). The implication is that *Exiles* fulfilled the promise and constitutes his contribution to the theatre movement. But even before *Exiles,* he thought of himself as belonging to the theatre movement. In a letter to Nora written after his return to Ireland in 1912, he told her that the Abbey Theatre was open and would be presenting plays by Yeats and Synge. Uttering a version of the idea that concludes *A Portrait of the Artist,* he adds, "You have a right to be there because you are my bride: and I am one of the writers of this generation who are perhaps creating at last a conscience in the soul of this wretched race" (*SL* 204). In this amusing bit of reverse cultural imperialism, Joyce supports his identification with the Abbey by projecting his own literary aims onto its playwrights. Yeats and Synge probably would have been highly surprised to learn of their interest in the conscience of the Irish. If anyone shared that interest with Joyce, it was the "intensely moral" Catholics whom he had attacked in "The Day of the Rabblement."

Joyce's concern with giving the Irish a conscience not only has nothing in common with the literary ideas of Yeats, Lady Gregory, or Synge, it also clashes with arguments he had been making since "Drama and Life" against the idea of literature having a moral function. Stephen makes a similar argument in *A Portrait of the Artist,* calling "kinetic" or "didactic" works "improper art" (*P* 205). Yet he hopes to forge "the uncreated conscience of [his] race."

In his attempts to convince Grant Richards to publish *Dubliners* as written, one of Joyce's main arguments was that the work had the potential to influence the moral life of Ireland. He told Richards, "I believe that in composing my chapter of moral history . . . I have taken the first step toward the spiritual liberation of my country." Repeating this notion in the following letter to Richards, he said, "I seriously believe that you will retard the course of civilization in Ireland [by not publishing *Dubliners*]" (*SL* 88, 90). Although this emphasis on the moral effect of *Dubliners* echoes Catholic precepts about literature, it also conflicts with the belief held by Catholic Revivalists that moral superiority was a key feature of Catholic identity. What Catholic Revivalists looked forward to was the restoration of their culture and the elimination of the inequities from which they suffered, not a "spiritual liberation" or a freshly minted conscience. Though his sense of the country's needs differed from Revivalists of both cultures, Joyce shared with them the fundamental Revival conviction that, as Yeats put it, Ireland was like "soft wax" and that even a single person could cause important changes in it.

His identification with the theatre movement is part of a broader sympathy toward Ireland that Joyce began to manifest shortly after he arrived on the continent. His sympathy initially took the form of an intense interest in Irish events, which he satisfied as nearly as possible through letters and Irish newspapers sent from home. It is not clear whether Joyce received copies of *The Leader,* though he refers to the paper in a letter to Stanislaus, suggesting that it might try to enliven an attack on Synge by digging up information about his life in Paris (*Letters II* 209). But he was sent a steady supply of Griffith's *United Irishman* and *Sinn Fein*. Joyce's 1902 review of Rooney's book shows little sympathy toward Griffith or his paper, but by 1906 that attitude has changed. He now calls the *United Irishman* "the only newspaper of any pretensions in Ireland" and adds that he believes "its policy would benefit Ireland very much" (*Letters II* 157–158). He faults Griffith for teaching "the old pap of racial hatred" but praises him for having revived "the separatist idea along modern lines," that is, with an emphasis on commercial independence. He speaks approvingly of Griffith's attempt "to inaugurate some commercial life for Ireland," and even allies himself with that effort, reminding Stanislaus of his own attempt at getting the agency for Foxford tweeds in Italy (*Letters II* 167). Also, like Griffith and most other Revivalists as well, Joyce says he has "no interest in parliamentarianism" (*Letters II* 157). When Stanislaus asks him what he would put in place of parliamentary agitation, he answers, "I think the *Sinn Fein* policy would be more effective," and goes on to say that, were it not for the insistence on the Irish language, "I suppose I could call myself a nationalist" (*Letters II* 187).

Joyce's burgeoning nationalist sympathies appear more explicitly in the 1907 essay, "Ireland: Island of Saints and Sages," which he gave as a lecture in Trieste, and in the series of articles he wrote between 1907 and 1912 for the Triestine newspaper *Il Piccolo della Sera*. There are occasional returns to the grim view of the Irish expressed in "The Day of the Rabblement" and "The Holy Office." In his 1912 article "The Shade of Parnell," as he had done before and would do again, Joyce treats the Irish as cowardly destroyers of their leaders. He says of the Irish response to Parnell's plea that they not throw him to the English wolves, "It redounds to their honour that they did not fail this appeal. They did not throw him to the English wolves; they tore him to pieces themselves" (*CW* 228). But the general tenor of his articles during this period is strongly nationalistic.

Joyce's nationalist sympathies were sufficiently intense that this supposed hater of all forms of violence wrote an article on "Fenianism," giving a completely favorable account of this "physical force" movement. In this article, Joyce all but openly endorses the Fenian commitment to violence, observing that "history fully supports" the Fenian assumption that England grants concessions to Ireland only "at the point of a bayonet." He also maintains, with less historical support, that until the leaders were arrested, the Fenians had been so successful that "the Republic was on the point of being established." He sees the Sinn Fein program as a direct outgrowth of Fenianism and calls Sinn Fein supporters "the new Fenians." The main aims of the program, he says, are "to make Ireland a bi-lingual Republic," to encourage "boycotts against English goods," "to develop industries throughout the entire island," and "to inaugurate a consular service in the principal ports of the world for the purpose of selling their industrial products without the intervention of England." He also emphasizes the Sinn Fein separatist doctrines that the Irish should "refuse to become [English] soldiers or to take the oath of loyalty to the English crown" and should withdraw financial support for the Irish representatives in the English Parliament (*CW* 188–192). Joyce's tone in describing these aims and doctrines is completely sympathetic.

Though his other articles dealing with Irish nationalism or politics—"Home Rule Comes of Age," "The Home Rule Comet," and "The Shade of Parnell"—don't mention Sinn Fein, they express ideas wholly in accord with the movement. In all of these pieces, Joyce supports separatist politics, portraying England as the determined enemy of Ireland. In "The Home Rule Comet," he reports that the Liberal government's abolition of the House of Lords' veto power, which in the past had been used to kill Home Rule bills, led an Irish political leader to claim that with the support of English democracy, Ireland at last would gain Home Rule. Forgetting the socialist principles he professed to believe in, Joyce argues that those who hope for any alliance between democratic forces in England and Ireland need to understand "that between the English nobles and the English workers there is a mysterious communion of blood; and that the highly praised Marquis of Salisbury . . . spoke not only for his caste but for his race when he said: 'Let the Irish stew in their own juice' " (*CW* 209–213). If Griffith promoted "the old pap of racial hatred," what is this reference to "communion of blood"?

Of all the Irish pieces Joyce wrote between 1907 and 1912, his 1907 essay/lecture "Ireland: Island of Saints and Sages" is by far the most substantial, detailed and comprehensive. It also contains his only discussion of the relationship between Catholics and Protestants. Anyone acquainted with Joyce's earlier attitude toward Ireland probably would conclude initially that the essay's title was ironic, like "The Two Gallants" or "Grace," but it is not. Joyce makes this clear right away, pointing out that "this exalted title" alludes to a time "when the island was a true focus of sanctity and intellect, spreading throughout the continent a culture and a vitalizing energy." He assures his audience that "this glorious past . . . is not a fiction based on the spirit of self-glorification" (*CW* 154–155). In his emphasis on Ireland's "glorious past," Joyce was echoing and endorsing a major premise of the Revival. He goes on to speak directly of the Revival, which he describes as "the Irish nation's insistence on developing its own culture," and "the demand of a very old nation to renew under new forms the glories of a past civilization" (*CW* 157). He gives a glowing picture not only of Revival aims but also of Revival achievements, particularly regarding the Irish language, about which he says,

> Now the Gaelic League has revived its use. Every Irish newspaper, with the exception of the Unionist organs, has at least one special headline printed in Irish. The correspondence of the principal cities is written in Irish, the Irish language is taught in most of the primary and secondary schools, and, in the universities, it has been set on a level with the other modern languages. . . . The League organizes concerts, debates, and socials at which the speaker of *beurla* (that is English) feels like a fish out of water. . . . In the streets, you often see groups of young people pass by speaking Irish (*CW* 155–156).

Later in the essay Joyce claims to be "an unprejudiced observer" rather than "a convinced nationalist" (*CW* 163), but the most fervent Gaelic Leaguer hardly could have presented a rosier account of the movement's success.

Though Joyce spends some time describing the glories of the medieval Ireland alluded to in his title, he focuses on the problems of contemporary Ireland. Reading Irish newspapers gave him a political awareness otherwise surprising in a person who had been away for nearly three years. His discussion includes an attack on sectarianism that at times sounds like a direct response to things Moran was saying in *The Leader*. Joyce begins his attack with a discussion of the twelfth-century English invasion and conquest of Ireland. It was a commonplace of nationalist rhetoric that the alien English culture introduced by this event commenced a long and disastrous erosion of Irish culture. Moran and other Catholics claimed that this alien English culture remained alive in contemporary Protestants, dividing them from Catholics and causing further damage to Irish culture. Joyce vigorously attacks this version of Irish history. He says that, rather than harming the culture of the native Irish, the invading Anglo-Saxons and Normans mixed with the Scandinavian and Celtic stock already there to produce "a new Celtic race" and at the same time caused a "renewing of the ancient body." As the chief evidence of this renewal he cites the battles against English rule, where Catholics and Protestants "made common cause, with the Protestant inhabitants (who had become *Hibernis Hiberniores,* more Irish than the Irish themselves) urging on the Irish Catholics in their opposition to the

Calvinist and Lutheran fanatics from across the sea" (*CW* 161). This description of intermarriage and cultural mixing in Ireland's early history, which parallels the one Hyde gives in "The Necessity for De-Anglicizing Ireland," lays the groundwork for Joyce's attack on contemporary sectarianism.

Focusing his attack on the racial basis of contemporary sectarianism, he claims that intermarriages make it impossible for any race to "boast of being pure today." "And no race," he adds, "has less right to utter such a boast than the race now living in Ireland" (*CW* 166). He insists, moreover, that most Irish accept the idea of a homogeneous Ireland. As evidence he cites the press response to an Irish politician who in a recent campaign speech "boasted that he was one of the ancient race and rebuked his opponent for being the descendant of a Cromwellian settler." Joyce says this speech "provoked general laughter in the press." He adds that rather than revering Catholics, "the new movement" takes as its heroes the Protestants Edward Fitzgerald, Wolfe Tone, Robert Emmet, Thomas Davis "and, finally, Charles Stewart Parnell, who was perhaps the most formidable man that ever led the Irish, but in whose veins there was not even a drop of Celtic blood" (*CW* 161–162).

The "new movement" Joyce refers to is clearly Sinn Fein, though the only thing particularly new about it was that a Catholic led it. Griffith emphasized his debt to the former leaders of Irish nationalism, but Joyce liked to think of himself as a champion of the new. While he doesn't explicitly support Sinn Fein in his lecture, he repeatedly echoes Griffith's position on the relationship between England and Ireland and between Catholics and Protestants. First, like Griffith, he denies the significance of sectarian differences in Ireland and insists that the only important difference is the one between England and Ireland, hence his point about Protestants and Catholics making "common cause" against England in the past. Second, he maintains that a "gulf" or "moral separation" still divides the Irish from the English (*CW* 163, 165). Third, he blames England for Ireland's economic troubles. "Ireland is poor," he says, "because English laws ruined the country's industries" (*CW* 167). And finally, Joyce echoes Griffith in blaming England for instances of sectarian tension in Ireland. Of England's behavior toward Ireland, he says, "She enkindled its factions," and again, "Her principal preoccupation was to keep the country divided" (*CW* 166).

For whatever reason, Joyce, like Griffith, offers no evidence that England caused sectarianism in Ireland. His most memorable example of sectarianism is that of the Catholic politician campaigning on the premise that Catholics are more Irish and patriotic than Protestants. While some papers may have found humor in the distinction drawn by this politician, many Irish people would have laughed at Joyce's picture of sectarian harmony in Ireland. And while it is true that Griffith was an admirer of the Protestant leaders of Irish nationalism, it is also true that Moran attacked them and that "The Pale and the Gael," which contained his most extended attack, was picked up and summarized by *An Claidheamh Soluis,* giving it what amounted to the Gaelic League stamp of approval.[7]

The nature and extent of Joyce's arguments against sectarianism suggest that he saw it as a growing problem among Catholics and was intent on combating it. Establishing that England promoted sectarianism was one way of discouraging Catholics from pursuing it. More directly to the point however, his claim that racial mixing has strengthened rather than weakened Irish culture denies the whole premise of Moran's distinction between Catholic and Protestant.

Despite his public posture, Joyce himself was not free of the Catholic sectarianism that he attacked in the "Saints and Sages" lecture. Sectarian feelings apparently triggered a significant if temporary shift of Joyce's sympathy from the Protestant dominated Abbey Theatre to the Catholic "Irish Theatre," founded by Edward Martyn. He told Stanislaus that even before the *Playboy* riots he knew that "there was a schism in the theatre" and cited as evidence the fact that "all of Columb's [*sic*] plays have been given by the 'Irish Theatre.' " He went on to say, "I believe Columb and the Irish Theatre will beat Y[eats] and L[ady] G[regory] and Miss H[orniman]: which will please me greatly . . ." (*SL* 144). A week later, still talking about the riots, he now shifted his attack to Yeats. Mistakenly believing that Yeats had appealed to the rioters as the author of *The Countess Cathleen,* which they disliked, rather than *Cathleen ni Houlihan,* which they liked, he told Stanislaus, "Yeats is a tiresome idiot: he is quite out of touch with the Irish people" (*SL* 147). Though this assessment of Yeats was based on a misunderstanding, Joyce seems quick to condemn him for not keeping in touch with the Catholic audience, especially given his previous criticism of Yeats in "The Day of the Rabblement" for attending too closely to that audience.

The influence of Joyce's Catholic heritage also is apparent in the "Saints and Sages" lecture and in his *Piccolo della Sera* articles. His remarks about the English, about Irish separation from England, and about the development of Irish industry are all typically Catholic. His Catholic heritage shows through again in the lecture when he refers to Protestants as "Calvinist and Lutheran fanatics." It surfaces even more tellingly when he says that as a result of the disestablishment of the Anglican Church in 1869, "the Irish populace, which is ninety percent Catholic, no longer contributes to the maintenance of the Protestant church, which exists only for the well-being of a few thousand settlers"(*CW* 169). This is the rhetoric and the arithmetic of Moran's brand of Irish Irelandism. Alert listeners in Joyce's audience must have wondered how it was that half a million Protestants, who had just been described as "more Irish than the Irish themselves," could be reduced suddenly to "a few thousand settlers"?

Joyce's Catholic perspective and sympathy is clearest in his article "Ireland at the Bar," which describes the trial of a seventy-year-old peasant, Myles Joyce, accused of murder in the small village of Maamtrasna. Since the old man spoke only Irish and the trial was in English, he was questioned through a translator, who then reported his answers to the court. According to Joyce, the old man gave extensive and animated replies, which the translator reduced to one-word responses. At the end the old man was convicted and subsequently hanged. "The figure of this dumbfounded old man," Joyce says, ". . . deaf and dumb before his judge, is a symbol of the Irish nation at the bar of public opinion." Completing the analogy, he likens English journalists to the translator, the former acting "as interpreters between Ireland and the English electorate, which gives them ear from time to time" (*CW* 198).

He also points out a symbolic importance in the peasant background of the accused. The Irish peasants, he explains, have been "reduced to misery by the brutalities of the large landholders" and occasionally "adopt violent methods of solution" to the agrarian problems, which they recognize as the source of their misery. He says that though silent about Ireland on all other occasions, the English journalists immediately report these instances of violence. The result is that English readers see the Irish "as highwaymen with distorted faces, roaming the night with the object of taking the hide of every Unionist" (*CW* 198–199). But it was specifically the Catholics, not the Irish generally, who were portrayed as violent, just as "Unionists" or Protestants would have been portrayed as the targets of the violence (*CW* 197–200). Both in its emphasis on the particular way English journalists misrepresent Ireland and in its portrayal of Irish peasants as the oppressed victims of brutal landlords, "Ireland at the Bar" is written from a Catholic perspective. It also presents Irish Catholics generally, and Irish peasants in particular, with a sympathy that is nearly melodramatic in its intensity.

The shift evident in Joyce's nonfiction from his early attacks on the Revival to the nationalist sentiments he expresses in the *Piccolo della Sera* articles is mirrored in his fiction. The harsh treatment of Irish nationalism in "Ivy Day" and "A Mother" gives way to a more positive view in "The Dead," *A Portrait of the Artist,* and *Exiles,* which were written in the same 1907–1912 period as the nonfiction articles or shortly thereafter. In *Ulysses,* however, Joyce returns to his unsympathetic treatment of Irish nationalism, particularly in the "Cyclops" chapter with its portrait of the Citizen. The Citizen sometimes is associated with Moran, but the connection doesn't go much beyond a shared taste for colorful rhetoric. What definitively sets him apart from Moran is his conviction that it is the English, not Irish Protestants, who are Ireland's worst enemies. In fact, he never mentions the problem of relations between the two Irelands. Only one character in Joyce shares Moran's acute awareness of that problem, Stephen Dedalus, who thinks about it in both *A Portrait of the Artist* and *Ulysses*.

If Joyce's work gives little hint of the sectarian tensions that marked Revival Ireland, neither does it show Protestants making "common cause" with Catholics as he describes in the "Saints and Sages" lecture. "Ivy Day in the Committee Room" makes the point that, like Parnell, the old tradition of the two Irelands uniting in opposition to England is dead. In *Ulysses,* Mr. Deasy's account of Protestant support of Catholic causes is so filled with errors that it calls into question whether such support ever existed. Though Deasy insists that he is Irish, he also strongly identifies with England and looks on Catholics as inferiors. Nor is there any sign in Joyce's fiction of a "new movement" whose followers admire the old Protestant leaders. Neither the student nationalists in *Stephen Hero* and *A Portrait* nor Miss Ivors in "The Dead" nor the Citizen ever mention any of the Protestant leaders, let alone express admiration for them. Though Joyce's fiction does not show the two cultures united against English rule, several *Dubliners* stories stress some sort of kinship between them. Even in these instances, however, Joyce carefully notes differences in power, position, and wealth between Catholic and Protestant characters. He also draws sexual and psychological distinctions.

Joyce's inclination to attack Catholics, apparent in "The Day of the Rabblement" and elsewhere, persists in *Dubliners*. It is especially obvious in "Ivy Day" because of the contrast between the reserved Crofton and the garrulous, hypocritical Catholics. Gradually, however, Joyce begins to portray Catholics in a more favorable light than the Protestant characters in whose company we see them. This pattern is especially pronounced in the narratives involving the English-accented probable Protestants. Of these characters, the old man in "An Encounter" and the nameless "captain" in *A Portrait* share oddly similar traits other than their accents (*D* 24–27 and *P* 228). Though not an obvious pervert like the old man, the captain is linked with sexual perversion in the form of incest. These two characters also share an appearance of physical decay that matches their decayed minds and decayed literary taste for romantic fiction by titled authors, Walter Scott in one instance, and Scott and Bulwer Lytton in the other. One example of an English accent being associated with decay and perversion might not mean much, but two such examples suggest that sectarian memories are at work. Tracing Joyce's treatment of the relationship between the two Irelands reveals those memories becoming more and more pronounced.

CHAPTER THREE

Dubliners

Insofar as Joyce wrote the stories in *Dubliners* with the idea that they would help transform the country, they all reflect a central notion of the Revival, but the movement itself also has a prominent place in the volume. The collection follows an arrangement that suggests the Revival's growth: the Revival is simply alluded to in "A Little Cloud"; and then later on, in "A Mother" and "The Dead," it appears as a major subject. Though the relationship between Catholics and Protestants might not be considered a major subject in *Dubliners,* this issue crops up early in the volume and ultimately figures in over a third of the stories. In these stories, as in his "Saints and Sages" lecture, Joyce gives contradictory views of the relationship, now emphasizing similarities between the two cultures, now differences. He does both in his characterization of Farrington and Alleyne in "Counterparts."

With a wife at "chapel," and a son who promises to say a Hail Mary for him, Farrington is clearly identified as Catholic, while Alleyne's name, along with his "North of Ireland accent" (*D* 86) and his partnership in the firm of Crosbie & Alleyne almost as clearly identify him as Protestant. The implied sectarian difference in "Counterparts" is juxtaposed with other contrasts so that the central characters are opposites in a variety of ways. Alleyne is the boss, Farrington the employee, Alleyne is from the North, Farrington from the South; Farrington is large, Alleyne is small (Farrington thinks of him as a "dwarf").

The critical point in the story comes when, in the presence of the other clerks and the attractive Miss Delacour, Alleyne loudly blames Farrington for two missing letters and when Farrington claims to know nothing of the letters says "Tell me, . . . do you take me for a fool? Do you think me an utter fool?" (*D* 91). Farrington's spontaneous response, "I don't think, sir, . . . that that's a fair question to put to me" wins him a temporary victory that turns to defeat as he is forced to make an "abject apology." Farrington recognizes, moreover, that from now on "his life [in the office] would be a hell to him" (*D* 92).

His later arm-wrestling match with the Englishman Weathers pits Farrington against the second of the two cultures with which Catholics traditionally have been in conflict. The onlookers who urge Farrington "to uphold the national honor" call attention to the cultural side of the match. Like the verbal clash with Alleyne, the arm-wrestling match with Weathers ends with Farrington's defeat. That he loses twice, after insisting on two out of three and, more importantly, that he loses to "a stripling," "a mere boy" (*D* 96, 97) leaves Farrington angered and humiliated. It also links him with Alleyne, who had been angered and humiliated by the retort of Farrington, a mere employee.

The two men also are linked by their shared habit of showing off in front of women. We see this habit in Alleyne's first scene with Miss Delacour, where Joyce describes him sitting with his right foot "thrown . . . jauntily on his left knee" and loftily dismissing Farrington with a flick of his finger (*D* 90). In the scene where he denounces Farrington for the missing letters, Alleyne is shown "glancing first for approval" at Miss Delacour (*D* 91) before asking the rhetorical question that will backfire on him. That she was present when Farrington made his retort and "began to smile broadly" (*D* 91) at it accounts for much of Alleyne's rage and humiliation.

Cheered by six shillings that he gained after work by pawning his watch, and remembering his brief victory over Alleyne, Farrington heads for a night of drinking. In a cruder version of Alleyne's behavior toward Miss Delacour (but much like T. S. Eliot's clerk with his "one bold stare"), Farrington walks along the Dublin streets, "staring masterfully at the office-girls" (*D* 93). Later in the pub he "gazed admiringly" at an attractive woman with a London accent (*D* 95). She seems to be returning his look and on leaving the pub "brushed against his chair and said O, pardon!" (*D* 95). But in another of the defeats he experiences this day, she leaves without looking back at him. Suddenly he is very angry and curses his "want of money," which is certainly one of his problems, though it hardly explains his lack of success with the woman.

The anger and humiliation he has experienced during the day leave Farrington with a feeling of "revengefulness" (*D* 96), which he vents on his son. This feeling provides the most striking link between Farrington and Alleyne, who exhibits his vengefulness when he forces Farrington to apologize and threatens him with dismissal.

The title "Counterparts" calls attention to the various ties between Alleyne and Farrington and suggests that Joyce means his readers to regard their similarities as having greater importance than the perhaps more obvious differences between the two men. The emphasis on parallels turns the story into a male instance of the Colonel's Lady and Judy O'Grady in Kipling's "The Ladies": the Catholic employee, Farrington, and the Protestant employer, Alleyne, turn out to be psychological brothers under their skins.

When the onlookers cast Farrington's match with Weathers as a matter of "national honor," they reveal a sense of history that Farrington lacks: he sees the match strictly as a personal matter. His pride in his size and strength dominates his perspective on his relationship with both Alleyne and Weathers. He never thinks of the former as a Protestant or Ulsterman or of the latter as an Englishman but regards the two men almost solely in terms of their physical presence. Except for Stephen, Joyce's other characters often have similarly limited perspectives, exhibiting only a vague awareness and little understanding of relations between Catholics and Protestants or between England and Ireland. Part of the comedy in "Ivy Day in the Committee Room" arises from this mutual obtuseness, where the Catholics in the story are in the dark about the political position of the Protestant Crofton and he is in the dark about theirs.

Joyce raises the issue of political relations between the two cultures in "Ivy Day" through Crofton's presence as a canvasser for Tricky Dicky Tierney. Identified in "Grace" as an Orangeman (*D* 165), Crofton appears here appropriately as a member of the Protestant supported Conservative or Unionist party, while Tierney is a candidate of the Catholic-supported Nationalist party. The party designations reflect an old political difference between Catholics, whose Nationalist party claimed Parnell as its founder, and Protestants, whose Conservative party opposed Parnell and everything he stood for. Catholics were in the habit of regarding this difference as evidence that they were more patriotic than Protestants. "Ivy Day," however, shows that the distinction no longer exists.

Joyce accounts for Crofton's presence by explaining that, its own candidate having withdrawn, the Conservative party has decided to support Tierney as "the lesser of two evils" (*D* 131), the greater in its opinion being Colgan, who represents the "labour classes." However reluctantly made, this decision of the Conservatives to support a Nationalist suggests that a political change has occurred somewhere. Joyce devotes the rest of the story to confirming that change has occurred and to revealing that it has occurred among the Catholics. His leading example is Henchy, who wants nothing to do with Parnell's policies but instead advocates keeping down the rates, promoting business, welcoming King Edward's visit, and defeating Colgan, all of which harmonize perfectly with Protestant politics. An illustration of this harmony is Henchy's report that he has won the votes of Parkes, Atkinson, and Ward, whose English-sounding names imply that they are Protestants. The point is made even clearer by Henchy's reference to Ward as a "[f]ine old chap . . . regular old toff, old Conservative" (*D* 131). Initially Ward was surprised at being asked to vote for a Nationalist, but Henchy claimed that nothing in Tierney's position conflicted with Conservative principles. Though this claim is made in the context of political canvassing, the story shows it to be exactly true.

The harmony has flaws, however. While admitting that Crofton is "a decent chap," Henchy complains that "he's not worth a damn as a canvasser. He hasn't a word to throw to a dog. He stands and looks at the people while I do the talking" (*D* 129). Crofton's taciturnity persists in the committee room, setting him apart from the garrulous Catholics. In a rare bit of authorial explanation, Joyce says that Crofton was silent partly because he had nothing to say and partly because he "considered his companions beneath him" (*D* 130). By showing the Catholic characters repeatedly directing their remarks at Crofton, Joyce indicates their tacit acceptance of this Protestant as their superior. Henchy points out that Parnell is dead, implying that this puts an end to previous political differences between the two cultures, and says that King Edward is "a jolly fine decent fellow" (*D* 132), implying Catholic sympathy with Protestant loyalists. Then, typically, he turns to Crofton, asking if he doesn't agree. Crofton simply nods. When Henchy presses further and proclaims in Crofton's direction that even the Conservatives respect Parnell now, Crofton temporizes with the first of his diplomatic remarks: "Our side of the house respects him because he was a gentleman" (*D* 132). Henchy clearly has presumed a closer bond between Protestants and Catholics than Crofton is willing to allow.

Crofton's second and most famous diplomatic remark, indirectly quoted, comes when O'Connor wants to know if Crofton isn't wonderfully impressed by Hynes' poem celebrating Parnell: "Mr. Crofton said that it was a very fine piece of writing" (*D* 135). Crofton's diplomacy is skilled but also comical, since he is carefully avoiding a political difference that no longer exists. While there is a residual political tension in the exchanges about Parnell, it is so slight as to resemble the gentle "pok" of the cork that flies out of Crofton's stout bottle immediately following Henchy's claim about Conservatives respecting Parnell.

"Ivy Day" recalls old political differences between Protestants and Catholics only to show that they no longer have any real validity, but it also contains a ghostly echo of the last occasion when, under Parnell's leadership, Catholic and Protestant could be said to have "made common cause" against English rule. In this shadow-filled story, the "tongue tied" Parnell, as Joyce called him (*E* 127), has his shadow in the equally tongue-tied Crofton, a lone Protestant among the Catholics in the "Ivy Day" committee room, as Parnell was nearly the lone Protestant among a crowd of Catholics in Committee Room Fifteen, where the vote against his leadership of the Irish Party took place. In Parnell's day, the common cause was against England and for Ireland; now it is against a representative of the workers and in behalf of a mercenary publican.

Their own mercenary interests have led both Catholics and Protestants to support Tierney, but pursuing those interests has not involved the Protestants in anything comparable to the Catholics' betrayal of their traditional party principles. Crofton himself exhibits not only a sharper mind but also a firmer attachment to principle than does anyone else in the story outside of Hynes, with his continued devotion to Parnell. As a result, Crofton becomes the chief exception to the rule that Protestants are more negatively portrayed than Catholics in Joyce's fiction.

In "Grace," Kernan's mention that he had gone with Crofton to hear a sermon by the famous Father Tom Burke raises the issue of religious differences, which for Catholics probably was a more sensitive topic than the supposed political difference between the two cultures. Puzzled and surprised at hearing that Crofton had attended a Catholic sermon, Mr. Power asks,

"But he's an Orangeman, Crofton, isn't he?" Kernan, a Protestant himself until his marriage, answers somewhat defensively, "'Course he is, and a damned decent Orangeman, too" (*D* 165). He goes on to report, apparently as evidence of this decency, that in a pub after the sermon, Crofton had said, "Kernan, we worship at different altars, but our belief is the same" (a surprisingly tolerant view for the man who was so careful in speaking about Parnell). Crofton's statement meets with the approval not only of Kernan, who thinks it "very well put," but also of Mr. Power, who says, "There's a good deal in that." McCoy chimes in, "There's not much difference between us." After a moment's pause to recollect exactly what the difference is supposed to be, he adds that both believe "in the Redeemer. Only they don't believe in the Pope and in the mother of God" (*D* 165–166).

This comic haziness about the two religions is resolved bluntly, if not very logically, by Martin Cunningham, who reminds his companions, "But, of course, our religion is *the* religion, the old, original faith" (*D* 166). At the end of the story, Father Purdon's retreat sermon, with its "text for business men and professional men" (*D* 174), exposes the nature of that "old, original faith": it is faith in money and position. As "Ivy Day" already has shown, Catholic and Protestant alike share this "old" faith. Thus in a way he would not have intended, Crofton was absolutely accurate when he said, "Our belief is the same."

Together, "Ivy Day" and "Grace" puncture two assumptions on which Catholics loudly prided themselves: that in politics they were more patriotic than Protestants and in religion more devout. In another version of the Colonel's Lady and Judy O'Grady trope, these two stories reveal that Catholics have become the political and religious brothers of Protestants. This revelation has the same satirical force as Milton's charge in "Areopagitica" that by instituting censorship, the Puritans were behaving like Catholics. At the conclusion of "Grace," however, Mr. Cunningham's list of supposedly distinguished people in the congregation is a comic reminder that although members of both communities are equally committed servitors of Mammon, Mammon has not rewarded them equally. The list, which Cunningham recites in an attempt at impressing the ex-Protestant Kernan, includes "Mr Harford the moneylender, . . . Mr Fanning, the registration agent and mayor maker of the city, . . . old Michael Grimes the owner of three pawnbroker's shops and Dan Hogan's nephew, who was up for the job in the Town Clerk's office . . . and poor O'Carroll . . . , who had been at one time a considerable commercial figure" (*D* 172–173). That this list impressed Mr. Kernan seems highly unlikely. While such a sundry group might well have been found in one of Dublin's Protestant churches, they hardly would have been the most distinguished members of the congregation, as they are in "Grace."

The differing economic circumstances of the two cultures, implied by Cunningham's list at the end of "Grace," becomes an important theme in "Araby," where it is dramatized by the contrast between the pinched circumstances of the narrator's family and the splendor of the Araby bazaar. Joyce suggests a Protestant connection with the bazaar by having the narrator's aunt say she hopes it is "not some Freemason affair" (*D* 32). Is he (or she) recalling that Araby is the third in a series of bazaars, the first of which was called the "Masonic Bazaar"?[1] In any event, her hope raises the possibility of Araby being a Protestant event, since at least in Ireland, the Freemasons were exclusively Protestants, Catholics being prohibited by the Church from belonging to secret organizations.

Several details about the bazaar would have made the aunt think it was not a Catholic enterprise. In the first place, being in aid of a hospital, Araby had the practical aim of Protestant charities rather than the pious purpose typical of Catholic charities. (The "Dublin by Lamplight" laundry, which appears in "Clay" and which was founded for the reform of prostitutes, is another instance of a practical Protestant charity.) More importantly, Araby, with its own special train, operated on a lavish scale uncommon among Catholic events. Joyce points out the humble level of Catholic charities by noting that the aunt's visitor, Mrs. Mercer, "collected used stamps for some pious purpose" (*D* 33). Both in its practical purpose and in its lavish scale, Araby is far removed from this simple example of a Catholic charity. That Mrs. Mercer's husband was a pawnbroker is a further reminder of the economic straits Catholics typically inhabited.

The narrator's aunt is surprised that he wants to go to Araby, probably because she understands the economic and cultural gulf between the bazaar and their world. The innocent narrator, however, associates the bazaar only with the "eastern enchantment" suggested by its name. He learns otherwise when he enters the bazaar and sees the *Café Chantant* where two men are "counting money on a salver" (*D* 34). These visual details tell him that he has entered an alien world of wealth and sophistication, not one of eastern enchantment. This message is underscored by the "porcelain vases and flowered tea sets" the narrator inspects at one of the few open stalls, and also by the people at the stall themselves. He says, "At the door of the stall a young lady was talking and laughing with two young gentlemen," then adds, "I remarked their English accents" (*D* 35). The three people are linked not only by their English accents but also by the narrator's significant designation of the men as "gentlemen" and the woman as a "lady" (repeated four times). The boy now realizes, without asking prices, that the goods here are beyond his reach.

There is no suggestion in "Araby" that the world the boy comes from and the bazaar are in any way "counterparts." The differences in this story are real, not imaginary as in "Ivy Day" and "Grace." Nor is there any suggestion of an under the skin sisterhood or brotherhood linking Mangan's sister and the narrator with the stall attendant and her two gentlemen admirers. The feeble sexual teasing carried on by the English-accented males is the antithesis of the narrator's passionate and idealistic devotion to Mangan's sister. Likewise, the stall attendant's coyness is far removed from the simplicity with which Mangan's sister accepts the narrator's adoration. There is the further contrast between the stall attendant's stale banter, "O, I never said such a thing!" and "O, there's a . . . fib!" (*D* 35) and the quiet simplicity and distinctly Irish phrasing of Mangan's sister's remark, "It's well for you" (*D* 32), which she makes apparently in reference to the narrator's going to Araby.

These contrasts resemble the conventional ones between the romantic relations of children and those of adults, as well as between those of the simple poor and the sophisticated rich. But the narrator and Mangan's sister are definitely Irish Catholics. We learn, for example, that she can't go to Araby "because there would be a retreat that week in her convent" (*D* 32). Moreover, by associating the girl with the name Mangan, Joyce calls up the image of Dark Rosaleen, the symbol for Ireland with which the poet Mangan is most closely identified.

The Araby bazaar is just as definitely not Irish or Catholic. A popular feature of Dublin social life at the time, *Cafés Chantants* were attacked repeatedly by both Moran and Griffith as examples of West Britonism.[2] Likewise, the English accents of the stall attendant and the two gentlemen make them seem to some extent alien. The contrast Joyce draws between the hollow sounding English-accented trio and the luminously attractive young Catholic pair suggests an attachment to his own culture that is not usually associated with him.[3]

The narrator in "Araby" confines himself to describing the present scene, much as Joyce does in writing *Dubliners*. We don't know whether he senses any significant differences between Mangan's sister and the stall attendant or between himself and the two gentlemen. In "Clay," however, Maria has a clear sense of the distinctions between Catholics and Protestants. Joyce tells us early in the story that Maria "used to have such a bad opinion of Protestants" (*D* 100) but changed her mind after working for them at the "Dublin by Lamplight" laundry. In language expressing Maria's formulation of this new opinion, Joyce writes that she now thinks Protestants "very nice people, a little quiet and serious, but still very nice people to live with" (*D* 100). She is particularly impressed by the matron, who is "such a nice person to deal with, so genteel" (*D* 100). The women who work in the laundry, on the other hand, most if not all of whom would have been Catholic, are not quiet or serious or genteel. On the contrary, we are told, "There was a great deal of laughing and joking" (*D* 101) while they ate their evening meal. When Ginger Mooney proposes a toast to Maria, the women all rattle their tea mugs on the table. Though Maria joins in the laughter, she looks down on Ginger Mooney for having "the notions of a common woman" (*D* 101). The clue to this assessment of Ginger lies in her wish for a "sup of porter" with which to drink to Maria's health. This wish exposes a level of diction and a taste in drink that are decidedly ungenteel.

Maria's own diction has telling peculiarities that reveal a desire to associate herself with her Protestant employers rather than her fellow Catholic employees. We must assume that she rooms at the laundry, which means that she would "live with" prostitutes, not Protestants. Her attempt at upgrading her living arrangement through a verbal fast shuffle has a comic pathos that is amplified at the end of the story when she sings, "I dreamt that I dwelt in marble halls." (A good deal is made of the verse she leaves out, but, given that she actually dwells in a laundry, the verse she sings should not be ignored.) Her impulse to associate herself with her Protestant employers also is revealed in her comment that the matron is nice to "deal with." For her, this phrase carries the pleasing suggestion of negotiations between equals rather than between employee and employer.

When Maria encounters the "colonel-looking gentleman" who makes room for her on the crowded tram (*D* 102–103) her soft spot for gentility is revealed again. Joyce writes that "she thought how easy it was to know a gentleman even when he has a drop taken" (*D* 103). Whether or not he is a Protestant, as Donald Torchiana claims,[4] Maria thinks he is very much like one and so approves of him even though he is somewhat drunk. Maria's loudmouth brother Joe, who drinks stout, brags about "the smart answer he made to the manager," and angrily asserts that "God might strike him stone dead if ever he spoke a word to his brother again," does not behave like a gentleman (*D* 104). The whole Hallow Eve party, particularly the crude trick played on her, clashes with the world of gentility to which Maria aspires. Readers frequently observe in Maria a barely hidden desire for romance and marriage. But if she could choose between married life and life as a Protestant-style lady, Joyce leaves little doubt which choice she would make.

With her impulse toward Protestant behavior and away from Catholic conduct, Maria exemplifies the type of Catholic that Moran castigated as West British. In the Doyles of "After the Race," Joyce gives an uncharacteristically bald account of this type. Almost immediately upon achieving success as a butcher, a trade Joyce associates with crudity, the senior Doyle dropped his "advanced Nationalist" views, which were commonly identified with Catholics. Next he subjected his son Jimmy to an educational routine typical of Protestants, sending him to England for his early schooling, then enrolling him in Trinity College Dublin, and finally sending him to Cambridge "to see a little life," that ineffable quality somehow not being available in Ireland. At school, Jimmy accumulated a number of debts, which his father mildly objected to, while being "covertly proud of the excess" (*D* 43). His pride stems from an understanding that this sort of excess is one mark of a gentleman, as it is in novels such as Lever's *The Martins of Cro Martin* and *Lord Kilgobbin,* both of which portray Ascendancy sons who have cosmopolitan friends with whom they dine, drink, and lose heavily at gambling. Joyce crams all these experiences into a single day, adding high-speed motorcars and a yacht to bring the story up to date. The parallels to Lever's work are so striking that "After the Race" has a slight air of parody, with Jimmy Doyle playing the part of Ascendancy wastrel, which in fact is what he is doing. The chief difference is that in Lever's novels, the

Ascendancy sons lose their money with aplomb or indifference, whereas there is little doubt that Jimmy will rue the losses incurred during his night of gambling.

Jimmy Doyle is a perfect example of what Moran called a "West British Snob," perhaps a bit too perfect. "An Encounter" contains a much more subtle and interesting treatment of this character type. Part of this story's appeal lies in the way it links the problem of West British snobbery with "the danger of 'human respect,'" which, as previously noted, Stanislaus Joyce says his brother's Jesuit teachers feared would assail their students when they met Protestants.[5] Though the old man encountered by the narrator and Mahony is not specifically identified as Protestant, his "good" accent suggests that he has gone to an English school, as Irish Protestants commonly did. The old man's talk about Sir Walter Scott and Lord Lytton suggests, though with a satirical twist, the cultivation associated with Protestants. (Also, Stanislaus tells us that his brother associated the old man's sexual perversion with English schools.)[6] In any event, the narrator would have been quick to conclude "Protestant" from the old man's bookish talk and accent just as the children in the previous scene immediately concluded "Protestant" from Mahony's cricket cap and badge.

As Stanislaus explained, the danger of seeking human respect is that it leads people to say or do things they might not otherwise say or do for fear of what people might think. This describes the narrator's behavior. He says he was "pained" at Mahony's ignorance of the Bulwer-Lytton books praised by the old man and goes on to explain, "I was afraid the man would think I was as stupid as Mahony" (*D* 25). His concern with earning the respect of this apparent Protestant leads him to the tacit lie of pretending to have read every book the old man mentions. More seriously, it leads him to the spiritual betrayal of his friend by trying to dissociate himself from him. From the narrator's proposal to use false names, where he assigns himself the non-Irish name of "Smith," while assigning Mahony the Irish name of "Murphy," we learn that he wants to dissociate himself not only from Mahony but also from Irish Catholics generally.

The narrator's West British leanings are hinted at in the earlier scene where the "ragged troup" of children mistake him and Mahony for Protestants (*D* 22). The narrator speculates that Mahony's cricket badge and cap caused this misapprehension; however, his own "frail canvas shoes" (*D* 21), which suggest yachting or lawn tennis, would have been just as eloquent a

Protestant symbol. Moreover, his having "diligently pipeclayed" them indicates a more active pursuit of such symbols than we see in Mahony. They set him apart from the troup of children, whose "ragged" clothing (mentioned twice) would have suggested immediately that they were Catholic. This episode also contains one of the rare instances of sectarian animosity in Joyce, when the children pursue the narrator and Mahony shouting, "Swaddlers! Swaddlers!" The point of the children's behavior, however, is not so much to show their animosity as to demonstrate their loyalty to their own culture, which they display by coming to the aid of the ragged girls whom Mahony was chasing. Mahony himself will exhibit a similar loyalty later on, when he comes running at the narrator's call.

While the narrator exemplifies the "danger of human respect," neither in this story nor in his other accounts of Jesuit schooling does Joyce show the teachers trying to arm their students against this danger, as Stanislaus claimed they did. Instead he portrays the Jesuit schools as fostering the very sense of Irish inferiority that would make their students especially susceptible to the danger. It is well known that the Jesuit education offered at Clongowes and described in *A Portrait of the Artist* followed the English public school system, emphasizing English (rather than Irish) games and English (rather than Irish) history. Mahony's cricket cap and badge indicate that the English public school pattern also was followed at Belvedere, which Dublin readers would have recognized as the school attended by the narrator and Mahoney in "An Encounter." Father Butler's name, which Torchiana notes is that of a famous family of English settlers,[7] adds to the Anglicized atmosphere of the school. As Moran kept insisting, such an atmosphere helped confirm the received idea that English, and by extension Protestant, ways were superior, and Irish (Catholic) ways were inferior. That is why he accused Clongowes and Belvedere of training West Britons.

A key moment in "An Encounter" comes when Father Butler catches Leo Dillon with a copy of *The Apache Chief* and remarks, "I'm surprised at boys like you, educated, reading such stuff. I could understand it if you were . . . National School boys" (*D* 20). Father Butler's message, stressed here by Joyce's carefully placed ellipsis, is that National School boys, which is to say the mass of Irish boys, are ignorant, and few things are worse than being like them.[8] This message, which would intensify rather than guard against the Catholic sense of inferiority, has made an impression on the narrator, who later on wants to tell the old man that he and Mahony are "not

National School boys" (*D* 27). It has planted or reinforced his wish to appear well read, along with his fear of being associated with Mahony, whose lack of sophistication suggests the National School boy. Father Butler's message also would have reinforced the narrator's wish to dissociate himself from Irish Catholics generally and from their stigma of ignorance and inferiority.

Though the ragged children are mistaken about Mahony and the narrator being Protestants, their mistake identifies a goal toward which the school is guiding its students. Encountered at the end of the boys' journey, the old man serves as a satirical representation of this Anglicized goal. He also offers a grotesque testimony to the narrator's progress when he says, "Ah, I can see you are . . . like myself" (*D* 25). For the narrator, the most significant part of the encounter occurs at the end, when he sees Mahony running to his call (just as the ragged boys had come to the aid of the girls) and suddenly feels penitent because he "had always despised [Mahony] a little" (*D* 28). Though the narrator blames himself for looking down on Mahony, Joyce shows Father Butler and the tenor of the school have had a share in shaping his attitude.

This story about a Catholic boy who observes two dramatic instances of Catholic loyalty and learns the error of despising a representative of his own culture may seem odd coming from the pen of a man who insisted that Irish Catholics were a rabblement and race of betrayers. But the Revival encouraged this sort of ambivalence. On the one hand, it singled out Catholics as the primary embodiments of a wonderful culture. On the other hand, that special position made them seriously culpable whenever they betrayed their culture. This Revival pattern runs through Moran's work, one side of which is devoted to denunciations of Catholics for becoming West Britons, while the other side treats them as superior to the Protestants and the English, as well as any other culture. A similar pattern of extremes occurs in Joyce. Occasionally even the terms are the same, as in "An Encounter," where the message that looking down on their own culture can have destructive consequences for Catholics echoes the premise of one of Moran's central texts. For whatever reasons, Joyce completely suppressed this covert sympathy with the Revival in the one story he wrote that focuses on the movement, "A Mother."

Joyce included this story, along with "Ivy Day" and "Grace," as one of the "stories of public life." It fits in that category partly because the concerts by the patriotically named Eire Abu Society are public events, like the election in "Ivy Day," and the retreat in "Grace," and partly because the Irish music featured at the concerts and the Irish language that Mrs. Kearney arranges for her daughter to study are aspects of culture, like nationalist politics and the Catholic religion, to which Catholics publicly proclaimed their devotion. "A Mother" also resembles "Ivy Day" and "Grace" in being thoroughly satirical. Following the pattern of those two stories, as well as that of "The Holy Office," "A Mother" portrays the supposed devotion of Revivalists to Irish language and music as a mummery, behind which lies a real devotion to Mammon or some other form of self interest. Mrs. Kearney's insistence that the Eire Abu Society pay in full for her daughter Kathleen's services at their concerts of Irish music is the central example of this type of self interest in "A Mother."

Kathleen's performance at the series of three concerts was due partly to Mrs. Kearney's earlier decision to have her daughter study Irish. Describing this decision so as to make clear that the spirit of the Revival had nothing to do with it, Joyce says, "When the Irish Revival began to be appreciable Mrs Kearney determined to take advantage of her daughter's name and brought an Irish teacher to the house" (*D* 137). The question is, what advantage did she anticipate? One obvious answer is that the Revival's emphasis on Irish music would open up jobs for pianists thereby allowing her to recoup some of the money spent on Kathleen's music lessons. She is a hardheaded woman who decided to marry a bootmaker when no more "romantic" option presented itself, and she is adamant about getting full payment. But, having attended "a high-class convent, where she had learned French and music" (*D* 136), she has come to value social status at least as much as money. She has persuaded her husband to cooperate fully with her social ambitions for their daughter. Besides sending Kathleen to a "good convent," where she learned the same socially appropriate subjects her mother had, he "paid her fees at the Academy," that is the Royal Academy of Music. Also, as she is careful to let her friends know, he regularly takes the family on July vacations to such proper places as "Skerries . . . Howth or Greystones" (*D* 137).

It is in the context of Mrs. Kearney's social ambitions that Joyce introduces her decision to have Kathleen study Irish. Mrs. Kearney imagines that an association with the Revival will promote her daughter's social standing, perhaps even provide her a more socially desirable husband than she herself married. Her arrangement that Kathleen be paid for the Eire Abu concert in guineas rather than pounds reflects her preoccupation with status, the salaries of great concert stars traditionally being given in that form.

It was also true that traditionally, Irish culture, including its music and language, was considered inferior, but Mrs. Kearney apparently has learned, as someone with her interests would learn, that the Revival was attracting middle or upper middle-class Catholics such as the students at UCD. She also might have been aware that the Revival had the support of distinguished or even titled Protestants such as Douglas Hyde and Lady Gregory.

Whatever the basis for her opinion, Mrs. Kearney expects the Eire Abu "Grand Concerts" really to be grand. She even makes expensive alterations in Kathleen's dress for the occasion. On the opening night of the series, however, the first thing she notices about the young men standing around the Antient Concert Rooms is that "none of them wore evening dress" (*D* 139). Expectations that this will be a socially prominent event are further chilled by the tiny opening night audience. Then signs that the concert series has lower-class connections begin to assail her. She particularly notices that the Eire Abu Society's secretary, Mr. Fitzgerald, has a pronounced Catholic or lower-class "flat" accent (*D* 139). Romantic possibilities for Kathleen appear in the form of two young men who are performing in the program and who are seen speaking together about her. But at least one of them, Mr. Duggan, clearly would be unacceptable to Mrs. Kearney since he is "the son of a hall porter in an office in the city." Piling it on, Joyce observes that, though a decent singer, Mr. Duggan "marred the good impression by wiping his nose in his gloved hand" and then adds further that Mr. Duggan "said *yous* so softly that it passed unnoticed" (*D* 142). The absence of any social profit in performing for the concert series, together with the more general realization that she has totally misjudged the advantages of being associated with the Revival, helps explain the fierceness of Mrs. Kearney's insistence that the contractual eight guineas be paid in full. It also helps explain her anger, which she only keeps from showing because "it would not be ladylike" (*D* 141).

Rather than being a story about the simple hypocrisy of a woman whose concern with money underlies her apparent interest in the Revival, as it sometimes is taken to be, "A Mother" dramatizes the more complex and amusing problem of what happens when someone who is fundamentally a

West British snob mistakenly gets involved in the Revival. Though Joyce does not suggest that any personal advantage motivates others in the story who have an association with the Revival, neither does he depict them as seriously committed to the movement. The interest that Kathleen and her "Nationalist friends" take in the Revival consists mainly of sending Irish postcards back and forth and saying "good-bye to one another in Irish" (*D* 137, 138). In one of several suggestions by Joyce that devotion to the Revival regularly was exaggerated, he reports that Kathleen became known as "a believer in the language movement" (*D* 138). It is this totally unfounded reputation that leads to her engagement for the concert series.

The minuscule audience at the concerts points to a lack of interest on the part of the general public. The reporter from the *Freeman's Journal,* a supposedly nationalist paper, adds further evidence of an uninterested public when he appears, only to announce, "he could not wait for the concert as he had to report the lecture which an American priest was giving in the Mansion House" (*D* 144). Though the patriotically named Eire Abu Society has sponsored the concerts, it has so little interest in their nationalist purpose that it has hired "Madam Glynn from London" as a featured performer. The Society has so little interest in the concerts themselves that it has left arrangements in the hands of the Society's incompetent "assistant secretary," Hoppy Holohan, whose efforts consist of standing "by the hour at street corners arguing the point and [making] notes" (*D* 136). Mrs. Kearney, who neither belongs to the Society nor professes any interest in the Revival, ends up making the arrangements, including the contract for eight guineas.

The Irish Revival is commonly credited with bringing new life to the spirit of Irish nationalism, which the fall and death of Parnell nearly had destroyed. Joyce gives no evidence of this rejuvenation in "A Mother." Spiritually, and in every other way, the people associated with the Eire Abu Society would be perfectly at home among the listless political canvassers of "Ivy Day in the Committee Room." It is altogether appropriate, then, that in "A Little Cloud" thoughts about the Revival should cross the mind of the dispirited Little Chandler, whose idea that he might write a poem full of melancholy about the houses along the Dublin quays reveals a faint aspiration to join the writers of the literary Revival. He is as indifferent as Mrs. Kearney to the nationalist aims of the Revival and, like her, is interested mainly in deriving personal advantage from association with the movement. His chief hope as a writer about Ireland is that his poems will appear in an English paper and be discovered by English critics, who "perhaps, would recognize him as one of the Celtic school" and detect in his work the "Celtic note" (*D* 74). His chief literary problem, he believes, is his name:

> It was a pity his name was not more Irish-looking. Perhaps it would be better to insert his mother's name before the surname: Thomas Malone Chandler, or better still, T. Malone Chandler (*D* 74).

The latter version of his name would appeal to Little Chandler because it highlights the Irish "Malone." It also is the classiest.

Gifford notes that when Chandler imagines being associated with the "Celtic school," he is using a phrase that English critics applied to Yeats and A. E.,[9] but this phrase, and more especially the expression "Celtic note," were applied repeatedly to Yeats by Moran. The presence of these terms in the story establishes a satirical link between Yeats and Chandler, who exhibits the same "floating will" and "instinct for adaptability" that Joyce attributed to Yeats. The melancholy mood that Chandler hopes to capture in his poem is a Yeatsian hallmark found in "The Stolen Child," where the "faery" speaker keeps asserting that "the world's more full of weeping than you / can understand."[10] Chandler's notion of extracting this mood from the land of faery and injecting it into an account of the houses along the Dublin quays suggests a comical but otherwise unpromising mixture of Yeats and Joyce.

Joyce's relentlessly satirical treatment of the Revival in "A Mother" and "A Little Cloud" would have contributed to the reservations about *Dubliners* that he began to feel during his 1906 sojourn in Rome and that he spoke of in an often cited letter to Stanislaus. In this letter, he confessed that perhaps his treatment of Ireland in *Dubliners* had been "unnecessarily harsh" and singled out Dublin's "ingenuous insularity and its hospitality" as especially important qualities that he had not shown in his stories. "The latter 'virtue,'" he said, "so far as I can see does not exist elsewhere in Europe." He mentioned the possibility of rewriting the book but added that "the perverse devil" of his satirical spirit probably would prevent much change (*Letters II* 166).

Instead of attempting to re-write *Dubliners,* Joyce began presenting more favorable accounts not only of Ireland generally but of Irish Revivalists in particular. These changes are especially apparent in his discussion of the Revival in the "Saints and Sages" lecture, which he delivered on April 27, 1907, shortly after returning to Trieste from Rome, and in his portrayal of Molly Ivors in "The Dead," which he completed later that same year. Whereas only two years earlier in "A Mother," Joyce had depicted the Revival as an anemic sham, in the lecture, as was noted previously, he claims that it is a vital and powerful movement with widespread support and significant results.

Molly Ivors, whose university education, interest in Irish, and association with the middle or upper middle class were typical of Catholic Revivalists, is portrayed as an isolated figure rather than as a member of a large and successful movement, but she remains a far more sympathetic character than Kathleen Kearney or the other pseudo-Revivalists in "A Mother." Though her brooch showing an "Irish device" and her good-bye in Irish (*D* 187, 196) might be taken as examples of the affectations practiced by Kathleen and her friends, and though she lists Kathleen among her companions on the trip to the Aran Islands, Joyce portrays Miss Ivors as a completely sincere follower of the Revival. He endows her with an intelligence that is not attributed to any of the characters in "A Mother," including Kathleen, and with a spirit and vitality that make her completely unlike the listless Little Chandler. Joyce's observation that "she did not wear a low-cut bodice" points to the Puritanism associated with Revivalists, but his description of her taking Gabriel's hand in "a warm grasp" and "laying her warm hand eagerly on his arm" (*D* 188, 189) shows that her Puritanism is not severe.

Rather than displaying the seriousness of the Puritan or zealot, Miss Ivors attacks Gabriel's West Britonism with good humor and even playfulness, as when she stands on tiptoe and whispers the charge in his ear (*D* 190). Her warmth toward him makes it clear that she does not object to Gabriel's writing a review for West British *Daily Express* strongly enough to alter her friendly feelings for him. She even says that "she liked the review immensely" (*D* 188). The frequency with which she echoes the language and ideas of Irish Ireland gives some justification to Gabriel's question, "Had she really any life of her own behind all her propagandism?" (*D* 192). Her life, however, is at least as much her own as Gabriel's is his own. If he is right in referring to her as "an enthusiast" (*D* 190), she is right in calling him a "West Briton" (*D* 188).

The sympathetic portrait of Miss Ivors contributes to a remarkable contrast between the views of the Revival in "A Mother" and in "The Dead." Whereas the earlier story portrays the Revival as little more than a fad, "The Dead" treats it seriously, as a movement dealing with important truths about the Irish, as well as important Irish problems. Joyce's comments about Irish hospitality in his letter to Stanislaus mesh with the Revival premise that the Irish possessed certain admirable traits that set them apart from other cultures. "The Dead" affirms this premise, though the admirable traits it emphasizes are different from those cited by Revivalists. This story also affirms a Revival premise by associating some admirable traits with the West of Ireland, but it contradicts Revival dogma by associating other admirable traits such as hospitality, with eastern and urban Dublin. Its attack on the Irish habit of scorning things Irish offers an even more striking instance of the story's harmony with Revival ideas. Gabriel has this habit, as is made clear in his outburst, "I'm sick of my own country, sick of it!" (*D* 189). Joyce portrays this disdain for Ireland as an important cause, if not the chief cause, of Gabriel's problems with Gretta.

There is one Revival issue that Joyce does not take, or at least does not treat, seriously in "The Dead": the relationship between the two cultures. He makes Protestant-Catholic relations a feature of the story by including the character of Mr. Browne, whom Mary Jane delicately identifies as "of the other persuasion" (*D* 194). The portrait of Browne demonstrates that Joyce was right about the "perverse devil" of his satirical spirit continuing to influence his pen, but in this story the chief victim is a Protestant. Giving Browne the role that Catholics traditionally had filled in Irish literature and still filled in many of the Abbey plays, Joyce, or his satirical spirit, made Browne the comic butt of "The Dead." Doubtless without knowing it, he thus answered Moran's call for work that would allow a "good laugh" at Protestants.

While Joyce had more reasons for including Browne than just to poke fun at Protestants, one has to go way back to John Kelleher's famous essay to find any significant discussion of them. Digressing from his examination of the story's mythic level (where he argues, not very convincingly, that Browne represents death), Kelleher points out that on the naturalistic level, the Morkans and most of their guests come from a small group of relatively well-off Catholics who emerged in Ireland at the end of the nineteenth century. He argues that prosperity among Catholics brought changes in the old relationship between Irish Catholic and Protestant and that Joyce dramatized these changes by portraying Browne as "the unwanted tilly" at the Morkans' party.[11] Perhaps, too, Joyce was making amends for the crude, ignorant Catholics that appear in his other stories by portraying a group of relatively well-off, educated, and sophisticated Catholics who are in every way superior to the one Protestant among them.

While Browne is a barely welcome guest at the party and a comic butt of the story, he is a more important figure than the term "tilly" implies. As Aunt Kate points out with her tart remark that "Browne is everywhere" (*D* 206), he is a major presence at the party, challenging Gabriel in prominence. Though the two never speak, Browne and Gabriel are closely linked through a series of parallels and contrasts, much as the Protestant Robert Hand and the Catholic Richard Rowan are in *Exiles*. The most obvious parallel between Browne and Gabriel is their difficulty in understanding women. Gabriel has been described as a man who misreads three women in a row. Browne does him one better, or worse, and misreads four. Browne's provincialism and Gabriel's cosmopolitanism produce some of the more obvious contrasts. These and other ties between the two characters are so extensive that Browne matches Michael Furey in importance as a foil to Gabriel.

According to a popular stereotype, the sophistication and social status of Protestant males made them powerfully attractive to Catholic women, as young Reggie Wylie is to Gerty MacDowell in *Ulysses*. Entering the story as if he were aware of this appeal, Browne announces, "I'm the man for the ladies" (*D* 182). Joyce then has Aunt Kate walk off as Browne is in the middle of explaining to her, "You know, Miss Morkan, the reason [women] are so fond of me is—." Unfazed by Aunt Kate's snub, he turns his attention to three young women, whom he conducts to the punch bowl. Then, badly miscalculating their sensibilities, he leans toward them "a little too confidentially" for their taste and tells a comic anecdote in "a very low Dublin accent" (*D* 183).[12] Such behavior might have flattered Gerty MacDowell, but these young women are refined (they include one of those pupils of Mary Jane's who "belonged to better-class families on the Kingstown and Dalkey line" [*D* 176]). They don't like to be reminded of their connection with the mass of less fortunate Catholics who speak with "low" accents. It is doubly offensive to be reminded by a Protestant. "With one instinct" they freeze into silence and thereafter pointedly ignore Browne.

In spite of snubs from four women in a row, Browne continues to behave as though he were a ladies' man. When it is time for Aunt Julia's song, he "gallantly" escorts her to the piano, introducing her in showman-like fashion as "my latest discovery," and when she mentions at dinner that the pudding is not brown enough, he replies waggishly, "Well, I hope Miss Morkan that I'm brown enough for you because, you know, I'm all brown" (*D* 192, 193, 200). We don't learn what sweet little Julia thinks of his gallantry, but the reactions of Aunt Kate and the three young women make it plain that he is badly mistaken about the ladies being fond of him.

In the scene at the dinner table (*D* 198–201), that traditional testing ground of *savoir faire,* Joyce skewers the image of the socially superior Protestant. There, with the sort of social ineptitude one might find in a stage Irishman, Browne announces in the presence of Dublin's leading tenor, Bartell D'Arcy, that contemporary tenors can't match those of the past. When D'Arcy asserts that excellent tenors still can be found, the thick-headed Browne asks, "Where are they?" D'Arcy answers, "In London, Paris, Milan," but Browne appears to know nothing about those cities (*D* 199). He doesn't even know Ireland well enough to understand the religious institutions and practices of the majority of its population. On hearing that the monks at Mount Melleray "never asked for a penny-piece from their guests," he says incredulously, "And do you mean to say that a chap can go down there and put up there as if it were a hotel and live on the fat of the land and then come away without paying a farthing?" He is even more baffled to learn that the monks sleep in their coffins and wonders why they don't choose "a comfortable spring bed" instead (*D* 200–201).

Rather than exhibiting the reserve commonly associated with Protestants, Browne is, as Aunt Kate remarks, "everywhere." In addition to escorting the three young women to the punch bowl and Aunt Julia to the piano, he takes charge of Freddy Malins, calling attention to his open fly and serving him a large and unwelcome lemonade (*D* 185). After Gabriel's speech, which Browne punctuates with loud cries of, "No, no!" and, "Hear, hear!" he quickly returns to center stage, and resumes his role as ladies' man, to lead the "for they are jolly gay fellows" song in honor of the Morkan women (*D* 202, 203, 205). In a last failure to display Protestant reserve, he leaves the party and the story boisterously laughing and shouting directions to the jarvey (*D* 209).

Except for the eloquent terminal "e" in his name, Browne lacks any of the traditional markers that would identify him as a member of the Ascendancy. Instead, Joyce has endowed this loud, garrulous, ignorant, provincial, obtuse confirmed bachelor and compulsive joker with key features of the Irish Catholic stereotype, including a fondness for alcohol. Browne's first words in the story, "And may we have some refreshment, too, Miss Morkan?" (*D* 182), establish his interest in drink. Within a few minutes of his appearance, he is asking people to "move aside" so he can reach the decanter, from which he pours himself "a goodly measure of whisky" (*D* 183). And after handing Freddy Malins the lemonade, he serves himself another whisky. In one of the many turnabouts in the story, Joyce shows none of the Catholic characters with whisky. Instead, he plants near Browne a group of abstemious young men drinking "hop bitters."

Browne's difficulties with the three young ladies also have to do with drink. Echoing the sentiment as well as the language of many a Catholic in Joyce's work, Browne says as he sips his whisky, "God help me, it's the doctor's orders." When one of the young ladies says that no doctor ever gave such an order, he gives a reply that offends them, telling them with heavily-accented voice, "Well, you see, I'm like the famous Mrs Cassidy, who is reported to have said: 'Now, Mary Grimes, if I don't take it, make me take it for I feel I want it' " (*D* 183). As was mentioned earlier, this episode encapsulates the theatre movement phenomenon of Protestant playwrights offending Catholic audiences by portraying Catholics as comic figures who have the pronounced Irish accent associated with ignorance. In accord with Hyde's call for Protestants to make themselves more Irish, Yeats, Synge, and Lady Gregory wrote their plays about the supposedly quintessential Irish from the West of Ireland. What they produced, however, seemed to many Catholics only a version of the Irish stereotype or stage Irishman. In Mr. Browne, Joyce presents a Protestant who, apparently having felt Hyde's call to become more Irish, has modeled himself on the Irish stereotype. The result is a comic example of those fabulous Protestants who became "more Irish than the Irish themselves."

Mistakenly convinced of his success at making himself more Irish, Browne feels perfectly at home in the Morkan household. Mary Jane says, "He has been laid on here like the gas . . . all during Christmas" (*D* 206). The trouble is that these middle-class Catholics do not fit the stereotype and in fact are trying to escape it. As a result, Browne remains a distinct outsider at the Morkan party. The only person with whom he has any rapport is Freddy Malins, the one Catholic at the party who comes close to the stereotype. In addition to being fellow drinkers, bachelors, and jokers, they have the same lowbrow tastes in music, so when Malins enters the discussion of opera to praise "a negro chieftain singing in the second part of the Gaiety pantomime," Browne approves. "It takes Teddy to find out the really good things," he says, without irony (*D* 198–199). Everyone else sits in mildly stunned silence until Mary Jane leads the conversation "back to the legitimate opera."

While the one item of Browne's clothing that is mentioned—a "long green overcoat"—has the appropriate color for someone aspiring to become more Irish, the coat's "mock astrakhan cuffs and collar" (*D* 206) suggest something fake about the results. Suspicions even about Browne's rapport with Freddy Malins are raised by his apparent confusion over Malin's first name, which he seems to think is "Teddy."

The cultural transformation implied in Browne's character serves as a precise counterpoint to the one that Gabriel has undergone. With his patent leather shoes (which, in a stage gentleman gesture, he deftly flicks with his muffler), his tip to Lily, his trips to the continent, his goloshes (which "everyone wears . . . on the continent"), his house in Monkstown where "better class" families live, his position at the university, and his stuffy speech decorated with classical allusions, Gabriel could be described as a Catholic who has become more Protestant than the Protestants themselves. True to Moran's law about prospering Catholics, the image of the "gentleman" has been Gabriel's magnetic North. Miss Ivors uses the appropriate term for the result when she calls him "West Briton." It is a measure of Gabriel's West Britonism that he knows nothing of the broad cultural meaning that the term took on during the Revival and so misunderstands it, thinking it refers only to politics (*D* 188).

In "After the Race," Joyce shows Jimmy Doyle embarking on the road to becoming a gentleman. Gabriel is the end result of a family that has followed this road for three generations. We glimpse an early stage in the progress when Gabriel tells the story about his grandfather, Patrick Morkan, who harnessed up the mill horse Johnny to "drive out with the quality to a military review in the park" (*D* 207). The "quality," of course, would have been mainly Protestants, and though Patrick would have resembled them in going out by horse and carriage to admire an English military review in the Phoenix Park, his use of a mill horse would have marked him as *nouveau riche* (or *shoneen*) like the Doyles in "After the Race." The lowly origins of Morkan's horse were revealed when it began going around and around King Billy's statue, located in the busy Dublin crossroads of College Green. The grandfather's exclamation, "Go on sir! What do you mean, sir? Johnny! Johnny! Most extraordinary conduct! Can't understand the horse!" (*D* 208) clearly was meant for the benefit of any onlookers, since he knew perfectly well that walking in circles was not extraordinary for the horse but something it did every day. The diction of Patrick Morkan's address to the horse, which is considerably more genteel than what one would expect from a Dublin mill owner under the circumstances, suggests the depth of his social ambitions. We learn from Gabriel that in spite of such setbacks as the episode with Johnny, his grandfather attained the end he sought and was "commonly known in his later years as the old gentleman" (*D* 207). Gabriel's repeated use of that title underscores its importance.

Patrick Morkan's daughter (and Gabriel's mother) continued to improve the family position by marrying "T. J. Conroy of the Port and Docks," whose job, Kelleher points out, was "good indeed, for the Port and Docks Board was very much an Anglo-Irish preserve."[13] Kelleher also points out that the family's rise is reflected in the Morkan sisters' Usher's Island address on the South, or Protestant, side of the Liffey and on a site formerly occupied by great Ascendancy houses.[14] An equally telling mark of Catholic prosperity is that their house, their party, and most of their guests are free from traits associated with Irish Catholics. It is significant that the Morkans don't have on their walls the pictures of saints or religious subjects typically found in Irish Catholic homes nor do they display pictures of Irish scenes or subjects. The pictures they do have, which show "the balcony scene in Romeo and Juliet" and "the two murdered princes in the Tower" (*D* 186), are both English. It is also significant that Mary Jane uses the piano to play a complex "Academy piece" rather than simply to accompany a singer; that Aunt Kate sings a demanding aria from Bellini rather than an Irish come-all-you; and that the dances at the party are waltzes and quadrilles rather than Irish jigs and reels. Most readers of Joyce will know that Irish nationalists objected to sports such as cricket and tennis as too English, but nationalists also objected to certain kinds of music and dancing on the same grounds. Arthur Clery claimed, "no one has ever yet ventured to waltz at an Irish college."[15] The Lancers, which Gabriel and Miss Ivors are dancing during their initial exchange, would have been equally repugnant to Irish nationalists.

Though possibly invented by a Dublin dancing master, the Lancers was commonly associated with the "nobility and gentry" and was featured at Queen Victoria's State balls.[16] Miss Ivors' early departure is not explained, but it is understandable since the dances and virtually everything else about the Morkans and their party clash with the ideals of Catholic Revivalists. Any Irish Irelander would have dismissed the whole affair as West British.

The Morkan's preference for non-Irish music, dances, and art was the sort of thing that Moran blamed on Protestant influences. In a pungent summary of the way those influences worked, Moran's follower, Daniel Corkery, said,

> The first article in an Ascendancy's creed is, and has always been, that the natives are a lesser breed and that anything that is theirs (except their land and their gold!) is therefore of little value. If they had a language and literature it cannot have been a civilized language, cannot have been anything but a *patois* used by the hillmen among themselves. . . . In the course of time the natives become tainted with these doctrines. . . .[17]

While there is no evidence that the Morkan sisters actively believe in this Ascendancy creed, Gabriel clearly does. True to the creed's doctrine that the native language is only a patois, Gabriel refuses to learn Irish. Instead he travels abroad every summer "to keep in touch with [European] languages" (*D* 189). True to the creed's premise that "the natives are a lesser breed," he looks down on the people at the party. On hearing "the indelicate clacking of the men's heels and the shuffling of their soles" as they dance, he reminds himself that "their grade of culture differed from his" (*D* 179). Later on he dismisses all the guests as "vulgarians."

Joyce is about as harsh on Gabriel as Corkery or Moran would have been, but the point he emphasizes about Gabriel's inclinations is that they are shallow, not that they are West British or stem from the Ascendancy. The "grade of culture" Gabriel has attained and sets such store by is that of an esthete whose sensibilities are offended by "indelicate" sounds, and whose love of books is centered in the feel of their covers and the look of their newly printed pages (*D* 188). His trips to Europe are the outings partly of a dilettante who wants "to keep in touch with" the languages and partly of a shopper for symbolic items such as goloshes (*D* 181). To put Gabriel's character in perspective one can think of Stephen Dedalus, who sees books as sources of knowledge and insight, who looks to Europe as a region of liberation for the accomplishment of great things, and who objects to the moral failings of the Irish rather than to their ignorance, vulgarity or indelicacy.

Of course, Gabriel is completely mistaken about his grade of culture being superior to that of the other people at the party. In at least one instance, his tastes turn out to be insufficiently advanced. He cannot appreciate Mary Jane's Academy piece, which he dislikes for the unsophisticated reason that it "had no melody" (*D* 186). One of the story's main points is that all these prospering Catholics share a fundamental cultural similarity. If the others at the party are vulgarians, so is Gabriel. As Browne feels at home among this gathering of Catholics because he mistakenly imagines that he has become just like them, so Gabriel feels like an alien because he mistakenly imagines that he has become different from them.

Gabriel's cultural aspirations produce a vein of social comedy in his relationship with the other guests, but they cause serious damage to his relationship with Gretta, who comes from the West and hence represents the unreconstructed, inferior "native." He once had been independent-minded enough to elope with her and still remembers angrily that his mother had referred to her in "slighting phrases" (*D* 187). Now, however, he himself is embarrassed about her origins so that when Miss Ivors asks if Gretta isn't from Connacht, he replies "shortly" that "her people are" (*D* 189), implying that she somehow isn't. His own behavior toward her now is slighting and worse. Following a habit that would have had special meaning for Joyce, who rarely went anywhere without his wife, Gabriel regularly leaves Gretta in the summer to go off to the continent with his male friends. And during the party we see him "coldly" rebuff her eager plea that he agree to the West of Ireland trip. Later, in the hotel room, his disregard for her reaches its paradoxical extreme in his wish initially "to be master of her strange mood" and then "to crush her body against his, to overmaster her" (*D* 217). Gabriel's attitude toward Gretta is a form of sexual West Britonism, recalling English attempts at mastering or overmastering Ireland. (In *A Portrait* Stephen makes similar connections between sex and Irish history when he uses the language of infidelity—"left him for another" [*P* 203]—to remind Davin of the way the Irish have treated leader after leader.)

Miss Ivors' charge that Gabriel does not know his own people is correct. Aside from failing to understand Lily, Miss Ivors herself, and practically everyone else at the party, he turns out to be completely ignorant of a major event in his wife's life. Having accepted the stereotype of Catholics as culturally inferior, Gabriel apparently has decided that they are not worth knowing. One reason he is taken aback by Lily, Miss Ivors, and Gretta is that they do not behave according to stereotype. Lily should have responded with some bland platitude to his query about her marriage prospects; Miss Ivors should have stood in awe of his having a review in the *Daily Express;* and Gretta should have responded warmly to his passion. Gretta's feelings about Michael Furey have a profound effect on Gabriel partly because they show that she is not the cipher he expects and partly because they reduce to meaninglessness the grade of culture he has attained and prides himself on.

Though Miss Ivors accurately assesses one of Gabriel's problems, she is too wrapped up in Revival dogmas to recognize that since Gretta comes from the West, he hardly needs to travel there to learn about his people. When Gretta tells him the story of Michael Furey and his love for her, Gabriel gains a shattering piece of knowledge about his people. Joyce sets up an implicit contrast between that knowledge and the Irish language, myths, and legends that Catholic Revivalists thought one should learn in the West. They considered these phenomena somehow central to Irish culture. Reflecting on Ireland from the vantage point of Trieste, Joyce concluded, however, that the important features of his country were its natural beauty and the hospitality and ingenuousness of its people (*Letters II* 166). Gabriel's after-dinner speech expands Joyce's meditation on the positive traits that are distinctively Irish, adding "those qualities of humanity, of hospitality, of kindly humour which belonged to an older day" (*D* 203). In the speech, as revenge for her calling him West Briton, Gabriel means to imply that Miss Ivors does not have these qualities, but he ends by condemning himself. In seeking revenge against a guest, Gabriel shows a complete lack of humanity, hospitality, and kindly humour. But he also lacks another, and even more important, Irish quality.

One of Joyce's notes to *Exiles* asserts that the relation between Parnell and Kitty O'Shea is "not of vital significance for Ireland" because "she was an Englishwoman" whose "manner of loving is not Irish" (*E* 127). The note does not define the Irish manner of loving; however, since Ireland was progressively Anglicized both geographically, beginning in the East, and chronologically, beginning with the earliest English invasions, it was a perfectly sound premise of the Revival that in order to find the Irish manner of doing anything one looked to the past and to the West. Located both in the past and in the West, Michael Furey's way of loving Gretta gets a double imprimatur as the Irish way.

Gabriel introduces the subject of love in Ireland, which well might be the main subject of "The Dead," when he asks Lily if she won't be marrying soon. Her blunt reply, "The men that is now is only all palaver and what they can get out of you" (*D* 178), turns out to be one of the shrewdest observations in the story. It pierces the two principal male characters with nicely sharpened mountingpins, Browne all palaver and Gabriel, particularly in the hotel room, all out for what he can get. The story of Michael Furey, whose only surviving words are that "he did not want to live" (*D* 221) if Gretta went away, confirms the precision of Lily's reference to the men "now": in the past, men were different. Revivalists bemoaned the disappearance of such things as the Irish language, Irish games, and Irish music. Joyce has Lily note the more significant loss of a way of loving. Another important feature of the people in "The Dead," aside from their being more sophisticated than the other characters in *Dubliners,* is that, with the exception of Gabriel and Gretta, they are all unmarried. This unmarried state, not only of the elderly Kate and Julia but also of the young or relatively young Mary Jane and Miss Ivors, seems a subtle commentary on the disappearance of the Irish manner of loving.

While the most overt link between Gabriel and Browne comes from their difficulties with women, the most overt contrast between them lies in their responses to the difficulties. Whereas Browne remains unaware that there are any difficulties, Gabriel exaggerates them. He overreacts first to Lily's retort about men, then to Miss Ivors' calling him "West Briton" and finally to Gretta's story about Michael Furey. Recalling the story, Gabriel thinks, "He had never felt like that himself toward any woman but he knew that such a feeling must be love" (*D* 223). Of course, as is made clear by the story of his elopement with Gretta and his memory of the way he caressed her first letter to him (*D* 213), it is not true that he had "never felt like that." The problem is that his feelings toward her have changed. If the change is partly a consequence of years of marriage, it also is a logical result of the cultural self-transformation that Gabriel has striven for. Erasing the stigma of his Irishness and entrenching himself in the exalted state of a gentleman has become more important for him than retaining either his love for Gretta or her love for him.

Gabriel's overreaction to Lily, Miss Ivors, and Gretta and his mistaken feeling that they are rebuffing him show that beneath his veneer of sophistication, he has some serious doubts about what he has become. Those doubts surface clearly in his fear that "he would only make himself ridiculous" by quoting poetry in his speech, and in his sudden sense that "[h]is whole speech was a mistake from first to last, an utter failure" (*D* 179). He also is rightfully uneasy with his assumption that Irish people and ways are inferior. His petulant outburst, "I'm sick of my own country, sick of it!" (*D* 189) is the response of a man who, as Miss Ivors recognizes, has no satisfactory defense for his feelings.

Gabriel's doubts and uneasiness about himself distinguish him from the imperviously self-satisfied Mr. Browne, much as Richard Rowan, who has "a deep wound of doubt" (*E* 112), differs from Robert Hand in *Exiles*. These doubts also enable his transformation at the end of the story when he undergoes a sort of conversion that involves a reassessment of his cultural aims and an acceptance of his Irish Catholic roots. The first evidence of this change comes with Gabriel's story about Patrick Morkan and the horse Johnny. Whereas earlier he had been very sensitive about Gretta's Galway origins, he minimizes his grandfather's position, saying that he was "a glue boiler" (Aunt Kate explains that he ran a starch mill). He also exaggerates the lowliness of his grandfather's address, placing it "somewhere near Back Lane" (Kate explains that "only the mill was there") (*D* 207–208). Though there is no sign that Gabriel recognizes any connection between his own ambition and his grandfather's, the story is the antithesis of his stilted after-dinner speech, where the allusions to the three graces and the Judgment of Paris show off his "level of culture." With its dependence on Dublin details, Gabriel's story is as distinctively Irish as Mr. Browne's patter about Mrs. Cassidy but less superficially so, being based on Gabriel's own family history. Infused with the "kindly humour" that Gabriel identifies as a quality of the older generation, it also signals an emerging sense of attachment to his people.

Gabriel's new cultural direction is manifested when the cab ride after the party takes him north, across the Liffey into territory that is traditionally Catholic. Here he immediately sees the presiding statue of that arch-

Catholic, Daniel O'Connell. Though O'Connell's grade of culture earned him Yeats' scorn as "the Great Comedian,"[18] Gabriel greets the statue with a friendly, "Good-night, Dan" (*D* 214). In a similar vein, he says of Freddy Malins, "Well, poor fellow, he's a decent sort of chap after all. . . . It's a pity he wouldn't keep away from that Browne, because he's not a bad fellow at heart" (*D* 216–217). Partly because it is made almost without thinking, while he awaits a sign of Gretta's mood, this comment reveals a significant cleavage in Gabriel's sympathies. If we look back at what happened at the party, we find that Browne took good care of Malins; nevertheless, Gabriel sides with the Catholic and blames the Protestant. (The people at the party respond in similar fashion, welcoming Gabriel in spite of his stuffiness and superior attitude, while they often give Browne the cold shoulder.)

Gabriel's new cultural direction also is reflected in the sound track or musical accompaniment that Joyce gives "The Dead." Having begun with Mary Jane's sterile Academy piece and Aunt Julia's complicated Italian aria, the accompaniment ends with Bartell D'Arcy singing "The Lass of Aughrim." Along with its setting in the West of Ireland, this simple ballad has, it seems to Gabriel, "an old Irish tonality" (*D* 210). When he asks Gretta why the song has had such a powerful effect on her, she explains that Michael Furey used to sing it (*D* 218–219); but the ballad also has a direct parallel to her current life, since she has been spiritually abandoned by the socially superior Gabriel Conroy, as the Lass of Aughrim was physically abandoned by the socially superior Lord Gregory.

The final push that moves Gabriel away from his West British ambitions and toward his Irish heritage comes from Gretta's story about Michael Furey, whose love for her—like the humanity, kindly humor, and hospitality that Gabriel praises in his speech—has nothing to do with "grade of culture." From the story of this boy in the gasworks, the sophisticated Gabriel learns that he not only has been ignorant of his people, as Miss Ivors claimed, but also has seriously underestimated them, while overestimating himself and overvaluing the image of the cultivated gentleman toward which he aspired. Chastened, he abandons his desire to overmaster Gretta and quietly withdraws, "shy of intruding on her grief" (*D* 221). In this self-sacrificing gesture, motivated by love, Gabriel imitates Michael Furey. He thus becomes more profoundly Irish than Browne or anyone else in the story, including Miss Ivors with her Gaelic jewelry and phrases. Gabriel thinks, "The time had come for him to set out on his journey westward"

(*D* 223), but spiritually he already has traveled a considerable distance on that journey.

For Douglas Hyde, as for Miss Ivors and other Revivalists, the main way to become more Irish was to learn the language; but for the Joyce of "The Dead," the way you love is more important than the language you speak. We can be fairly certain that when Gabriel sets out on his journey westward, it will not be to follow Miss Ivors' belief that he should study Irish. The story also conflicts with the standard Revival view of West Britonism. Whereas Revivalists condemned West Britonism because it damaged Irish culture, the point in "The Dead" is that Gabriel's West Britonism has damaged his relations with Gretta, in other words, his manner of loving.

The story does not attack West Britonism itself. There is no suggestion that anything is wrong with the Morkans having English pictures on their walls or failing to have Irish music and dances at their party. Likewise, Joyce's West of Ireland figures, Michael Furey and Gretta Conroy, are equally far removed from the pious, Irish-speaking peasants inhabiting the West imagined by Catholic Revivalists and from the quaint comic peasants of the Abbey stage. The story clashes most obviously with Revival dogma by revealing the presence of positive Irish traits in urban Dublin as well as in the rural West. For all his fame as a hater of Ireland, Joyce produces in "The Dead" a more broadly sympathetic picture of the country than appears in the work of Yeats, Synge, Lady Gregory, or the other writers normally identified with the Revival.

In a memorable phrase, Richard Ellmann calls "The Dead" Joyce's "first song of exile" (*JJII* 253). "Araby" and "An Encounter," are important preludes to that song. Even more than Michael Furey's love for Gretta, the narrator's devotion to Mangan's sister in "Araby" reveals a facet of splendor in Irish Catholic culture. The loyalty of the ragged children and Mahoney in "An Encounter" exposes another such facet. The parallels between "An Encounter" and "The Dead" are particularly striking, the uncultivated Irish Catholics in both stories displaying qualities that make them in ways superior to the cultivated central characters, who previously had looked down on them.

If "The Dead" is Joyce's first song of exile, it also is his last. From now on he will aim for a more balanced account of Ireland and the Irish. Never again will he recall the Irish with the strong sympathy that colors "The Dead," but neither will he treat them with the relentless harshness characteristic of "A Mother" and "Ivy Day" or "The Two Gallants." With respect to one issue, this balance darkens the picture of Ireland. Whereas *Dubliners* is almost entirely free of examples of sectarian animosity, in Joyce's subsequent works, instances of such animosity begin to appear along with occasional allusions to past episodes of sectarian violence and bloodshed. The Protestants who appear, however, are shown living in relative harmony with Catholics.

CHAPTER FOUR

Stephen Hero and *A Portrait of the Artist*

The published pages of *Stephen Hero* contain a nearly complete version of the part of the novel that Joyce called "the University College episode" and that he later condensed into Chapter V of *A Portrait of the Artist*. The episode, which often focuses on the manifestations of the Revival within UCD, contains Joyce's most extensive account of the movement. It distinguishes a Griffithite political strain of cultural nationalism from an apolitical strain such as Moran advocated. Perhaps because Joyce inclined toward Griffith rather than Moran, the political strain figures more prominently in *Stephen Hero* and is treated more sympathetically. For the most part, however, the novel criticizes the Irish Revival whatever its form. Composed in early 1905, the novel attacks the movement and its followers with much the same satirical harshness found in "A Mother," which Joyce wrote later that year. This attack on the Revival is closely linked to an even harsher one on the Catholic Church, whose ties with the Revival Stephen sees as extensive and insidious.

The assessment of the Revival in *Stephen Hero* comes mainly from Stephen, who at this stage in the book's development is essentially Joyce's mouthpiece. Like Joyce, he also is full of contradictions. On the one hand, he claims indifference to the Irish problems that preoccupy the UCD student nationalists and Revivalists. We are told that "he could not take to heart the distress of a nation, the soul of which was antipathetic to his own, so bitterly as the indignity of a bad line of verse" (*SH* 146). In the next sentence, however, we are told that he "wished to express his nature freely and fully for the benefit of a society which he would enrich." This plan to "enrich" his society—presumably Ireland—puts him close to, if not in, the camp of Yeats and other literary Revivalists who thought of their work as contributing to the country.

The information that Stephen might be considered "an ally of the collectivist politicians" (*SH* 147) gives a possible clue to the sort of enrichment he had in mind, but this suggestion that he is an incipient socialist borders on the preposterous. Stephen shows no interest in, or even awareness of, an Irish working class or labor movement. Though he recognizes that there are gross inequities of power and wealth in Ireland, he does not relate them in any way to capitalism nor does he show any interest in seeing them corrected. The forces in the country that most occupy his mind are not capitalism and socialism but Irish nationalism and the Catholic Church. What concerns him most about these two forces is their relationship to intellectual freedom, which he prizes above all else. When he speaks of enriching his society through expressing his nature, he apparently means promoting intellectual freedom through some sort of autobiographical writing.

One of Stephen's main objections to the Revival is that it does not aim at providing this sort of freedom. Alluding to efforts at reviving the Irish language and to a related habit of wearing items of Gaelic clothing, like Miss Ivors' brooch with the "Irish device," he dismisses the liberty desired by Revivalists as "mainly a liberty of costume and vocabulary" (*SH* 61). According to Joyce, rather than being simply indifferent to freedom of thought, the Catholic Church has waged a powerful and effective war against it, turning the Irish into intellectual slaves and cowards. In a long passage describing Stephen's reaction to the depressing scenes he observes in walks around Dublin, Joyce summarizes the church's effect on the Irish:

> These wanderings filled [Stephen] with deep-seated anger and whenever he encountered a burly black-vested priest taking a stroll of pleasant inspection through these warrens full of swarming and cringing believers he cursed the farce of Irish Catholicism: an island [whereof] the inhabitants of which entrust their wills and minds to others that they may ensure for themselves a life of spiritual paralysis, an island in which all the power and riches are in the keeping of those whose kingdom is not of this world, an island in which Caesar . . . confesses Christ and Christ confesses Caesar that together they may wax fat upon a starveling rabblement . . . (*SH* 146).

Allusions to the church in this passage have all the rhetorical violence of an Irish nationalist denouncing England. It is not only the rhetoric of Stephen's assessment that is reminiscent of Irish nationalism but also the nature of the indictment itself. Joyce's charges that the church controls the nation's wealth and power and turns the people into slaves are the same ones that Moran made against Protestants and that traditional Irish nationalists made against England. The forces of Irish nationalism appear to have influenced Joyce in ways he perhaps did not realize.

The above lengthy assessment of the church's effect on Ireland explains Stephen's conviction that in attacking England, Irish nationalists missed the real enemy. As Joyce puts it, "The Roman, not the Sassenach, was for [Stephen] the tyrant of the islanders" (*SH* 53). Joyce shows that, rather than being attacked by the Revival for its tyranny over the Irish, the church had become a powerful influence within the movement. He reports that the public meetings of the Gaelic League "were largely patronised by priests," who "made speeches of exhortation" to those present (*SH* 61). He also notes the presence of a young priest in the Gaelic classes that Stephen attends for a while to get closer to Emma. Stephen himself particularly notices that Emma often converses with the young priest (*SH* 65–66). Her reaction is perhaps meant to illustrate the power of the church over Irish minds, but Stephen's anger at her behavior makes sexual jealousy seem the main issue.

Concluding that the church was a friend of their movement, Revivalists made the defense of this hallowed institution part of their program. They adopted the watch cry "Faith and Fatherland," Joyce says, and thus simultaneously called for Irish freedom and lent support to a tyrannical church (*SH* 53). In a scene at the nationalist Daniels' household underscoring the incongruity of this alliance, Joyce writes that while Mr. Daniels recited "national pieces," presumably celebrating Ireland's struggle for freedom, "Stephen's eye never moved from the picture of the Sacred Heart which hung right above . . . the reciter's head" (*SH* 44). Another scene at the Daniels', this one featuring a "little fat white priest," illustrates Stephen's claim that the interest of the church in Irish nationalism and the Revival is only pretense. The priest, who is the guest of honor and the center of attention, says that he is "greatly interested in the new Gaelic revival and in the new literary movement in Ireland." A moment later, however, we hear him agreeing that Gladstone "was the greatest man of the nineteenth century." To Joyce's mind, a true Irish nationalist might think Parnell deserved that ranking but would never grant it to an English politician, especially not to one who helped bring down Parnell. Though Stephen would recognize that the priest's praise of Gladstone "shows forth" the falsity of his professed interest in Irish matters, no one else appears to have noticed the epiphany. Joyce tells us that "when [the priest] spoke the room was all ears" and that Mr. Daniels was "glowing with pride" at having "so honorable a guest" (*SH* 156–157).

The Revival's alliance with the church results in a doubly strong coercive force. Joyce illustrates the coercive nature of the partnership at the meeting of the Literary and Historical Society where Stephen reads his paper celebrating Ibsen and continental drama. On the one hand, the students attack his paper on xenophobic grounds inspired by Irish nationalism, claiming that it promotes "the decadent literary opinions of exhausted European capitals." On the other hand, they accuse his essay of being "hostile to the spirit of religion" and claim that it is contaminated "by atheistic poisons" (*SH* 102–103). Whether deriving from mainly religious or mainly nationalist sentiments, the responses to Stephen's paper reveal that the UCD Revivalists are energetic allies of the church in its battle against intellectual freedom.

While the scenes at the Daniels' and at the Gaelic League meetings criticize the Revival generally, Joyce's main target in *Stephen Hero* is the UCD Revivalists. He charges them with two main faults besides the inclination toward intellectual coercion that they display in their attacks on Stephen's paper. One of these faults is that they are ideologues who prefer Revivalist and nationalist dogmas to freedom of thought. Stephen refers to them as "the compact body of national revivalists" and distinguishes them from the small "intelligent center" of the College, where people "had certain ideas of their own" (*SH* 38–39). The compact nature of the group is apparent in their united attack on Stephen's paper as well as in their shared belief in the received ideas of the Irish Revival that make up the terms of their attack. The second main failing of the UCD Revivalists is that, like Mr. Daniels and the priest and others we meet at the Daniels' house, they are mummers or hypocrites whose commitment to the Revival is largely a pretense. Pouncing on their duplicity with strange ferocity, Stephen describes the UCD Revivalists as "fit to inhabit the fraudulent circles [of Dante's *Inferno*] where hidden in hives of immaculate ice they might work their bodies to the due pitch of frenzy" (*SH* 158–159). In the most common manifestation of their fraudulence they profess a detestation of everything English while preparing themselves for positions in the civil service, which, Stephen points out, means that they will be "pledged to the [English] government and paid by the [English] Government" (*SH* 64).

Joyce singles out for special attention two leading student Revivalists, Hughes and Madden. Based on Louis J. Walsh, who was one of the chief attackers of Joyce's paper on "Art and Life," Hughes comes from Armagh, as did Walsh, and speaks with "a cutting Northern accent," nearly always the sign of an unsympathetic character in Joyce.[1] Laying it on, Joyce describes Hughes as "having a very sick-looking smile and a very crooked mouth." The main exemplar of UCD's "national revivalists," Hughes teaches a sparsely attended Irish language class, which he pelts with Revival clichés, denouncing "seoninism" or West Britonism and those Irish "who would not learn their native tongue." Following Revival doctrine, he explains that English is "the language of commerce and Irish the speech of the soul" (*SH* 59). He also regularly attends the Friday night public meetings of the Gaelic League, where he gives speeches full of similar clichés. He attacks the Irish Parliamentary Party, for example, because its members "had taken oaths of allegiance to the Queen of England," which he says a true patriot never would do (*SH* 60).

Like Kathleen Kearny, Hughes is known by "everyone" as "a great enthusiast" of the Irish language. Joyce explains, however, that when Hughes spoke at League meetings he used English "as he did not know enough Irish." That he used the language of the enemy did not bother the League audience, who, we are told, "always loudly applauded" his speeches (*SH* 60).

As he does at the Gaelic League meetings, Hughes takes a vocal part in the L & H meeting where Stephen reads his paper. A number of students attack the paper, but Joyce says that the "climax of aggressiveness was reached when Hughes stood up." Hughes proceeds to barrage Stephen with a battery of commonplace Revival charges, claiming that the ideas in his paper were "foreign filth" and a menace to "the moral welfare of the Irish people," condemning him for ignoring the "glorious literature" of Ireland, and finally calling him a "professed cosmopolitan" and "renegade from the Nationalist ranks" (*SH* 103).

As was mentioned earlier, Walsh was an enthusiastic follower of Moran. Though Moran's name is not mentioned anywhere in *Stephen Hero,* Walsh's attachment to Moran is reflected in Hughes' attack on Trinity College.

Yeats and other Revivalists criticized Trinity for its West British scorn of Irish culture; but like Moran, Hughes objects to it on sectarian grounds, proclaiming that "he could not regard as a national university an institution which did not express the religious convictions of the majority of the Irish people" (*SH* 59–60) Also, like Moran, Hughes advocates the revival of Irish culture but not political separation from England.

While the triteness of his opinions and of his charges against Stephen calls in question the sincerity of Hughes' belief in the Revival, Stephen's discovery that Hughes is studying for a career in law provides the chief evidence of his fraudulence. Stephen points out that Hughes not only is preparing himself to administer "English law" but also that in order to administer it he will have to take the same oath of allegiance to the Queen of England that he condemns Parliamentary Party members for taking.

Based on Joyce's college friend George Clancy, whose nationalist politics probably contributed to his murder by the British Black and Tans in 1921, Madden is identified as "the spokesman of the patriotic party" (*SH* 39). Why Joyce describes the party this way is not clear, but the party has as one of its leading members a figure based on Michael Cusack. This person holds court in a tobacco shop, as did Cusack, where various people come to report, among them Madden and also "the editor of the weekly journal of the irreconcilable party" (*SH* 61). This editor, of course, was Griffith and the journal, *United Irishman*. Joyce says that these irreconcilables or separatists took as their chief inspiration "the case of Hungary," which Griffith explained in a series of articles holding up Hungary as a model for Ireland to follow (*SH* 62).

Hughes and Madden, then, reflect the two conflicting strains of Revival nationalism in UCD and Ireland at the time: the apolitical cultural nationalism of D. P. Moran, and the separatist political nationalism of Arthur Griffith. Unlike Moran and Griffith, the two young men are portrayed as friends, (in a conversation with Madden, Stephen refers to Hughes as "your friend"[*SH* 63]). Madden also admires Hughes' poetry, several examples of which he carries about with him and shows to an unimpressed Stephen (*SH* 82–83). Though their friendship further justifies the description of UCD Revivalists as a "compact" body, Joyce gives Hughes and Madden sharply contrasting personalities. Hughes is a loudmouthed hypocrite and Madden an example of the eager, sincere Revivalists whom Joyce described in the "Saints and Sages" essay. Madden also becomes one of Stephen's closest friends. The first day they meet we see them walking across the green together: Stephen, in an extraordinary gesture of kindness, has taken Madden under his wing and is conducting him to the library (*SH* 25).

The completely negative portrait of Hughes and the decidedly sympathetic one of Madden doubtless stem in part from a difference in Joyce's feelings about their real life models. These characterizations may also stem in part from Joyce's underlying attraction to separatist politics. In *Stephen Hero,* as in *A Portrait of the Artist,* Joyce keeps any such attraction well hidden. In fact, he shows Stephen denouncing the independence from England advocated by Madden and other separatists as "a poor scarecrow of liberty," because it aims at mere political freedom while ignoring the intellectual tyranny exercised by the church (*SH* 61).

In the scenes with Madden, Joyce shows Stephen dispatching a series of other Revival dogmas and practices, among them the Revival's alliance with the church. Madden claims that the alliance is "politic." "If the least infidelity were hoisted on the standard," he says, "the people would not flock to it." He admits that in the past the church had opposed rather than helped nationalist movements but claims that now the priests are "on the side of the people" (*SH* 53). Stephen counters that the priests have no real interest in the Revival but "encourage the study of Irish that their flocks may be more safely protected from the wolves of disbelief." "[T]hey consider it is an opportunity to withdraw the people into a past of literal, implicit faith," he says (*SH* 54). Here, as throughout the novel, Joyce presents Stephen's opinions in such a way as to make them always appear the true ones.

Having dispatched the notion that the church was a friend to the Revival, Stephen next takes on Revival dogma about Irish peasants. When Madden claims that the Irish peasant is free from "the gross materialism of the Yorkshire peasant," Stephen replies, "One would imagine the country was inhabited by cherubim." He adds, "Damme if I see much difference in peasants. . . . The Yorkshireman is perhaps better fed." When Madden defends the "simple life" of the peasant, Stephen responds, "Yes, a life of dull routine—the calculation of coppers, the weekly debauch and the weekly piety—a life lived in cunning and fear between the shadows of the parish chapel and the asylum!" Finally, when Davin argues for the superior chastity of the peasant and the Irish generally, Stephen agrees that "my countrymen have not yet advanced as far as the machinery of Parisian harlotry" and then explains "because they do it by hand." Madden has no response to this blunt charge except for a feeble, "O, Daedalus!" (*SH* 54–55).

Though Madden is free of Hughes' militant intolerance, the members of his "party" aren't, particularly when it comes to any criticism of Griffith's Hungarian plan. Joyce writes that they became "aflame with indignation at any young sceptic who was aware of the capable aggressions of the Magyars upon the Latin and Slav and Teutonic populations" (*SH* 62). The awareness of this young sceptic, presumably Stephen, calls attention to some harsh facts that Griffith omitted from his inspirational account of Hungarian politics and that his followers also presumably ignored.

In one of the few positive remarks about Revivalists in *Stephen Hero,* Joyce says that the students in the Irish language class "learned quickly and worked very hard" (*SH* 60). This presumably includes Emma Clery, whose presence in the class drew Stephen to it; however, her eagerness to let him know on their first meeting that "she always signed her name in Irish" implies that her interest in the language is not deep. There is a suggestion of the "compact body" not only in her devotion to the Irish form of her name but also in her decision to go to the Aran Islands "with a Gaelic party," as Miss Ivors proposes in "The Dead" (*SH* 161–162). There is a similar suggestion when at the Daniels' she is observed "in deep conversation with Hughes" and asks Stephen to sing an Irish song. Joyce writes, "When the song was over she applauded loudly and so did Hughes." This further linking of her with Hughes is not complimentary. She goes on to say, "I love the Irish music" and then, "inclining herself towards him with an air of oblivion," adds, "it is so soul-stirring." The nicely calculated "air of oblivion" does not contribute to faith in her sincerity. Stephen finishes the job by reflecting that he has been unable to find "a spiritual principle in her worthy of so significant a name as soul" (*SH* 155–156).

Although in the "Saints and Sages" essay Joyce makes a point of acknowledging and attacking the anti-Protestant side of Catholic nationalism, he ignores it in *Stephen Hero,* except for Hughes' sectarian remark about Trinity College. But Stephen does exhibit a pronounced bias, though it takes a different form from that found among Catholic nationalists. While they typically focused on cultural and economic differences between Protestants and Catholics, Stephen dwells on intellectual and spiritual differences. Joyce writes that Stephen's abandonment of the formal practice of

Catholicism resulted in his paying more attention to Jesus but did not lead him to "a consideration of the merits of Protestantism." Stephen "was quite sure," Joyce explains, "that behind the enigmatic utterances of Jesus there was a very much more definite conception than any which could be supposed . . . discoverable behind Protestant theology" (*SH* 113). The implication, of course, is that Catholic theology is superior because it has this "definite conception." Summing up the lack of rigor in Protestantism, Stephen says, "Protestant Orthodoxy is like Lanty McHale's dog: it goes a bit of the road with everyone" (*SH* 112). Again, the implication is that Catholicism is more rigorous than Protestantism and hence superior.

Joyce elaborates on this contrast later when he shows Stephen meditating on his relationship to the Catholic Church and on the position of both the Catholic Church and the Protestant Church with regard to the issues of art and "human liberty." Concerning the first issue, Stephen asks himself rhetorically, "[D]uring the formulation of his artistic creed, had he not found item after item upheld for him in advance by the greatest and most orthodox doctor of the church?" The obvious answer to this question, with its allusion to Aquinas, is, "Yes." The answer is resoundingly confirmed in Stephen's acknowledgment that "the entire theory, in accordance with which his entire artistic life was shaped, arose . . . out of the mass of Catholic theology." Joyce amplifies this line of reflection by having Stephen conclude, "The Puritan, the Calvinist, the Lutheran were inimical to art and to exuberant beauty: the Catholic was the friend of him who professed to interpret or divulge the beautiful" (*SH* 205). What is perhaps most remarkable about Stephen's praise of Catholicism is that it clashes sharply with the many passages in the book denouncing the church and its priests. Joyce seems to have held the not easily reconcilable opinions that, while the Catholic Church in Ireland was tyrannical and destructive, in general, it was a virtually flawless institution.

Stephen's views on the relationship of the two denominations to the question of human liberty revolve around a similar contrast. We are told that he rejected Protestantism because "he knew that the liberty it boasted of was often only the liberty to be slovenly in thought and amorphous in ritual." According to Joyce, Stephen also knew that even "the most rabid enemy" of the Catholic Church could not accuse it of those failings (*SH* 205). Stephen alludes to this contrast in response to Cranly's criticism of him for asking Emma to go to bed with him. Stephen says that Lynch would not have objected if he had asked her to marry him. Lynch agrees: "Marriage is a custom," he says, and "to follow a custom is a mark of sanity." Stephen retorts, "It is a mark of ordinariness." Apparently it is Cranly's willingness to follow custom, like Lanty McHale's goat, that leads Stephen to tell him, "Your everyday life is Protestant: you show yourself Catholic only when you discuss" (*SH* 201).

Of the changes Joyce made in rewriting *Stephen Hero* as *A Portrait of the Artist,* one of the most extensive was to greatly reduce attention to the Revival. He eliminated all passages about the supposed alliance between Revivalists and the church. He also eliminated those about Hughes and his crude revivalism and, along with them, reflections of the split at UCD between the followers of Moran and of Griffith. Madden reappears with few changes as "Davin." Described as having "sat at the feet of Michael Cusack, the Gael" (*P* 180), Davin follows one of the Revival leaders Madden admired, but has no links with Griffith, who is not referred to anywhere in *A Portrait of the Artist*. These changes produce a far more sympathetic picture of the Revival than appears in *Stephen Hero*.

Another of Joyce's important changes was to make Stephen an independent character rather than the author's mouthpiece, and also to make him a more complex character. Stephen no longer simply divorces himself from Ireland as in *Stephen Hero,* but instead he takes his Irish heritage seriously. Offended by Davin's question, "Are you Irish at all?" Stephen says, "Come with me now to the office of arms and I will show you the tree of my family" (*P* 202). Because he takes his heritage seriously, the decisions he makes regarding his relationship to Ireland become major events in the novel. These decisions, in turn, often have to do with central issues of the Revival.

One such issue is the relationship between the two Irelands, which figures in *A Portrait* from the time Stephen is a small child until the end of the novel when he announces his bold literary plan: "I go to encounter for the millionth time the reality of experience and to forge in the smithy of my soul the uncreated conscience of my race" (*P* 253). The problem of this relationship is introduced immediately in Chapter I, where we learn that, like Joyce, Stephen had an early experience with sectarianism. Joyce's experience came when his courtesy aunt, Mrs. Reardon, told him that he would go to hell if he played with his Protestant friend Eileen Vance. If the young Joyce blithely ignored this warning, as Ellmann says (*JJI* 25), he nevertheless remembered the episode twenty years later and patterned his depiction of Stephen's first encounter with sectarianism on it. We hear of the encounter during the Christmas dinner episode, where it comes up in an apparent *non sequitur* that effectively conveys the irrationality of sectarianism as well as Stephen's difficulty in making sense of the division between the two Irelands. Recalling his father's description of Dante as a "spoiled nun," Stephen muses, "Perhaps that made her severe against Parnell. And she did not like him to play with Eileen because Eileen was a protestant and when she was young she knew children that used to play with protestants and the protestants used to make fun of the litany of the Blessed Virgin" (*P* 35). If the original warning carried a threat of hell, as Ellmann reports, Joyce made the fictional version more intensely sectarian by substituting the story about Protestants making fun of a particularly important part of Catholic liturgy.

The news about Dante's warning is related to an earlier passage that also turns on an apparent *non sequitur*. The well-known passage runs, "When they were grown up [Stephen] was going to marry Eileen. He hid under the table. His mother said: 'O, Stephen will apologise.' Dante said: 'O, if not, the eagles will come and pull out his eyes' " (*P* 8). The later information that Eileen was a Protestant and that Dante did not like Stephen to play with Protestants, allows us to fill the narrative gap with a likely sequence of events. Apparently the news that Stephen intended to marry Eileen elicited some warning from Dante, possibly the one he recalls at the Christmas dinner, and he retorted in a way thought to require an apology. Whatever happened, the text implies (and many readers assume) some connection between Stephen's friendship with a Protestant and his first traumatic experience. It is logical for Stephen to recall the sectarian key to this episode during an argument where Catholics are debating the issue of loyalty to a Protestant leader.

The sectarian undercurrent to the Christmas dinner argument first surfaces when Dante accuses Simon and Mr. Casey of being "renegade catholics" and using language that "the blackest protestant in the land would not speak" ("black" Protestants being those who hated Catholics and/or the Catholic Church) (*P* 34–35). Joyce makes it clear that Dante is not the only one at the table who has strong sectarian feelings. They are intense enough even in the outspoken anti-cleric Mr. Casey that he flushes when he denies Dante's charge (*P* 35). His allusion to the time when "we [Catholics] gave up our lives rather than sell our faith" is a reminder of the deep roots those feelings have in Irish history. (It also points to an important component of the Catholic ancestral memory.) The exchange between Dante and Mr. Casey establishes the context for Stephen's recollection of Dante's warning.

The warning passage seems less of a *non sequitur* when its two elements are arranged in chronological order—Dante "did not like him to play with Eileen because Eileen was a protestant," and she was "severe against Parnell." If Stephen knew that Parnell also was a Protestant, he would have recognized that sectarian feelings probably had as much to do with Dante's severity against Parnell as did either her being a spoiled nun or her professed obedience to the priests of the Catholic Church. A Catholic who thinks Catholic children should not play with Protestants cannot be altogether comfortable supporting a Protestant as leader of the country. Dante's departing cry of victory over the fallen Protestant, "Devil out of hell! We won! We crushed him to death! Fiend!" (*P* 39) removes any doubt about the sectarian feelings behind her attitude toward Parnell. Though Joyce enjoyed blaming Parnell's fall on some mysterious compulsion of the Irish to betray their leaders, his treatment of the Christmas dinner quarrel acknowledges what Roy Foster has called "the ineluctable sectarian reality of Irish politics." [2]

Sectarian animosity is implicated in two especially painful episodes of young Stephen's life: the demand that he apologize to Dante and the Christmas dinner quarrel, which left him "terrorstricken" (*P* 39). Presumably these episodes contribute significantly to the formative process that he later refers to when he says, "This race and this country and this life produced me" (*P* 203). In a scene back at Clongowes after the Christmas dinner Joyce dramatizes the influence on Stephen that Dante's warning about playing with Protestants has had. Having recalled that Eileen's hands were "like ivory" and decided, "That was the meaning of *Tower of Ivory,*" Stephen thinks, "but protestants could not understand it and made fun of it" (*P* 42). Dante's story about Protestants has lodged in Stephen's mind as a fact about them, giving him the initial contours of a bigot. Of all the reasons for leaving Ireland that are developed in Chapter I, the country's capacity for molding bigots is among the most persuasive.

Ireland's long history of troubled relations with England offers an equally potent motive for leaving. This history dominates the Christmas dinner quarrel over Parnell but is featured elsewhere in the chapter through allusions to nationalist leaders such as Michael Davitt, Wolfe Tone and Tone's friend, Hamilton Rowan, whose flight from British soldiers intrigues young Stephen (*P* 10).

Following Chapter I, allusions to Ireland and its problems disappear from the novel until Chapter V. There, true to the "chiastic" structure noted by Hans Walter Gabler, Ireland once again becomes an important focus.[3] But it is a different Ireland. In the ten years or so between the two chapters, the Irish Revival has been born. Contrasts between Chapters I and V dramatize the resulting changes. In Chapter I, for example, we find the boys playing the English games of rugby and cricket, neither of which is even mentioned in Chapter V (*P* 8, 59). Instead, we find there that the games are Irish hurling and handball (*P* 182, 203–204). Likewise, in Chapter I Parnell and Tone are admired as nationalist leaders, but in Chapter V Stephen alone remembers them (*P* 20, 203). And whereas the political nationalists of Chapter I, Simon Dedalus and Mr. Casey, are anti-clerical and admire the old Protestant leaders; Davin, who is *the* nationalist of Chapter V, is a devout Catholic and never mentions Tone, Parnell or other Protestant nationalists. Instead, Davin has been inspired by the Catholic Michael Cusack (*P* 180).

Ireland becomes a major subject of Chapter V because for the first time Stephen thinks about his country and his relationship to it. This development would be natural for a person his age who finds himself in the midst of the Revival: it would be almost unavoidable for someone like Stephen, who also was a student at UCD, surrounded by fervent Irish Irelanders. We get an insight into Stephen's thoughts about various features of Ireland early in the Chapter during the long Bloom-like walk that he takes through Dublin on his belated way to classes at UCD. A repeated trait of these thoughts is that they resemble Revival or Irish Ireland dogmas while at the same time differing in key respects. A typical example is Stephen's reaction as he walks by Trinity College and begins "striving this way and that to free his feet from the fetters of the reformed conscience" (*P* 180). The effect of this Protestant institution on Stephen, which must have astonished onlookers, might be taken as evidence that Dante's bigotry has left its mark on him, but during the Revival, Trinity also was under attack from Revivalists, who denounced it as a bastion of English influences. While Stephen clearly shares the Revivalists' negative view of Trinity, it is not because he sees the college as a source of English influence. Neither does he attribute to Trinity the anti-Catholic sentiments that Dante and other

Catholics associated with Protestants. In addition to revealing a highly individualized bias against Protestantism, Joyce's description of Stephen's reaction to Trinity introduces the issue of "conscience," which will have a central place in Stephen's literary plan to forge "the uncreated conscience" of his race (*P* 253).

One might expect Stephen to find his own Catholic college a comforting contrast to Trinity; instead it seems to him even more sinister (*P* 184). He identifies UCD with "a corruption other than," though apparently not less than, "that of Buck Egan and Burnchapel Whaley," two Protestants whose lives are associated with the earlier history of the college building and whose notorious behavior provided Catholics with one of their favorite evidences of Protestant immorality, as opposed to their own presumed moral purity. According to Stephen, the contrast between Protestants and Catholics is not between the corrupt and the uncorrupt but between different kinds of corruption. A clue to the kind Stephen associates with UCD comes in his conversation with the dean of studies, who urges him to work hard and get his degree. "It may be uphill pedalling at first," the dean says. "Take Mr Moonan. He was a long time before he got to the top. But he got there" (*P* 190). Readers will remember that in Chapter I Moonan was identified as "McGlade's suck" and also was one of those caught "smugging" (*P* 11, 42). This memory exposes a chill irony in Stephen's "quiet" response to the dean, "I may not have [Moonan's] talent" (*P* 190). The corruption Stephen associates with UCD may explain his depressed feeling on entering the college that "the Ireland of Tone and of Parnell [had] receded in space" (*P* 184). This feeling, however, also is appropriate for someone entering an institution where Moran's spirit reigned.

When a strange sense of being watched by the walls of the college building leads Stephen to wonder if this Jesuit house were "extra territorial" and he "among aliens," he calls in question the cherished Catholic notion that their church was somehow native while the Protestant Church was alien (*P* 184). The association of aliens with UCD, rather than with Trinity, sounds capricious or perverse, but Joyce quietly lends it support by seeing that the first person Stephen meets in the college, the dean of studies, is an English convert, whose accent and vocabulary differ from Stephen's (*P* 188–189). The nail is clenched later in the diary entry about the Italian Ghezzi, where Stephen carefully remembers that "his country and not mine . . . invented what Cranly the other night called our religion" (*P* 249).

During his walk Stephen meditates on other important features of Ireland beside the two colleges, among them Thomas Moore. Observing Moore's statue across the street from Trinity, Stephen senses that "sloth of the body and of the soul crept over it like unseen vermin, over the shuffling feet and up the folds of the cloak and around the servile head" (*P* 180). Though extreme, this reaction to Moore is not particularly unorthodox for a Catholic during the Revival. That Moore had attended Trinity, where he was enrolled as a Protestant (apparently to qualify for scholarships, which were not open to Catholics), and that he had married a Protestant would have offended many Catholics during any period of Irish history. Catholic Revivalists, however, would have been especially upset that this "national poet of Ireland" spent most of his career in England entertaining the English. The story is told of a group of Revivalists who were so offended by Moore's behavior that they withdrew from a Gaelic League club when the members persisted in singing Moore's songs. What Stephen most objects to is the aspect of Moore's character reflected in the statue's "servile head." Just a few minutes before coming to the statue, Stephen had imagined "the heads of his classmates meekly bent as they wrote in their notebooks the points they were bidden to note," while "his own head was unbent" (*P* 178). Stephen's association of servility with Catholics turns up again in his recollection of Davin, whom he thinks of by an initially puzzling association with Moore.

The association is puzzling since, in contrast to Moore, Davin is a militant nationalist, not only prepared to take up arms for Ireland but also set steadfastly against "whatsoever of thought or of feeling came to him from England or by way of English culture" (*P* 181). Stephen's persistent references to Davin as a "peasant" signal an even more fundamental contrast with Moore. In the rhetoric of Irish Irelanders as well as of other nationalists during the Revival, the peasant was the polar opposite of the West Briton, and as Moore is the archetypal West Briton, Davin's unquestioning faith in the Catholic church, moral purity and knowledge of things Gaelic make him the model peasant of Irish Irelandism. Joyce even endows him with the same "inbred courtesy" that Moran claimed for Irish peasants. But Davin's attitude toward Ireland and the Catholic church, which Stephen defines as that of "a dullwitted loyal serf," links him firmly to the servile Moore as well as to the UCD students with their bent heads (*P* 181). Moran and other Catholic nationalists railed against Catholics for the same servility that Stephen associates with them. But whereas Moran in particular objected to the servility in Catholics because it allowed Protestants to walk over them, Stephen objects to it because it reveals the absence of a proper pride. He thinks that simple self-respect requires one to stand up and be independent in thought and act. His main exemplars are those "honorable and sincere" men, Tone and Parnell (*P* 203). His admiration for Tone emerges when his walk brings him to the top of Grafton Street and the stone slab in memory of this nationalist leader. There he angrily recalls the "tawdry tribute" paid to Tone when the stone was laid (*P* 184). His admiration for both leaders is emphasized when he finds the corrupt atmosphere of UCD antithetical to them.

Though full of objections to Davin's serflike devotion to faith and fatherland, Stephen has been powerfully impressed by the story he told about the half undressed and possibly pregnant peasant woman who brought him a mug of milk, then held him in conversation, though her breasts were bare, and finally took his hand, saying, "Come in and stay the night here. You've no call to be frightened. There's no one in it but ourselves" (*P* 182–183). The story of this woman, which "rings in [Stephen's] memory," probably has greater significance to him and to the novel than does the famous rococo vision of the "bird girl" at the end of Chapter IV. He sees this peasant woman as "a type of her race and his own, a batlike soul waking to the consciousness of itself in darkness and secrecy and loneliness and, through the eyes and voice and gesture of a woman without guile, calling the stranger to her bed" (*P* 183). Stephen's association of racial identity with this woman is the first glimmer of the place race will play in his literary plan at the end of the novel.

This sense of racial identity, which flatly contradicts Joyce's position on race in the "Saints and Sages" lecture, takes a strange twist concerning "E. C.," whom Stephen thinks of as a type of "her race," but not of his (*P* 220). Does he share the Irish Ireland idea that a Dublin girl like E. C., who has grown up in the Protestant pale, would be less purely Irish than a peasant woman? Certainly Stephen's sense that a peasant typifies his race accords with the ideas of Moran and most other Revivalists about the peasantry. The woman in Davin's story, however, has little in common with the spartan and pious figure celebrated by Moran. Aside from her gender she also has little in common with traditional representatives of the Irish such as Yeats' folk tale Cathleen ni Houlihan or Mangan's mystical Dark Rosaleen, the "virgin flower" with "holy delicate white hands." Unlike these women who appear to know all, Joyce's peasant woman is "waking." Also, whereas Cathleen ni Houlihan and Dark Rosaleen call men to sacrifice themselves for Ireland, she calls them to bed. Moreover, since English invaders were known in Ireland as "the strangers," the image of her "calling the stranger to her bed" suggests that, like Irish women in history and also like Molly Bloom and Anna Livia Plurabelle, she may call foreigners.

Stephen's diary entry for 14 April could be taken as evidence that he completely rejected Revival ideas about the peasant. This entry tells of one John Alphonsus Mulrennan visiting the west of Ireland and speaking Irish with a peasant in a nonsensical conversation "about [the] universe and stars." The entry concludes with Stephen saying of the peasant, "I fear him. I fear his redrimmed horny eyes. It is with him I must struggle all through this night till day come, till he or I lie dead . . ." (*P* 251–252). If there is anything in this passage beyond an exercise in writing hyperbolical prose, it is hard to see what it might be. In any event the diary entry is more than balanced by Stephen's fondness for Davin, whom he regularly thinks of as a peasant, and by his sympathetic and repeated view of the peasant woman as the purest embodiment of his race.

Stephen's reverie about Davin's peasant woman is shattered by the cry of a girl selling flowers in Grafton Street. His encounter with this girl, who wears a ragged dress and has "damp coarse hair and hoydenish face" and who offers herself to him as "your own girl" (*P* 183), is a grotesque Pale version of Davin's experience with the peasant woman. The girl's plea that he buy some flowers and his repeated assertion that he has "no money" also continues the economic motif established in the chapter's opening picture of Stephen's impoverished home. His poverty, which is never far from his mind, represents one half of the unbalanced economic equation that Clery argued was a central issue in Catholic/Protestant relations. The contrast between the massive "grey block" of Trinity College that Stephen passes in his walk and the ramshackle UCD that is his destination would remind anyone familiar with the city of the full equation. During the walk, Stephen touches on a likely consequence of his poverty and the meager university designated for Catholics. We are told, "It wounded him to think that he would never be but a shy guest at the feast of the world's culture" (*P* 180). At this point he comes to Trinity and the statue of Moore, as if to remind us of the Irish Catholics who have sought access to the world's culture or its wealth by enrolling in Trinity.

As both an aspiring poet and a moneyless Catholic, Stephen is in a good position to sympathize with Moore. He sympathizes at least to the extent of looking at Moore's statue "without anger . . . since it seemed humbly conscious of its indignity" (*P* 180). This indignity is the one Stephen identifies more explicitly in *Ulysses* when he finds himself treasuring material for Haine's chapbook. It is the indignity of a poet serving as "a jester at the court of his master, indulged and disesteemed, winning a clement master's praise" (*U* 26). At the moment in *Ulysses* it is the Protestant Mr. Deasy rather than the Englishman Haines who has the position of Stephen's master. Having served a similar master and having once planned a singing tour of English seaside resorts to make money, Joyce was in a good position not only to sympathize with Moore but also to understand the problems he faced. Stephen's encounter with the flower seller in Grafton Street, just beyond Moore's statue, obliquely dramatizes one of those problems. After telling the girl that he has no money, Stephen hurries off, "wishing to be out of her way before she offered her ware to another, a tourist from England or a student from Trinity" (*P* 184). Stephen's complex reaction here exposes a dilemma that historical and economic circumstances have created for Irish Catholics who wish to dispense wares (and they could be literary as well as floral): offering them to other Catholics is futile since they have no money, yet it is somehow wrong, nearly a betrayal, to offer them to Englishmen or to the Protestant students from Trinity. The only way to escape this dilemma, which hinges in part on making the same identification between Irish Protestants and the English that Moran made, is via Holyhead.

Stephen's most explicit comments on Ireland come in response to Davin's plea for him to "be one of us" by becoming an Irish nationalist. Stephen first replies:

> My ancestors threw off their language and took another. . . . They allowed a handful of foreigners to subject them. Do you fancy I am going to pay in my own life and person debts they made? What for?

Davin's explanation, "For our freedom," prompts Stephen's second and more histrionic, as well as more than a little inaccurate, response:

> No honourable and sincere man . . . has given up to you his life and his youth and his affections from the days of Tone to those of Parnell but you sold him to the enemy or failed him in need or reviled him and left him for another. And you invite me to be one of you. I'd see you damned first.

Stephen, who is by this time "following his own thoughts," utters his third response:

> When the soul of a man is born in this country there are nets flung at it to hold it back from flight. You talk to me of nationality, language, religion. I shall try to fly by those nets.

What Stephen calls "nets," are, of course, the central pillars of Catholic nationalism. He concludes his rejection of them by calling Ireland "the old sow that eats her farrow" (*P* 203).

These loud denunciations of the Irish as spineless and self-destructive betrayers are frequently quoted as straightforward expressions not only of Stephen's views but also of Joyce's. But the denunciations are an example of what Joyce describes as "the violent or luxurious language in which Stephen escaped from the cold silence of intellectual revolt" (*P* 181). Stephen's revolt against Irish nationalism, however, is not so much against its basic premises, with many of which he agrees, as against the serflike acceptance of them that he finds in Davin. Stephen insists on finding his own way; in the end, that way will lead him to become as much a patriot as Davin, though of a different kind.

Stephen's responses to Davin's plea to become "one of us" echo things that Joyce himself said about the Irish. On the other hand, Joyce's sympathetic portrayal of Davin gives a more positive picture of an Irish nationalist than appears anywhere else in his work. On discovering that Davin has signed the peace petition, Stephen asks if he will now throw out the military drill manual that he keeps in his room and that reveals his sympathy with physical force nationalism. Davin replies, "That's a different question. . . . I'm an Irish nationalist, first and foremost" (*P* 202). Everything about Davin points to the truth of this claim. The antithesis of the mumming and fraudulent nationalists in *Stephen Hero* and "A Mother," Davin, as a sympathetic portrayal of Irish nationalists, falls in the same category as Miss

Ivors. Of course, Davin has his flaws. Apparently believing that all poets are mystics, like the two most prominent examples from the Revival, A. E. and Yeats, Davin tells Stephen, "Ireland first, Stevie. You can be a poet or mystic after" (*P* 203). This comic misunderstanding of Stephen, who is not at all a mystic, may reveal in Davin the influence of Catholic nationalist attacks on Yeats for his mysticism. Or it may simply illustrate what Stephen calls Davin's "grossness of intelligence" (*P* 180). But to call Stephen a mystic is an innocent error. Whatever Davin's faults, his complete sincerity, innocence, friendliness and even such small things as his delight in Irish games make this Catholic nationalist one of the most appealing characters in the novel.

The episode where Stephen recalls the protests against *The Countess Cathleen* may not give a strongly sympathetic picture of Catholic nationalists, but it is certainly far less damning than the ones in "The Day of the Rabblement," "A Mother," or *Stephen Hero*. The episode reports the students shouting, "A libel on Ireland! Made in Germany! Blasphemy! We never sold our faith! No Irish woman ever did it! We want no amateur atheists. We want no budding buddhists" (*P* 226). Oddly for someone who is supposed to be an artist, Stephen does not recall any detail about the play itself, not even its title or the name of its author. Rather, it is the Catholic protesters who dominate Stephen's recollection, making their presence at the opening seem the most important feature of this historic event.

The protests have a clear sectarian cast. The complaint, "We never sold our faith," is obviously Catholic, while the cry, "We want no budding buddhists," alludes to Yeats' interest in Indian mystics. "We want no atheists," apparently refers to the supposed blasphemy of the play and beyond that probably to the fact that Yeats was not a church-going, orthodox Christian. In general the protests (is Joyce quoting actual examples or making up his own version of their substance?) are comic. "We want no budding buddhists" shows a touch of verbal wit, while "No woman ever did it" manages a double entendre in its reference to the Countess Cathleen selling her soul. The protests may appear silly but the protesters themselves seem light-hearted, mildly witty college students. Certainly the episode doesn't imply that they are the frauds Stephen accuses the UCD Revivalists of being in *Stephen Hero* or the militantly narrow minded philistines that Joyce describes in "The Day of the Rabblement."

In spite of Stephen's often sour view of Irish Catholics and their institutions, and his unqualified admiration for Tone and Parnell, there is no mistaking his primary attachment to his own culture. While he thinks of the Catholic Church as alien and venal, he still regards it as superior to its Protestant counterpart. When Cranly asks if Stephen intends to become a Protestant, he replies,

> I said that I had lost my faith but not that I had lost selfrespect. What kind of liberation would that be to forsake an absurdity which is logical and coherent and to embrace one which is illogical and incoherent? (*P* 243–244).

The novel's most explicit illustration of the pull that Catholic culture exerts on Stephen comes in his long meditation inspired by Maple's Hotel. In the account of Stephen's walk to school, Joyce tells us that Grafton Street prolonged the "moment of discouraged poverty" that Stephen experienced with the flower seller (*P* 184). Later on, however, after the library episode, when Stephen glances across Kildare Street at Maple's Hotel, his discouragement gives way to more volatile feelings:

> The name of the hotel, a colourless polished wood, and its colourless quiet front stung him like a glance of polite disdain. He stared angrily back at the softly lit drawing room of the hotel in which he imagined the sleek lives of the patricians of Ireland housed in calm. They thought of army commissions and land agents: peasants greeted them along the roads in the country: they knew the names of certain French dishes and gave orders to jarvies in highpitched provincial voices which pierced through their skintight accents (*P* 238).

It is clear enough from the context that by "patricians of Ireland," Stephen means those landholding Protestants usually called the Anglo-Irish or the Ascendancy. That he doesn't think of them as Catholic is made definite a few lines later when he distinguishes their "race" from "the race to which he belonged."

In a letter to Stanislaus, Joyce once sketched a scene portraying the difficulties of his life in Trieste and titled it "The Anarchist" (*Letters II* 206). The image of the angry, envious, and resentful Stephen looking at Maple's Hotel might be titled "The Rebel." It could be taken as a forecast of the time five years after the publication of *A Portrait* when Catholic anger erupted in attacks on the big houses of Ireland's "patricians." But this scene is nearly as comic as the one that depicts Stephen struggling to escape those invisible fetters of Protestantism as he walked past Trinity College. There is too much wobble between envy and scorn and far too much made over the knowledge of French dishes for Stephen to be taken with complete seriousness. Besides, as Joyce pointedly reminds us, Stephen's vision of the Maple's Hotel Protestants is "imagined."

A few pages earlier, Joyce supplies an instructive example of the way Stephen's imagination works. As Stephen, Cranly, and Dixon are leaving the library they encounter the "captain," a grotesque, dwarflike person who is not quite all there and who, like the twin figure in "An Encounter," enjoys reading Walter Scott. "I love old Scott," he says. "I think he writes something lovely. There is no writer can touch sir Walter Scott." The captain's uncertain grammar, which throws considerable doubt on his literary judgment, is carefully noted by Stephen. He also notes that the captain has a "genteel accent" and then goes on to wonder, "Was the story true and was the thin blood that flowed in his shrunken frame noble and come of an incestuous love?" At this point Stephen's imagination takes over, conjuring up a detailed scene in which a brother and sister embrace. But he discovers that his mind has cast Davin, rather than the captain, as the incestuous brother. Displeased, Stephen suspects that this misrepresentation shows the degree to which "Davin's simplicity and innocence [had] stung him" (*P* 227–228). Learning here that Stephen's imagination plays curious tricks with things that have "stung" him, we should be on the alert when Joyce tells us that the sight of Maple's Hotel "stung" Stephen.

The scene with the captain does more than demonstrate the unreliability of Stephen's imagination. It also introduces a character whose genteel accent, along with his military title and rumored noble blood, mark him as a patrician, but he differs from Stephen's imagined patricians in much the same way that the French aristocracy portrayed by Flaubert differ from those imagined by Emma Bovary. The captain looks like a literary brother to Flaubert's drooling, senile Duke du Laverdière. He also looks like the sort of revenge an angry Joyce might take on the Ascendancy.

For all Stephen's anger, he has no interest in taking literary, incendiary or any other kind of revenge on the sleek lives of these patricians of Ireland. Instead, he wonders, "How could he hit their conscience? . . ." Here Joyce introduces the earliest form of Stephen's idea about forging the conscience of his race. The idea is a version of one attributed to Thomas Moore, who supposedly hoped that by performing his Irish songs before English audiences he could hit their conscience about Ireland. Whatever Moore's success, if the dwarf captain's literary tastes are any indication, Stephen would have small chance of hitting the Ascendancy's conscience with anything he might write. Immediately, however, Stephen's idea changes shape. Still thinking of the patricians he wonders how he might "cast his shadow over the imaginations of their daughters, before their squires begat upon them, that they might breed a race less ignoble than their own?" (*P* 238). Though it later would be taken seriously by William Butler Yeats, in *A Portrait* this notion of promoting better breeding through literature serves as one of the more comical reminders that the novel depicts the artist as a young man. Apparently himself attracted by the idea of influencing Ascendancy women, Joyce has Richard Rowan try it with Beatrice in *Exiles,* and get nowhere. He finally dismisses it with a comic flourish in *Ulysses,* where Bloom is accused of writing letters to the Ascendancy ladies, Mrs. Yelverton Barry, Mrs. Bellingham, and the Honorable Mrs. Mervy Talboys urging them to ambitious programs of sexual experimentation (*U* 15:1014–1074).

Stephen's speculations about influencing the Ascendancy are stopped by a sudden upwelling concern with "the thoughts and desires of the race to which he belonged." He goes on to associate his race not with the streets and buildings of the Dubliner but with the "dark country lanes" and "pool mottled bogs" of the Irish peasant. More specifically he associates it with the "woman who had all but wooed [Davin] to her bed." He sees her as the repository of the thoughts and desires of his race. He also may recognize that, apparently already pregnant, she is a more promising breeding prospect than are Ascendancy daughters. Stephen believes she was drawn to Davin because he "had the mild eyes of one who could be secret." Aware that he himself lacks Davin's innocent mildness of eye or mind, Stephen feels cut off from her and hence from his race. Still, it is "his" race and has a hold on him that overwhelms his momentary preoccupation with the "ignoble" race of the Ascendancy (*P* 238).

The Maple's Hotel episode brings Stephen to the threshold of the literary aim he announces at the end of the novel. The episode makes clear that, in spite of his elaborately developed literary theory with its insistence that didactic works belong among the "improper arts," he has a powerful impulse toward didacticism. Going beyond the Stephen of *Stephen Hero* who wants to "enrich" his society, the Stephen of *A Portrait* wants to improve it morally. Stephen's careful distinction between his race and the "ignoble" race of the Ascendancy also makes clear that when he alludes to "my race" he means Irish Catholics.

Stephen's decision to leave Ireland is not a denial of the commitment to his race. "The shortest way to Tara," he tells Davin, "is via Holyhead" (*P* 250), and it is Catholics, not Protestants, who have descended from the ancient Ireland of Tara. Stephen's references to Tara, and above all to race, leave no doubt that his penultimate diary entry, "I go to . . . forge in the smithy of my soul the uncreated conscience of my race," states an intention to aim his writing at Catholics rather than at Protestants. According to *A Portrait of the Artist* ancestral memories of their treatment by Protestants does not necessarily inspire Catholics to noise and violence, as Daniel Corkery said, nor do they lead to the hate Clery spoke of, but they cannot be erased.

Stephen's literary aim clashes with the Irish Ireland premise that Catholics were morally superior to all other peoples. On the other hand, in devoting himself to improving the welfare of his race, Stephen stands next to Davin as an Irish patriot. The difference is that Stephen wants to give his people a conscience rather than political independence, a revived language, and restored games and music. One might expect some ironic undercutting of Stephen's ambitious aim, were it not that in the letter to Nora, quoted earlier, Joyce expressed the same aim. Even if the older Joyce of *A Portrait of the Artist* saw an element of overweening in Stephen's aim, it reminds us that the country might have greater needs than the revived culture sought by Catholic nationalists or the elevated taste desired by their Protestant counterparts.

CHAPTER FIVE

Exiles

In his 1952 introduction to *Exiles,* Padraic Colum took issue with critics' habit of dwelling on the play's debt to contemporary continental drama, particularly Ibsen. The situations in Joyce's play, he said, "being motivated by a Catholic and not by a Protestant conscience, are different from the situations in an Ibsen play" (*E* 8). The preoccupation with Joyce's interest in Ibsen has obscured not only the Catholic elements in *Exiles* but also the play's connections with the Irish theatre movement, the Revival, and Ireland generally.

The stage directions identify the setting of *Exiles* as the "suburbs of Dublin" in the "summer of the year 1912" (*E* 13). The play itself tells us that Richard and Bertha recently have returned to Ireland from Italy, where they went eight years earlier, in 1904. These are significant dates in Joyce's life, 1904 being the year he and Nora Barnacle left Ireland for what he called "exile," and 1912 the year that he returned to Ireland for the last time. They also coincide with the first eight years of the Abbey Theatre. As was noted in Chapter 2, Joyce thought of himself as belonging to the literary movement represented by the Abbey and contributed *Exiles* to the theatre. As also was noted, the play was returned to him with a rejection letter from Yeats explaining that it was "too far from the folk drama" normally done at the Abbey (*JJII* 401–402). Indeed, *Exiles* was far removed from the usual Abbey play. It replaced the comic peasants of Synge and Lady Gregory with two complex and intelligent Catholics. Whereas the most famous of the comic peasants, Christy Mahon, "never left [his] own parish" until the "murder" and was such a dunce that he "never reached his second book" in school, Richard Rowan has just returned from eight years abroad, has published a book, and has sufficient academic qualifications to be a candidate for a university chair in Romance literature.[1] Although Bertha insists that she is "simple" (*E* 52), she holds her own in conversations with Robert and with Richard.

Exiles also breaks with the Abbey tradition of keeping Protestants off the stage. A Protestant stationmaster makes a brief appearance in Lady Gregory's *Hyacinth Halvey;* otherwise one would never gather from the plays of Yeats, Synge, and Lady Gregory that there were two Irelands. *Exiles,* however, puts Protestants on the stage as principal characters. At the same time, it upends the stereotypical distinction between the two cultures by making the Catholic pair, Richard and Bertha, in almost every respect the superiors of the Protestant pair, Robert and Beatrice.

Of at least equal importance, rather than looking to the old Ireland of the past, as Abbey plays consistently did, *Exiles* is set in the present and looks to the new Ireland of the future. The theme of Ireland's future surfaces in Act One when Robert proclaims to Richard, "If Ireland is to become a new Ireland she must first become European" (*E* 43). Later we learn that as young men living together, Robert and Richard thought of themselves as pioneers of a new Ireland. Robert reminds Richard, "Our house was not only a house of revelry; it was to be the hearth of a new life" (*E* 41). The theme of a new Ireland is underscored by contrast when Richard says to Bertha as she enters Robert's cottage, "Welcome back to old Ireland" (*E* 72).

While Joyce may have viewed *Exiles* as a corrective to the Abbey plays, it follows well-established patterns in his other work. Like "The Dead" and *A Portrait of the Artist,* it is heavily autobiographical, and like Gabriel Conroy and Stephen Dedalus, Richard has much in common with the bright, well-educated Catholic, James Joyce. Robert and Beatrice simply continue Joyce's practice of writing about Protestants. They even resemble some of the Protestant characters in his previous works. Robert, for example, shares several important traits with Mr. Browne. The play's concern with Ireland's future also reflects a long-time interest of Joyce. *Exiles* is the first time he explicitly refers to a "new Ireland," but, as was pointed out in Chapter 2, from the beginning of his career he had thought of his work as contributing to its realization.

In his textual study of *Exiles,* John MacNicholas reports that in the final version of the play Joyce dropped half-a-dozen allusions to Ireland that appeared in early drafts. Commenting on these changes, he says it is clear that Joyce "wished to subdue the play's references to Ireland, specifically to Irish politics."[2] *Exiles* is in part a serious study of sexual and psychological phenomena, which perhaps Joyce did not want overshadowed by Irish politics. It is just as likely, however, that he did not want Irish politics to obscure the play's domestic and cultural themes. Judging from his treatment of those themes, Joyce believed changes in Irish domestic life to be even more important than any changes in Irish politics.

In spite of the deletions, significant references to Ireland not only remain in *Exiles,* they also appear in the notes that Joyce wrote about the play and that usually are published with it. In one such note he says, "Perhaps the new Ireland cannot contain both [Richard and Robert]." He adds, "Robert will go" (*E* 123). For Moran, as for many other Catholics, achieving the new Ireland meant ridding the country of the political and economic inequities between themselves and Protestants as well as ridding it of the Anglicizing influence of Protestants. Whatever Joyce had in mind when he wrote, "Robert will go," it probably had little if anything to do with the problems of inequity and the Anglicizing of Ireland.

These problems are not mentioned in the notes and are only barely alluded to in the play. The news at the end of the play that Robert is going to visit his cousin Jack Justice in England suggests the English sympathies often attributed to Protestants. Likewise, Robert's ability to influence Richard's chances at being appointed to the chair of Romance literature at the university typifies the power held by Irish Protestants. But if Robert has English sympathies, they are not a significant theme in the play, and his apparent power becomes a moot issue since Richard is indifferent to the university position and does not attend the dinner at the vice-chancellor's that Robert arranges.

As their address in the "Dublin suburbs" establishes, Richard and Bertha, like Gabriel and Gretta Conroy, are part of the rising Catholic middle class who have become the social and economic equals or near equals of Protestants. Making them the central characters in the play practically eliminates the issue of inequities. There is even a suggestion in Beatrice's position as a piano teacher, and Robert's as a journalist, that this Protestant couple may be less well off than Bertha and Richard, who appear to live on money inherited from his family. The play also discounts the significance of the religious bigotry that is commonly associated with relations between Irish

Catholics and Protestants. Richard reminds Beatrice that his mother used to call her "'the black protestant,' the pervert's daughter" (*E* 24). However, like Dante's bigotry in *A Portrait of the Artist,* this slur, where "pervert" simply means a Protestant, is voiced by a representative of the older generation, suggesting that it is a thing of the past.

Of the usual distinctions between the two cultures, only class difference has any notable role in the play. Accepting as true one of the typical class-related distinctions between the two cultures, Bertha believes that Beatrice is far more intellectual and sophisticated than she is. Bertha also assumes that Richard is attracted to Beatrice as a result. During a heated exchange in which she accuses him of wanting to go off and "have an intellectual conversation" with Beatrice, she angrily calls Beatrice "her ladyship," a class designation that Joyce repeats in a note (*E* 74, 117). Bertha returns to this distinction in the last act, where she remarks to Richard, "[Beatrice] is everything that I am not—in birth and education" (*E* 103). None of the other characters appear to share Bertha's sense of a class difference between Catholics and Protestants, but according to a long and complex note about *Madame Bovary,* Joyce expected his audience to be aware of it.

Joyce opens the note by observing that since the publication of *Madame Bovary,* "the centre of sympathy appears to have been esthetically shifted from the lover or fancyman to the husband or cuckold." This shift in sympathy, he argues, is a stable one due to "the gradual growth of a collective practical realism," which he attributes to "changed economic conditions in the mass of the people who are called to hear and feel a work of art relating to their lives." Joyce goes on to explain that the shift in sympathy "is utilized in *Exiles*" to counteract any ill feeling towards Richard on account of his irregular union with Bertha so that the "spiritual revolt of Richard . . . can enter into combat with Robert's decrepit prudence with some chance of fighting before the public a drawn battle" (*E* 115–116).

The shift in sympathy that Joyce refers to has a class dimension of special relevance to *Exiles,* where the traditional class distinction between its Protestant seducer, Robert, and Catholic husband, Richard, parallels the one in *Madame Bovary* between its upper-class seducer, Rodolphe, and middle-class husband, Charles Bovary. Though people all over Europe experienced "changed economic conditions," the only group that fits the context of Joyce's note is the Irish Catholic middle class. This group is the only one that would bring to the theatre an awareness of the class distinction between the Catholic husband and Protestant seducer that Joyce counted on to produce the initial sympathy for Richard. Whatever Joyce means by "collective practical realism," it is clearly not a term of esthetic appreciation; rather, it seems to describe the belief held by a group that a work of art should have some application to their lives. As he attributed to the theatre movement didactic aims that in fact were his own, so he now attributes to this presumed Catholic audience a desire for the sort of didactic work that he intends to write.

Joyce's portrayal of both Robert and Beatrice makes his concern over the object of the audience's sympathy seem comically misplaced. Perhaps influenced by his didactic aims, Joyce left little opportunity for an audience to sympathize with either of the Protestant characters, both of whom come close to fitting Father Finlay's description of Protestants as an "effete aristocracy," though they are perhaps closer to a decayed aristocracy. Since they are first cousins, Robert and Beatrice's former engagement and continuing close relationship has about it the same air of incest associated with the decrepit "captain" in *A Portrait of the Artist*. Beatrice also suffers from weak eyes and other physical debilities. After Richard and Bertha eloped she developed some mysterious illness, which she says brought her "near to death" (*E* 21). She now describes herself as "convalescent" (*E* 22), but Bertha still calls her, "The diseased woman!" (*E* 54). If she has regained her physical health, she continues to have psychological problems that Robert attributes to her religion. Commenting on her recent visit to her father's house, he says, "She goes there on retreat, when the protestant strain in her prevails—gloom, seriousness, righteousness" (*E* 30). But she suffers more obviously from profound inhibitions and appears to be a study of someone trapped in those "fetters of the reformed conscience" that Stephen struggles against in *A Portrait of the Artist*.

Her entrapment in these fetters especially concerns Richard, who somehow has inherited Stephen's peculiar desire to "cast his shadow over the imaginations" of Ascendancy daughters. We learn in the opening scene that while in exile, he sent Beatrice chapters of his book, which he implies was inspired by and written for her. He asks her, "with some vehemence," if the book and letters and also his "character and life" expressed "something in your soul which you could not"? She agrees, when he presses her, and also agrees that she could not because she "dared not," and that she dared not "for want of courage" (*E* 20). A moment later, he proceeds to identify a related weakness when he explains why she is wrong in believing that she could find peace in a convent if her religion had such institutions. "You could not give yourself freely and wholly," he says (*E* 22). Alluding to the same problem, he accuses her of having "held back" from him as well as from Robert, whose engagement to her she has allowed to lapse. He repeats his observation that she cannot give herself "freely and wholly." Again she agrees (*E* 22).

Joyce reinforces Richard's assessment of Beatrice by having Bertha echo it in even harsher terms. After noting that he has "given that woman very much," Bertha adds, "You will get very little from her in return—or from any of her clan. . . . Because she is not generous and they are not generous" (*E* 55). The reference to Beatrice's "clan" is delicately ambiguous, extending the charge beyond her immediate family without specifying Irish Protestants in general. If Richard hoped for anything from her it probably was some sort of psychological support. His main interest, however, seems to have been to liberate her from her fears and inhibitions, and this he has failed to do. She clearly will not contribute to any new Ireland.

Robert has rejected "the asthmatic voice of protestantism," as he calls it (*E* 30), and consequently he has escaped becoming a type of his religion, like Beatrice. Instead he has become a type of his class, the gentleman seducer. He is a more sophisticated version of Browne, the Protestant ladies' man, and a less crude type than Blazes Boylan, the dolled-up, bottom-slapping Catholic seducer in *Ulysses*. The details of the cottage where Robert arranges the assignation with Bertha indicate that seduction is habitual with him, as tepid gallantry toward ladies is with Browne. The habitual nature of his behavior is reflected in his gestures and language, which are full of borrowings from the romantic lovers of nineteenth-century literature and are as hackneyed as the overblown roses he carries when he first appears. A hilarious example of his seduction style comes in the first act just after Bertha has granted him his kiss:

> ROBERT, *sighs:* My life is finished—over. . . . Over, over. I want to end it and have done with it.
>
> BERTHA, *concerned but lightly:* You silly fellow!
>
> ROBERT, *presses her to him:* To end it all—death. To fall from a great high cliff, down right down into the sea.
>
> BERTHA: Please, Robert . . .

> ROBERT: Listening to music and in the arms of the woman I love—the sea, music and death (*E* 35).

One of the most convincing evidences of Bertha's simplicity is that she doesn't break out laughing at this accumulation of romantic clichés.

Referring to the problem of Richard's irregular union with Bertha, Robert says, "Everyone knows that you ran away years ago with a young girl . . . not exactly your equal." He quickly excuses himself, explaining, "That is not my opinion nor my language. I am simply using the language of people whose opinions I don't share" (*E* 39). As his exchanges with Bertha make clear, using the language and opinion of others has become as much a habit with him as seduction. He uses others' words while purportedly arguing for Richard's welfare and also in attempting to seduce Bertha. This facility links him with Flaubert's habitual seducer, Rodolphe, who draws heavily on the language and opinions of others, particularly Goethe's great lovers, during the famous scene at the agricultural fair when he says to Emma,

> Duty, duty! Ah! by Jove! as if one's real duty were not to feel what is great, cherish the beautiful and not accept all conventions of society. . . . Why cry out against the passions? Are they not the one beautiful thing on earth? . . . There are two moralities, the petty one, the morality of small men that constantly keeps changing . . . , the other, the eternal, that is about us and above. . . .[3]

We hear Robert's version of this speech in the seduction scene at his cottage when he "warmly" tells Bertha,

> I am sure that no law made by man is sacred before the impulse of passion. Who made us for one only? It is a crime against our own being if we are so. There is no law before impulse. Laws are for slaves (*E* 87).

To make plain the literary kinship of the two gentlemen seducers, Joyce supplies Robert with Rodolphe's green velvet jacket (*E* 79).

Joyce's Irish seducer differs from Flaubert's French version in one important respect. The fat, cliché-spouting Robert with his overblown roses and slapstick perfume pump is primarily a laughable figure, who must confer with the husband before his assignation with the wife and who finds that, contrary to all the rules of seduction, she has told her husband everything while he himself has remained in the dark. More profoundly funny than Browne, the character of Robert presented the Abbey directors with an opportunity to put on their stage one of those comic Protestants that Moran chided them for never showing. It is hardly surprising that they found the opportunity resistible.

While in some ways Beatrice and Robert are marked by their Protestant heritage, they are also, like Browne, ironic examples of Protestants who have become more Irish than the Irish themselves. Again as with Browne, Robert's typically Irish role as a comic figure is a clue to this transformation. But whereas Joyce made Browne more Irish by endowing him with all the details of the Irish stereotype, he gave Robert the negative traits that he himself associated with the Irish, the most obvious one being a proclivity for betrayal, which Robert demonstrates in attempting to seduce his friend's wife. Robert also is guilty of the mummery or hypocrisy that Joyce attributed to the Irish in "The Holy Office," then dramatized in *Dubliners* and elsewhere, and that Robert himself admits to in his remark about using the language and opinion of others. Robert means to imply that this use is restricted to his remark about Bertha, but Richard specifies, "Writing one of your leading articles, in fact" (*E* 39). The article on Richard confirms this accusation that Robert's career is built on hypocrisy. The part Richard reads aloud is made up almost exclusively from the language and opinions of others. Its clichéd description of Richard as someone who left Ireland "in her hour of need" (*E* 99) not only is an example of Robert using the language and opinions of others but also exposes an animosity underlying the article's surface friendliness. The implication that Robert himself is concerned with the needs of Ireland reveals a hypocritical stance that Richard alluded to earlier in his ironic reference to Robert as a "patriot" (*E* 51). The man who claims, as Robert does, that what Ireland really needs are cigars and black coffee is concerned with no needs but his own.

Though Beatrice's reserve is linked to her Protestant heritage, it also is a trait that Joyce associated with certain Irish or Catholic women, most memorably in the *Dubliners* story "Eveline," where at the last minute Eveline abruptly holds back from Frank. Beatrice's inhibitions have turned her into a nun-like figure who is formally contrasted with the rakish Robert. The two have one trait in common, however—paralysis—which Joyce at one time thought of as typically Irish and intended to portray in *Dubliners*

(*Letters I* 55). Beatrice most obviously reveals her paralysis when she admits that she wants to change but can't. That he apparently continues to live with his mother suggests that Robert is as much a victim of arrested development as of paralysis (*E* 36, 50). In any event, his life as outlined in the play is a completely static one. When he proclaims to Bertha during their meeting at the cottage that nothing is as "sacred" as "the impulse of passion," he is repeating an idea that he and Richard shared years ago when they lived in the cottage. That is why Richard says to Bertha when she enters the cottage, "Welcome back to old Ireland!" (*E* 72). That Robert still maintains the cottage, still uses it as he did years ago, and still utters the same idea about passion drives home the lack of any change or development in his life. Joyce claimed to find exactly the same sort of stasis in Francis Sheehy-Skeffington and Richard Sheehy, making his 1907 visit very much a return to "old Ireland." He told Stanislaus that the two men appeared to have "just been taking a walk around themselves since October 1904" (*SL* 147). The paralyzed Robert and Beatrice also have gone nowhere. Their only change has been to deteriorate. Beatrice suffered her mysterious ailment and, according to her, Robert also went downhill. "His life, his mind, even, seemed to change," she says. She explains that he became "a pale reflection" of Richard and adds "then that too faded" (*E* 21).

In every respect, Joyce's Catholic couple is the direct opposite of the Protestant pair. Bertha notes, and perhaps exaggerates the importance of, the contrast between her simplicity and Beatrice's intellectual sophistication. While Joyce gives little evidence of Beatrice's intellectual sophistication, his portrait of Bertha repeatedly emphasizes her simplicity along with the related traits of openness, directness, and frankness. Though apparent in her exchanges with Beatrice, Bertha's simplicity is most vividly dramatized in the scenes with Robert, where it provides a comic counterpoint to his elaborate mummery. When he asks, "May I kiss your eyes?" she does not respond with any of the coyness, coquetry or moral outrage conventional for such situations but says bluntly, "Do so" (*E* 35). And when he says, "Little Bertha!" she replies, "But I am not so little. Why do you call me little?" (*E* 35). These simple responses leave Robert at a comic loss, with all the romantic air let out of his stolen tires.

Bertha also is the psychological opposite of Beatrice. Where the inhibited, ungenerous Beatrice held back from Robert, allowing their engagement to lapse, the uninhibited, generous Bertha gave herself "freely and wholly" to Richard, eloping with him without even being asked. Whether she gives herself freely and wholly to Robert the night at his cottage is left unanswered, but she hardly shies away from him any of the times we see them together. Neither does she hold back from Beatrice, in spite of some acute feelings of jealousy. In the final scene between the two women, Bertha "impulsively" reaches out to Beatrice and says she wants them to be friends. Beatrice answers with a restrained, "We will try to be." Undamped, Bertha embraces and kisses Beatrice and, in a long confessional, tells her that she often thought about her while in Rome. Beatrice's only reply is, "Really?" (*E* 102). They part, with Bertha "pressing" Beatrice's hand and Beatrice "disengaging" it as she says a cool, "Good morning" (*E* 102). It is hard to tell whether Beatrice behaves as she does because of inhibitions or lack of generosity, but there is no doubt about Bertha's generosity toward the woman she thinks of as a rival. This quality in her is illustrated once again in the play's last scene where we see her comforting Richard, in spite of the pain he has caused her by refusing to take any stand on the question of her visit to Robert (*E* 112).

The contrasts between Richard and Robert are even more marked and more extensive than those between the two women. Joyce's notes draw a number of explicit contrasts, identifying Richard as "an automystic" and Robert as "an automobile," Richard as a masochist and Robert as a sadist, Richard as a man in "spiritual revolt" and Robert as the practitioner of a "decrepit prudence" (*E* 113, 116, 124). The play dramatizes these as well as other contrasts. Where Robert admits to using the language and opinions of others, Richard says, and means, "I don't take my ideas from other people"(*E* 53). Where Robert is a hypocrite, Richard is militantly honest. Bertha calls attention to this contrast, claiming that Richard is different from other men, who are "all false pretenders" (*E* 54). Joyce alludes to it in a note, observing that Richard is "unfitted for adulterous intercourse with the wives of his friends because it would involve a great deal of pretence on his part rather than because he is convinced of any dishonourableness in it" (*E* 125). The contrast between the two characters' views on this issue is dramatized in the scene where Richard tacitly rejects Robert's proposal to set afloat a rumor that Richard and Bertha are married (*E* 39).

Beyond showing Richard's commitment to absolute honesty, his refusal to go along with any attempts to mislead people about his relation with Bertha illustrates what one of the notes refers to as his "delicate, strange, and highly sensitive conscience" (*E* 116). Richard's sensitive conscience also is demonstrated by his refusal to accept money from his mother because she disapproved of his relationship with Bertha (*E* 23–24). Indeed, Richard's conscience is illustrated throughout the play, so that, with the possible exception of Stephen Dedalus, Richard becomes the most complete example of what Joyce probably had in mind when he spoke of creating a conscience in the Irish.

Several of Richard's key decisions regarding his relationship with Bertha reflect a conscience that not only is acute but that also functions according to Catholic doctrine. As this doctrine is explained in the Vatican Edition of *The New Catholic Dictionary,* conscience sometimes can be "certain" and sometimes "doubtful," sometimes "true" and sometimes "erroneous." A conscience is "certain," when "it dictates something as right or as wrong, without experiencing any reasonable fear of the opposite being true." Failure either to do or to omit doing something dictated by a certain conscience is a sin. A conscience is doubtful when one has reasonable fear that its dictates may be wrong. "A person is never allowed to act with a doubtful conscience." Conscience is "true" when "its dictate as to what is right or wrong is correct; erroneous, when it judges what is really right as wrong or vice versa." The church maintains that even though one's conscience may be erroneous it "must be followed." If an erroneous conscience leads one to conclude that "he is obliged to perform or to omit a certain act, then he commits sin if he fails to perform or to omit it, as the case may be."[4]

Catholic and Protestant views of conscience are much alike; however, the Catholic doctrine requiring obedience even to an erroneous conscience adds weight to the necessity of following one's conscience. Though it is not clear why Joyce thought his "race" in particular should have no conscience, his characters often have none. Like Stephen in *A Portrait of the Artist,* Richard is one of the rare exceptions to Joyce's rule of the conscienceless Irish. Fond of taking precepts from Catholic doctrine and giving them secular applications that the church hardly would approve, Joyce depicts Richard's elopement as an act of conscience. Robert calls it "an act of impulse" (*E* 38), but Richard explains to him that, on the contrary, it was based on "a certitude as luminous as that of my own existence" (*E* 63). Here Richard describes the "certain conscience" that the Catholic Church says it is a sin not to follow. When he goes on to admit that he no longer has the luminous certitude, he provides one reason for his refusal to express any opinion on whether Bertha should or shouldn't visit Robert. In sticking to that refusal he follows the Catholic injunction against acting on a "doubtful" conscience.

Robert is Richard's opposite on the issue of conscience as on everything else. When Richard makes the startling assertion that he would "go away" if he became convinced that Robert had the same luminous certitude about Bertha that he himself once had, Robert responds, "A nice little load on my conscience!" (*E* 64). To say that his conscience would be burdened if he openly did something about which he had a luminous certitude reveals Robert's confused understanding of conscience. It also is a patent falsehood since someone who secretly attempts to seduce his friend's wife is hardly burdened by a conscience.[5]

The difference between the coolly rational Richard and the warmly impulsive Bertha provides one more example of contrasts in Joyce's play. But the Catholic couple also has important things in common. Unlike the paralyzed Beatrice and Robert, Richard and Bertha have a readiness to act and to change. Bertha notes this quality in herself during an angry exchange with Richard where she accuses him of being in love with the intellectual Beatrice. She claims that he didn't ask Beatrice to elope with him because he knew she would refuse. When Richard points out that he hadn't asked Bertha either, she replies, "Yes. You knew I would go, asked or not. I do things" (*E* 75). Later she observes that Richard, too, "is able to do something" (*E* 100). They are distinguished from the Protestant pair by their capacity not just to "do things" but to do things that require boldness and daring. While Robert and Beatrice stayed at home, allowed their engagement to lapse, and remain essentially sterile, Richard and Bertha eloped, went abroad, and had a child. Similar contrasts on both large and small matters dot the play. Whereas Beatrice has a hard time mustering the courage to visit the Rowan house, even though she has the legitimate pretext of giving Archie piano lessons, Bertha boldly goes alone to visit Robert in his cottage.

Robert pretends to boldness, proposing that women should be free to try many men. He goes on to say, "I wanted to write a book about it. I began it . . ." (*E* 65). While he can echo other people's opinions in articles for the newspaper, it is clear that his book, like his sentence, will remain uncompleted. Richard not only has completed and published his book but also hints that "some new thing is gathering in [his] brain" (*E* 19). Joyce emphasizes the intensity with which Richard is pursuing this new project. In Act One Brigid tells Beatrice, "He is wearing himself out about something he is writing. Up half the night he does be" (*E* 16). Then in Act Three, Bertha tells Beatrice that Richard "is writing very much since he came back." Pointing to the study she adds, "He passes the greater part of the night in there writing. Night after night" (*E* 96). These references call attention to the contrast between his vigorous determination and Robert's limpness.

Among the more important things Richard has done is change his thinking. In their long Act Two debate at the cottage, Robert says to Richard,

> The blinding instant of passion alone—passion, free, unashamed, irresistible—that is the only gate by which we can escape from the misery of what slaves call life. Is not this the language of your own youth that I heard from you so often in this very place where we are sitting now? Have you changed? (*E* 71).

Richard admits that it is the language of his youth and says, "Yes," he has changed.

One major change in Richard's thinking is revealed earlier in the cottage discussion when he responds to Robert's remark that in moments of "intense passion for a woman" one wants "only to possess her" (*E* 63). Presumably this also is the language of Richard's youth. It is clearly implied that he acted in accord with this youthful language and used the cottage to possess women (*E* 50). Now, however, Richard uses quite different language. "I am afraid that that longing to possess a woman is not love," he says. Echoing Dante, he goes on to explain that to love a woman is "To wish her well" (*E* 63).

Further evidence of Robert's malfunctioning conscience, as well as of his paralysis, is that he still sees nothing wrong with the use to which he has put the cottage. He says of his affairs, "I have no remorse of conscience." Richard's comment, "For you it was all quite natural?" implies that for him it was not at all natural but some sort of aberration. Richard and Robert's opposing views on the relations between men and women are reflected in their subsequent disagreement over the significance of a kiss. While Robert calls it a simple "act of homage" to beauty, Richard says, "it is an act of union between man and woman" (*E* 41). This minor dispute is related to a far more important difference in the way they regard the "union of man and woman."

Robert's multiple affairs and his attempt at seducing Bertha make it clear that he sees no particular importance in that union. He argues that what is most important or "sacred" is passion. On the other hand, Richard's profound commitment to his relationship with Bertha demonstrates his belief in its paramount importance: for him, the union between man and woman is sacred. It is easy to see reflected in his attitude the Catholic doctrine that marriage is a sacrament. Robert's most serious offense in attempting to seduce Bertha is that he attacks a form of this sacrament, not that he betrays a friend.

Richard's shift from a belief in passion and possession to a belief in love and wishing the other well, which presumably was triggered by his meeting with Bertha, parallels the change Gabriel undergoes in "The Dead." There is, however, one significant difference between the two characters. Whereas with Gabriel the change was limited to his relationship with his wife, Richard's transformation has had wider consequences. His belief in wishing the other well has prompted an attempt to "cast his shadow" over the imagination of the Ascendancy daughter Beatrice as well as that of the native daughter Bertha. He could say of Beatrice the same thing he said of Bertha: "I tried to give her a new life" (*E* 67). Confirming the implication of *A Portrait of the Artist* that the imaginations of native daughters are more fertile fields than those of Ascendancy daughters, the play shows that whereas Richard's attempt failed with Beatrice, it succeeded with Bertha. He gave Bertha a new life not only as her companion in Italy and as the father of Archie but also as an encourager of new degrees of honesty and frankness such as we see in their exchange about what went on when Robert kissed her. She admits her debt to Richard for this development, remarking, "I think that Dick is right. . . . Why should there be secrets?" (*E* 80). In refusing to hinder her relation with Robert, Richard leaves the door open for her to have yet another new life.

In Act Three, Bertha concludes that whatever Richard is writing "must be about something which has come into his life lately—since we came back to Ireland. Some change." She goes on to ask Beatrice, "Do you know that any change has come into his life?" (*E* 96–97). Though Beatrice avoids answering, in Act One she herself says to Richard, "Something has changed you since you came back three months ago" (*E* 25). He does not reply to Beatrice's query about the recent change, but since returning to Ireland he has learned, among other things, that his irregular union with Bertha will make living there difficult. Referring bitterly to his mother's opposition to his relation with Bertha, he says, "On account of her I lived years in exile and poverty too, or near it" (*E* 23). He returned to Ireland only after his mother had died, apparently hoping that his relationship with Bertha would not cause a problem with others. His first conversation with Robert reveals that in fact there are problems, which Robert proposes to allay by setting afloat the rumor that Richard and Bertha have gotten married. He implies that otherwise people will make life difficult for the two of them. We learn in the last act that the Irish reaction to her relation with Richard has in fact made life difficult for Bertha. Speaking of the Irish, she says to Beatrice, "Do you think I am a stone? Do you think I don't see it in their eyes and in their manner when they have to meet me?" She adds, "I am in such suffering" (*E* 100–101). This confession echoes, and by doing so throws light on, Richard's exclamation to Beatrice in the first act, "O, if you knew how I am suffering at this moment!" (*E* 22).

Though the cause of Richard's suffering, like the nature of his change, is left unexplained, it is not hard to understand. He faces a painful dilemma. On the one hand, allowing people to believe that he and Bertha are married, he says, would be "to give the lie to my past life" (*E* 39). Regularizing their marriage would have the same effect. On the other hand, insisting on disclosing the real nature of their relation will cause Bertha pain and so clash with his love for her. How can he wish her well while at the same time remaining true to his past life and his conscience? His rejection of Robert's plan makes it clear that he has decided to remain true to his past life and to the act dictated by his conscience. His awareness of the pain that this decision will cause Bertha helps explain his outburst, "And now I pray that I may be granted my dead mother's hardness of heart! For some help, within me or without, I must find" (*E* 22). It may also explain his apparent loss of the luminous certainty about his relation with Bertha.

In its domestic source, Richard's anguish resembles Gabriel Conroy's, but Joyce's perspective in *Exiles* is altogether different from his viewpoint in "The Dead." Though Gabriel speaks bitterly of Ireland and the Irish, the story focuses on his faults, placing the blame for his problems on his own failings, rather than on Ireland. Conversely, the setting of *Exiles* just after Richard and Bertha have returned to Ireland portrays the country as primarily responsible for the problems the couple experiences. The play itself continues the attacks on Ireland and the Irish that Joyce had begun with

"Day of the Rabblement." The destruction of the initial edition of *Dubliners* by its printer just two years before the writing of *Exiles* prompted Joyce to launch a new attack on Ireland in "Gas from a Burner." An important part of the play's subject is stated succinctly when the speaker of the broadside refers to Ireland as:

> This lovely land that always sent
> Her writers and artists to banishment
> And in a spirit of Irish fun
> Betrayed her own leaders, one by one.
> 'Twas Irish humour, wet and dry,
> Flung quicklime into Parnell's eye (*CW* 243).

In his newspaper article, "The Shade of Parnell," written the same year as *Exiles,* Joyce dwelt on the Irish mistreatment of Parnell, but that episode long had been his favorite example of Irish iniquity. Believing that he himself had been or was about to be betrayed, Joyce identified with Parnell and associates Stephen with him in *A Portrait of the Artist*. In many ways, beyond being a victim of betrayal, Richard, too, resembles Parnell as Joyce saw him. The description of Parnell in Joyce's article as a "strange spirit" with a "cold and formal bearing" and a tendency to melancholy fits Richard equally well. Also like Parnell, who Joyce says refused a post in the English government, Richard effectively refuses the university position. Finally like Parnell, who according to Joyce "died of a broken heart," Richard is shown at the end of the play suffering from "a deep wound of doubt" and with the appearances of a broken heart.

Of all the ways that Richard resembles Parnell, his irregular union with Bertha is probably the most important. It has the same intensity for which Parnell's relation with Kitty O'Shea is famous. Bertha and Richard's relationship also aroused a milder form of the public outrage described in "The Shade of Parnell." Referring to Parnell and Kitty O'Shea, Joyce reports in his article that "the Irish press emptied on him and the woman he loved the vials of their envy."[6] On one key point, however, Joyce's Catholic pair differs from Parnell and Kitty O'Shea. It will be recalled that in his note about this pair he says, "The relations between Mrs. O'Shea and Parnell are not of vital significance for Ireland—first, because Parnell was tongue-tied and secondly because she was an Englishwoman." He adds furthermore that Mrs. O'Shea's "manner of loving is not Irish" (*E* 127). The implication of the note is that the relations of Richard and Bertha *are* "of vital significance for Ireland," presumably because, in contrast with the Protestant Parnell, Richard is not tongue-tied and, in contrast with the Englishwoman Mrs. O'Shea, Bertha is an Irishwoman with an Irish manner of loving.

In "The Dead," the Irish manner of loving involves sacrificing oneself for the beloved, like Michael Furey, who Gretta believes died for her. *Exiles* presents the related idea that Irish loving means giving oneself "freely and wholly." This manner of loving is epitomized in an elopement, the significance of which Bertha defines when she says of her elopement with Richard, "I gave up everything for him, religion, family, my own peace." She reaffirms this meaning at the end of the play when she tells Richard, "I gave you myself—all. I gave up all for you." Mrs. O'Shea did not give up "everything" for Parnell, but kept her family, her reputation, and also the financial support of her wealthy aunt. Joyce portrays Beatrice as incapable of giving up anything for a man. Bertha's angry outburst about Beatrice's "clan" suggests that Protestants generally are incapable of generous self-sacrifice. On the other hand, Richard's point that joining a convent requires giving oneself freely and wholly is a reminder that this sort of self-sacrifice is something that Irish Catholics have been demonstrating for centuries. If Bertha's is an Irish manner of loving, then it is a manner that an Irish audience would be capable of emulating and might be inspired to adopt, hence her significance for Ireland. Being a writer, Richard can describe his and Bertha's relationship and thereby influence the relationships of other Irish men and women as the tongue-tied Parnell could not.

Joyce gives us only clues about Richard's writing. As we learn from their opening exchange, Richard has let Beatrice know that she plays an important role in his work. Thinking that she might be offended, he says, "If I were a painter and told you I had a book of sketches of you you would not think it so strange, would you?" (*E* 18). The Dante connection suggested by her name also is developed in this conversation when Richard implies that she has inspired him (*E* 19). What emerges most clearly from the conversation, particularly Richard's preoccupation with the effect his book has had on her, is that he has written it with the didactic intention of helping Beatrice overcome her crippling inhibitions. The *Comedy* also is strongly didactic, but in it, of course, Dante is the one who needs help from Beatrice;

in Joyce's and presumably Richard's version, however, it is Beatrice who needs the help. There is the further contrast that whereas it was Beatrice's perfection that inspired Dante, it is the need of Joyce's Beatrice that apparently inspired Richard, much as Stephen's assumptions about the needs of Ascendancy daughters momentarily inspire him.

Coming in the play's first moments, the conversation between Richard and Beatrice plants impressions that easily could lead to overestimating her importance to him and his work, as Bertha does later on when she accuses him of preferring Beatrice to her (*E* 74). In fact, after their first scene, Richard barely thinks of Beatrice. For the rest of the play, it is Bertha and his relationship with her that dominate his thoughts and feelings. She has held this place of importance in his mind from the very beginning. Recalling Richard when he was first falling in love with Bertha, Brigid, the family servant, tells her, "I can see him sitting on the kitchen table, swinging his legs and spinning out of him yards of talk about you and him and Ireland" (*E* 90).

While, as noted in the previous chapter, Lily's assessment of contemporary Irish males is the shrewdest comment on the men in "The Dead," here, Brigid's recollection of Richard's feelings for Bertha is probably the most reliable clue to his current thought and work. It imputes to him a conviction that his relationship with Bertha has the "significance for Ireland" that Joyce says Parnell and Kitty O'Shea's relationship lacked. Presumably, the book he wrote in Italy described his relationship with Bertha. Apparently his current work deals with what has happened to the two of them since their return to Ireland. In other words, it apparently is very much like *Exiles,* which, like his talks with Brigid, is about Richard, Bertha, and Ireland.

Perhaps allowing its continental inspiration to excessively influence his reading of *Exiles,* Harry Levin says that an issue for Richard is whether he should "settle down at home, accept a professorship of Romance languages [*sic*] at his old university, and attempt to Europeanize Ireland?"[7] But it is Robert who proposes a Europeanized new Ireland. He treats Richard as a pawn in his design to make the country more European, telling him, "[T]hat is what you are here for." In *Ulysses,* Buck Mulligan endows Stephen with a similar role in his equally specious plan to Hellenize Ireland. Joyce gives no more credit to Robert's idea than he does to Mulligan's. "The

Dead" completely undercuts the aim of Europeanizing Ireland, just as it does the aim of becoming more Irish by learning the language, visiting the West, or otherwise obeying the dogmas of Irish Ireland.

Lily's observation about contemporary Irish men being all palaver or out for what they can get fits Robert (who combines both faults), as well as Gabriel and Mr. Browne. Her observation also reveals a key difference between Joyce's views and those of most Revivalists about what needed changing in Ireland. For the Joyce of *Exiles* as well as of "The Dead," it is not the relations between England and Ireland, or Catholic and Protestant, that need changing but those between Irish men and women. In the story and in the play, Joyce places the same high value on Irish culture that Revivalists did, only for him, reviving the Irish manner of loving was more important to the new Ireland than reviving the Irish language, de-Anglicizing the country, or any of the other Revivalist aims. Unless Joyce radically changed his literary aims in the two years since he wrote to Nora about his dealings with the Abbey Theatre, he viewed *Exiles* as helping to mold an Irish conscience. According to the play, the presence of a conscience in the Irish would lead them to practice the Irish manner of loving exemplified by the union of Richard and Bertha, and so take a key step toward realizing the new Ireland. Robert would be out of place in this new Ireland not just because he lacks a conscience or because his relations with women are the antithesis of that manner of loving but also because he appears incapable of change.

It was mentioned earlier that at the end of the play Richard resembles the broken-hearted Parnell described by Joyce, but Richard's heart is not altogether broken. In their final scene Bertha says to him, "If you wish to go away now I will go with you." He replies, "I will remain. It is too soon yet to despair" (*E* 111–112). In their continuing devotion to one another and their determination to stay in Ireland, Bertha and Richard demonstrate a tenacity and toughness that is perhaps what most distinguishes them from the Protestant pair. Robert, at least, has found them too tough and daring for comfort and has fled to the less harrowing company of his English cousin, while Beatrice presumably has returned to one of the family retreats she favors. Though hardly triumphant, Richard and Bertha remain in command of the stage as possible seeds for a new Ireland.

Joyce asks in one of his notes, "Why the title *Exiles?*" The answer follows: "A nation exacts a penance from those who dared to leave her payable on their return" (*E* 114). Though their suffering may be seen as the penance required of Bertha and Richard for having left, Joyce would have seen in Richard's betrayal by Robert a link with all the betrayed Irish leaders and martyred heroes, including Robert Emmet, Edward Fitzgerald and Wolfe Tone, as well as Parnell. As Joyce was just beginning *Exiles,* Yeats published his poem "September 1913," in which he celebrates Emmet, Fitzgerald, and Tone, calling them "exiles" because no one around them shared their heroic spirit.[8] Richard also is an exile in Yeats' sense, set apart from others by the boldness of his ideas and the strength with which he pursues them. In making him the protagonist of *Exiles,* Joyce provided a Catholic hero to match the old Protestant ones, Parnell, Emmet, Fitzgerald, and Tone. He also provided a different kind of hero in that Richard's struggle is against the bonds of conventional morality and conventional thinking rather than against the bonds imposed by English rule.

That the idea of heroism appealed to the young Joyce is reflected in the title *Stephen Hero*. Shortly after arriving on the continent, however, he wrote Stanislaus, "Do you not think the search for heroics damn vulgar?" He added, "I am sure . . . that the whole structure of heroism is, and always was, a damned lie . . ." (*SL* 53–54). Subsequently, in rewriting *Stephen Hero* as *A Portrait of the Artist* he undermined Stephen's stature with his use of persistent irony. With *Exiles,* his early attraction to the idea of heroic achievement apparently reasserted itself so that his portrayal of Richard is free from any hint of irony. The play might well be called *Richard Hero*. Irish history provided the irony that Joyce left out. Following the treaty in 1922, when members of the rising Catholic middle class became the country's leaders, they avoided anything resembling the new Ireland represented by Richard and instead imitated the decrepit prudence that Joyce associated with the Protestant Robert, approving a constitution that outlawed divorce and birth control and practicing a level of censorship probably unmatched outside the more stringent Islamic states.

CHAPTER SIX

Ulysses

Richard and Robert's youthful attempt to create a new life in Ireland resembles the moments in Irish history that Joyce cites in his "Saints and Sages" lecture when Protestants and Catholics joined forces in a national cause. Their alliance also exemplifies the popular Revival vision of the two cultures working together to reshape the country. The implication of *Exiles,* however, is that, whatever their relationship may have been in the past, the two cultures have become so divided that cooperation between them no longer is possible. In *Ulysses* Joyce lays greater stress than ever before on that division. Nowhere in the book are there signs of the kinship between Irish Catholic and Protestant that Joyce celebrated in his "Saints and Sages" lecture and that had been an article of faith for many Revivalists, Moran being one notable exception. Neither are there signs of any serious hope for an altered Ireland, not even the faint hope expressed by Richard at the end of *Exiles*. The Stephen Dedalus of *Ulysses* seems to have abandoned the plan he had at the end of *A Portrait of the Artist* for creating a conscience in his race. The similar plan that had lingered in Joyce's mind since *Dubliners* also appear to have vanished. The idea of a new Ireland is mocked in "Cyclops," where the Narrator tells of the blowhard Citizen going on and on about "a new Ireland and new this, that and the other" and adds, "Talking about new Ireland he ought to go and get a new dog so he ought" (*U* 12.483–484). Other ideas for a reformed Ireland, from Buck Mulligan's Hellenized version to Bloom's vision of "the new Bloomusalem in the Nova Hibernia of the future" (*U* 15.1544–1545), are treated as jokes.

The novel is equally devoid of the narrowly circumscribed, but once apparently strong, sympathy toward Revival ideas that Joyce expressed in *Exiles, A Portrait of the Artist,* and "The Dead." Throughout *Ulysses,* he treats the movement with the same relentless satire found in his early attacks on it in "The Holy Office," "A Mother," and *Stephen Hero*. The main difference is that Joyce has enlarged his target. Whereas he aimed his early attacks primarily at the literary Revival and cultural nationalism, in *Ulysses,* he satirizes all versions of Irish nationalism, from the literary Revival back to the old separatist politics of Wolfe Tone, Edward Fitzgerald, and Robert Emmet. More importantly, rather than limiting himself to exposing the hypocrisy of people involved in nationalist movements as he had in the past, he now also examines problems with nationalism itself.

As was mentioned earlier, Joyce objected to Griffith for "educating the people of Ireland on the old pap of racial hatred" (*SL* 111). Moran, too, taught this "old pap." Though he targeted Irish Protestants, and Griffith the English, the common thread of racial hatred united them in the anti-Semitism that becomes a major theme of *Ulysses*. In his "Saints and Sages" lecture, Joyce made a special issue of the racist tenor in Revival rhetoric, but *Ulysses* is his first work of fiction to show racism in action. While examples of racial hatred appear throughout the novel, particularly in the form of anti-Semitism, they culminate in Joyce's archetypal Irish nationalist, the Citizen.[1] In the Citizen's attack on Bloom, Joyce takes the further step of linking racial hatred with violence.

A conclusion that Irish nationalism inevitably was flawed by racism and violence perhaps explains Joyce's attack on Irish nationalists in *Ulysses*. His attack may also have been motivated by the Easter Rising of 1916, which was an obvious culmination of nationalist fervor aroused by the Revival and which occurred at an early stage in the book's composition.[2] In his poem "Easter 1916," Yeats dwelt on the transformative effect this event had on his own views. Whereas he had once thought of the people in the Rising as worth only "a mocking tale or a gibe," he now saw them as transformed into heroic martyrs, who would be recalled "Now and in time to be, / Wherever green is worn . . ."[3] It is highly unlikely that Joyce shared Yeats' view of the Rising. He attacks the whole notion of patriot heroes in "Cyclops," where his fiercely satirical treatment of Robert Emmet's public execution reads like a reflection on the all but public execution of the Rising leaders. What the Rising would have shown Joyce was that Catholic nationalists were not the essentially harmless hypocrites that he typically portrayed; rather, they were capable of triggering widespread violence and destruction.

Following his usual practice of introducing important themes immediately, Joyce commences his satirical treatment of Irish nationalism and includes an instance of anti-Semitism in the opening chapter of *Ulysses*. The example of anti-Semitism comes during Haines' observations about relations between England and Ireland. "We feel in England," he tells Stephen, "that we have treated you rather unfairly. It seems history is to blame" (*U* 1.648–649). He adds, "Of course I'm a Britisher, . . . and I feel like one. I don't want to see my country fall into the hands of German jews either. That's our national problem . . ." (*U* 1.666–669). The "either" is a puzzle. Does Haines mean to imply a kinship between the English and the Irish in that both fear the Jews taking over their countries? Has he been reading about the anti-Jewish riots that occurred in Limerick during 1904 and that were written about extensively in the Irish press?[4] In any event, Haines' speech introduces not only the theme of anti-Semitism but also that of the relationships between the Jews and the Irish.

The novel's examination of Irish nationalism begins with the episode involving Haines and the old milkwoman. This episode upends two Revival dogmas: that Irish peasants epitomized Irish culture, and that the English were its enemies. Joyce reminds us of what the peasant is supposed to represent when he has Stephen associate the milkwoman with the traditional symbols for Ireland, "Silk of the kine and poor old woman" (*U* 1.403). Contrary to Revival dogma, the Englishman Haines displays no animosity toward Irish culture but instead is the only person in the chapter who can speak Irish. Equally contrary to Revival dogma, the milkwoman is so ignorant of the Irish language that she can't even recognize it when Haines speaks it to her. As Stephen does in *A Portrait of the Artist,* she assumes that knowledge of French goes with privilege and so guesses that French is what Haines is speaking. When she is put right, she says, "I thought it was Irish" (*U* 1.428), displaying a moral flexibility that clashes with Revival notions about the rigorously upright Irish peasant.

The novel's most extended treatment of Irish nationalism comes in "Cyclops," where Joyce endows the Citizen with a compendium of nationalist beliefs. Like the cultural nationalists, the Citizen champions Irish literature, art, music, and sports, along with the Irish language. Like the more extreme political nationalists, he favors the use of physical force to wrest political independence from England and admires the United Irishmen of 1798, the Fenians of 1867, the more recent Invincibles, and others who, as the Narrator of the chapter comically puts it, "were hanged, drawn and transported for the cause by drumhead courtmartial" (*U* 12.482–483).

Like traditional Irish nationalists, the Citizen attributes Ireland's problems mainly to the English. In particular he blames "the yellowjohns of Anglia . . . for our ruined trade" and looks forward to a time when Ireland's "harbours that are empty will be full again" (*U* 12.1255, 1301). A thriving foreign trade and a generally improved economy appear to be the leading features of the Citizen's "new Ireland" (*U* 12.483–484). In his focus on the Irish economy, and in virtually every other way, the Citizen remains a typical Catholic nationalist. One does not find Yeats, Lady Gregory, or other Protestant Revivalists advocating improvements in Ireland's trade or demanding independence from England or talking about a "new Ireland." Likewise, one does not find the Citizen being concerned about English periodicals corrupting Irish taste as Yeats and other Protestant Revivalists were. Judging from their response to the *Police Gazette,* neither the Citizen nor his cronies would have worried about the style of popular periodicals being a threat to Ireland. Like the one-eyed Cyclops who is his Homeric counterpart, the Citizen has a limited vision that excludes, among other things, any knowledge of the literary Revival. In spite of its focus on current nationalist activity, neither the Citizen nor anyone else in the chapter mentions either the literary Revival or any of its Protestant leaders.

Besides giving him a typically Catholic perspective on national issues, Joyce associates the Citizen with the three most prominent Catholic nationalists of the Revival—Michael Cusack, D. P. Moran, and Arthur Griffith. As is well known, the Citizen was based on Cusack, even bearing his name in early drafts. Joe Hynes specifically identifies him as "the man that made the Gaelic sports revival" (*U* 12.880). The Narrator reports that the Citizen talked "about Irish sports and shoneen games the like of lawn tennis and about hurley and putting the stone and racy of the soil and building up a nation once again" (*U* 12.889–891), all of which are topics associated with Cusack. Among the Citizen's links with Moran are his use of the Irish word "raimeis," which means something like "hot air" and was a favorite with Moran (*U* 12.1239). The Citizen's use of the word involves a now somewhat arcane joke since Moran typically applied it to just the sort of patriotic rhetoric that the Citizen spouts and that according to Moran most Irish nationalists substituted for effective action. The Citizen applies the term to Bloom's talk but it actually fits his own much better. The Citizen's attack on *The Irish Independent* for giving space to English social events represents a further connection to Moran, who made the same charge against this paper (*U* 12.220–237).[5] A reference to the Guinness brothers as "Bungiveagh and Bungardilaun" (*U* 12.281–282), also recalls Moran, "bung" being the term he coined to refer to the liquor trade in his crusade against alcohol.

The Citizen, of course, is no enemy of drink. Neither is he an enemy of Protestants; for him, England is Ireland's enemy. In his insistence on that point, he allies himself with traditional Irish nationalism and with Griffith, who was its chief contemporary spokesman and whose movement is recalled when the Citizen utters the old rallying cry, "*Sinn Fein! Sinn Fein amhain!*" (*U* 12.523). The Citizen's closest links, however, are to Joyce's "Saints and Sages" lecture, important parts of which, including the title, now come from the mouth of the Citizen. In his lecture Joyce dwells on Ireland's past greatness and alludes to its notice in ancient sources, mentioning Plutarch and Festus Avienus, while the Citizen names "Tacitus and Ptolemy, even Giraldus Cambrensis" (*CW* 156, *U* 12.1251). The problem of Irish emigration, which Joyce mentions in his lecture, is expanded on by the Citizen, who asks, "Where are our missing twenty millions of Irish [who] should be here today instead of four, our lost tribes?" (*CW* 172; *U* 12.1240–1241). Also as the Citizen does in "Cyclops," the lecture envisions a future Ireland that will be an "enterprising island with its own commercial fleet, and its own consuls in every port of the world" (*U* 12.1241–1257; *CW* 173). The most numerous parallels have to do with England. The Citizen's denunciation of the English as "bloody thicklugged sons of whores' gets" and "tonguetied sons of bastards' ghosts" (*U* 12.1198–1201) has a vituperative eloquence unmatched in the lecture; his account of the way they have treated Ireland simply expands Joyce's description of that treatment as "cruel" and "cunning," characterized by use of "the battering-ram, the club and the rope" (*CW* 166). Both accuse England of having destroyed Irish industry, while Joyce's description of "Anglo-Saxon civilization" as "almost entirely a materialistic civilization" is echoed pungently in the Citizen's attack on English civilization or "syphilisation," and his claim that the English have "No music and no art and no literature worthy of the name" (*CW* 173; *U* 12.1197–1200).

The glowing portrait of the "enterprising island" that Joyce presents in the "Saints and Sages" lecture is part of his laudatory account of the effects of Irish nationalism. While many details of this account reappear in "Cyclops," that the Citizen voices them raises serious doubts about their accuracy. Also, the chapter presents a broader examination of Irish nationalism than appears in the lecture, revealing negative sides to it, the most serious of which is that it leads not only to "national hatred," as Bloom calls it, but also to racial hatred and to violence. While England's treatment of Ireland might justify Irish nationalists hating England, Joyce depicts the Citizen's national hatred as leading him to condemn the English for matters having nothing to do with their treatment of the Irish, as in his attack on their "syphilisation." (Did Joyce realize he had done the same thing in his lecture?) According to Joyce, another problem with national hatred is that it quickly spreads, as when the Citizen easily turns from attacking England to denouncing the French for being a "[s]et of dancing masters" who were "never worth a roasted fart to Ireland" (*U* 12.1385–1386). Illustrating how the virus of national hatred proliferates, Joyce shows it infecting even the decent Joe Hynes, who refers to "the Prooshians and the Hanoverians" as "sausageeating bastards" (*U* 12.1390–1391).

Irish nationalism's connection with racial hatred, particularly anti-Semitism, is less well known than its link with hatred of England, yet this aspect of Irish nationalism is clearly visible in articles that appeared in both *The Leader* and the *United Irishman*. The articles stress two main points about Jews: that they are behind many of the country's economic problems, and that they are aliens. These are the themes in Griffith's heated defense of Father Creagh, who led the months-long anti-Semitic campaign in Limerick. Griffith writes,

> In all countries and in all Christian ages [the Jew] has been a usurer and a grinder of the poor. The influence he has recently acquired in this country is a matter of the most serious concern to the people. In Dublin half the labourer population is locked in his toils. Father Creagh deserves the thanks of the Irish people for preventing the poor of Limerick being placed in a similar predicament. The Jew in Ireland is in every respect an economic evil . . . and he remains among us, ever and always an alien.

The allusion here to Jews as aliens is expanded on in another article, where Griffith says,

> I would insist that the exclusion of Jews in Germany, Russia, and Austria has nothing to do with religious beliefs. It is rather a question of Patriotism. The Jew has at heart no country but the Promised Land. He forms a nation apart wherever he goes. He may be a German citizen today, and a British subject tomorrow. He is always a Jew Nationalist bound by the most solemn obligations and the fiercest hopes to the achievement of National Restoration and Revenge.[6]

The same twin themes turn up in *The Leader* where an article on "The Jew Question in Ireland" talks of the "innate usurious proclivities" of Jews. The author writes particularly about "the extension of the Jew system to the rural parts [of Ireland], as in Russia." He says, "It is the falling of the farmer—the man of some property and fixed abode—into the hands of the Hebrews that I dread."[7] The point of this dread is that the farmer, like the peasant, is thought to embody essential Irish traits so that to threaten him is to threaten the foundation of Irish nationalism. In the initial issue of *Dana,* Joyce's acquaintance Frederick Ryan (Stephen remembers him as "Fraidrine" [*U* 9.1084]) attacked a "weekly Dublin journal," apparently *The Leader,* because it demanded justice for Catholics while denying it to Jews and supporting anti-Semitism.[8]

It hardly takes a second look at these attacks on Jews to notice that they closely parallel nationalist attacks on the English. The link between the English and Jews was easy for people in Ireland to make because of the belief, expressed by Haines, that Jews were a dominant force in England. Jewish domination of England is a common theme of anti-Semitic articles in both the *United Irishman* and *The Leader*. Moran objected that the uniforms an Irish railroad ordered from England would be "made by Jews in the slums of Manchester," and Griffith attacked "the Anglo-Jew news-agencies and newspapers."[9] When he attacks Griffith for feeding the Irish with "the old pap of racial hatred," it is hard to know whether Joyce has in mind the campaigns against Jews or those against the English. In the "Saints and Sages" lecture, however, it is clear, that his attack on racist thinking is aimed at its presence in Irish nationalism. This attack marks probably the most significant difference between the Joyce of the lecture and the Citizen, who is Joyce's most prominent example of that kind of thinking.

The examples of the Englishman Haines and Protestant Deasy early in the novel establish that anti-Semitism isn't limited to Irish nationalists. In "Cyclops" the Orangeman Crofton provides another example. Referring to Bloom, Ned Lambert asks, "Is he a jew or a gentile or a holy Roman or a swaddler or what the hell is he?" and Crofton, speaking as a Protestant, responds bluntly, "We don't want him" (*U* 12.1631–1634). But the Citizen is at once the most intensely nationalistic character in the novel and the most intensely anti-Semitic. In remarks clearly aimed at the nearby Bloom, the Citizen denounces Jews for "coming over here to Ireland filling the country with bugs." He also accuses them of "[s]windling the peasants . . . and the poor of Ireland" and ends by proclaiming, "We want no more strangers in our house" (*U* 12.1141–1142; 1150–1151). Here the Citizen not only makes the usual point about the economic ravages caused by Jews but also, in calling them "strangers," he firmly links them with the English. In his portrait of the Citizen Joyce shows that, as with Moran and Griffith, an Irish nationalist's hatred extends to Jews as easily as it does to England.

The connection between racial hatred and violence is introduced in "Cyclops" through the *Police Gazette* picture, which carries the cut line, "*Black Beast Burned in Omaha, Ga*." and which the Narrator describes as showing "a lot of Deadwood Dicks . . . firing at a Sambo strung up in a tree with his tongue out and a bonfire under him" (*U* 12.1324–1326). The picture and text prepare for the chapter-ending combination of racial hatred and violence when the Citizen pursues Bloom, shouting, "By Jesus, I'll brain that bloody jewman for using the holy name. By Jesus, I'll crucify him so I will" and then throws a biscuit tin at Bloom (*U* 12.1811, 1853). The chapter is peppered with other examples of violence, most of which have some association with Irish nationalism. They range from the mock newspaper account of the boxing match between the Irish Myler Keogh and the English Percy Bennett (*U* 12.960–987) to Alf Bergan's allusion to the hanging of Joe Brady, who was executed for his part in the Phoenix Park murders, when the new Chief Secretary of Ireland, Lord Frederick Cavendish, and an official from Dublin Castle, Thomas Burke, were stabbed to death by members of an underground group called the Invincibles. These examples culminate in the mock epic account of the Irish hero sentenced to be hanged, drawn, and quartered, which is based on the execution of Robert Emmet for leading a rebellion against the English and which forms the centerpiece of the chapter (*U* 12.525–678).

The Citizen announces his faith in violence when he proclaims that Ireland's lot will be improved only when "the first Irish battleship is seen breasting the waves with our own flag to the fore" (*U* 12.1307–1308). His attraction to violence is underscored through his implicit parallel with the savage Cyclops and his explicit parallel with the mythical Irish giant, who has beside him a "couched spear of acuminated granite" and who quietens his dog by "blows of a mighty cudgel rudely fashioned out of paleolithic stone" (*U* 12.199–205). Describing a similar treatment of Garryowen, the Narrator says that the Citizen "took the bloody old towser by the scruff of the neck and, by Jesus, he near throttled him" (*U* 12.149–150).

The Citizen's rationale for an Irish battleship repeats the standard nationalist argument that violent means were necessary to make the English change their treatment of Ireland. In *A Portrait of the Artist* this is Davin's justification for his apparent involvement in an underground military organization (*P* 218). As was noted earlier, in his essay "Fenianism," Joyce himself defended the use of violence for a national cause, claiming that "history fully supports" the Fenian argument that concessions from England always have been "granted unwillingly, and, as it is usually put, at the point of a bayonet" (*CW* 188). In "Cyclops," however, he undercuts this traditional defense by suggesting that racial hatred, rather than any concern over the country's welfare, may lie behind nationalist violence.

He further undermines Irish nationalism by introducing a pronounced streak of fraud and hypocrisy into the Citizen's makeup. On entering Barney Kiernan's, the Narrator says of the Citizen, "There he is, in his gloryhole, with his cruiskeen lawn and his load of papers, working for the cause" (*U* 12.122–123). It is not clear what work for the cause the Citizen is doing, or can do, sitting by himself in a pub. Implying none at all, the Narrator explains that "the citizen [was] up in the corner having a great confab with himself and that bloody mangy mongrel, Garryowen, and he waiting for what the sky would drop in the way of drink" (*U* 12.119–121). Later on, apropos the Citizen's nationalistic talk, the Narrator comments acidly, "All wind and piss like a tanyard cat" (*U* 12.1311–1312). He is accusing the Citizen of indulging in *raimeis,* but he identifies a greater fault when he reports, "As much as [the Citizen's] bloody life is worth to go down and address his tall talk to the assembled multitude in Shanagolden where he daren't show his nose with the Molly Maguires looking for him to let daylight through him for grabbing the holding of an evicted tenant" (*U* 12.1312–1316). In the Irish nationalist calendar of sins, land grabbing was second only to informing.

The contrast between the Citizen and the other Irish nationalists that Joyce had most recently portrayed, Miss Ivors and Davin, offers further evidence of Joyce's changed attitude toward the movement. He depicts both Miss Ivors and Davin as perfectly honest and sincere nationalists, however misguided they may be. The fraudulent, hypocritical Citizen is a reversion to the type of nationalist found in "Ivy Day," "A Mother," *Stephen Hero,* and other early work. Among other signs of Joyce's dramatic loss of sympathy for Irish nationalism is the chapter's long episode based on the execution of Robert Emmet, possibly the most cherished of Ireland's patriot martyrs. It would be hard to find a greater affront to the tradition of Irish nationalism than turning Emmet's execution into a comic event as Joyce does in "Cyclops." If such an affront exists it is the loud fart that Bloom looses at the end of the "Sirens" episode, while gazing at a picture of Emmet and reading his famous last words (*U* 11.1284–1294).

Discussing possible Irish responses to *Ulysses,* Joyce told Frank Budgen, "I don't want to hurt or offend those of my countrymen who are devoting their lives to a cause they feel to be necessary and just."[10] It is difficult to square this sentiment with his portrayal of the Citizen and his comic treatment of the Emmet figure. There was a sufficient residue of national feeling in Joyce, however, that he shows Irish violence to be less egregious than its English counterpart. During "Circe" there is a brief but memorable allusion to Irish nationalist violence when Old Gummy Granny holds out a dagger to Stephen and, referring to one of the two British soldiers menacing him, says, "Remove him, acushla. At 8:35 a.m. you will be in heaven and Ireland will be free" (*U* 15.4737–4738). Her plea grotesquely repeats a theme of self-sacrificing violence that is common in the literature of Irish nationalism and that Yeats promotes in *Cathleen ni Houlihan*. But the main emphasis in the episode is on British violence, when Private Carr punches Stephen in the face (*U* 15.4746–4748). Its closest Irish counterpart is the Citizen's futile attempt at hitting Bloom with the biscuit tin. Even if the Citizen had succeeded, little harm would have resulted since the tin was empty. Private Carr actually hits Stephen and hits him hard enough to knock him down. It is the most violent act to occur on June 16. Though the episode about the execution of the Emmet figure mocks a hero of Irish nationalism, it also gives a vivid example of English violence. In mentioning that the English soldier in charge of the execution "had blown a considerable number of sepoys from the cannonmouth without flinching" (*U* 12.671–672), in introducing the letter of an accomplished English hangman (*U* 12.415–431), and in various other ways, Joyce makes the point that when it comes to violence the English outdo even the most fervent Irish nationalists. This point, however, does not alter the chapter's negative view of Irish nationalism.

The isolation of the Citizen when we first see him, sitting alone in Barney Kiernan's, suggests that Irish nationalism does not have a wide following. The rest of the novel supports this suggestion. Only one other character shares the Citizen's interest in political nationalism. That is the keeper of the cabman's shelter, who, as Bloom notes, talks "the same identical lingo" as the Citizen (*U* 16.1079). As for cultural nationalism, news that the Dublin City Council is discussing the Irish language leads the Citizen to say of the language, "It's on the march" (*U* 12.1190), but there is nothing in *Ulysses* to support his claim. In "Wandering Rocks" we learn from Jimmy Henry, the assistant town clerk, that the discussion at the Council meeting was violent and, apparently, fruitless. In disgust he refers to "their damned Irish language" and again to the "Damned Irish language," adding with apparent sarcasm, "language of our forefathers" (*U* 10.1007–1012). The only time the Citizen himself speaks Irish, beyond the occasional popular term, is to his dog (*U* 12.705). Amusingly, the other character to speak it is Haines, one of those Englishmen whom the Citizen dismisses as "bloody brutal Sassenachs."

In accord with his Thersites-like character, the Narrator of "Cyclops" paints the harshest picture of Irish cultural nationalism, describing a Revival musical evening that emphasized temperance, along with the Irish language and Irish music. "There was a fellow with a Ballyhooly blue ribbon badge spiffing out of him in Irish," he says, "and a lot of colleen bawns with temperance beverages and selling medals . . . and a few old dry buns." He adds that the musical part of the evening included "an old fellow . . . blowing into his bagpipes and all the gougers shuffling their feet to the tune the old cow died of." The whole was overseen by some priests on the lookout for any unsuitable behavior between the sexes (*U* 12.686–696). The one exception to the generally bleak picture of Irish nationalism given in "Cyclops" comes in a brief passage about Joe Hynes. His characterization in "Ivy Day in the Committee Room" as the one sincere supporter of Parnell is recalled in "Hades" when he proposes a visit to Parnell's grave (*U* 6.918). In "Cyclops" we learn that he has become a "wellknown and highly respected worker in the cause of our old language" and that at Barney Kiernan's he "made an eloquent appeal for the resuscitation of the ancient Gaelic sports and pastimes" (*U* 12.907–909). The Citizen's prominence in the chapter, however, suggests that hypocritical blowhards who promote violence have a greater appeal to the Irish than do sincere and "highly respected" people like Joe Hynes.

Given the concern of Catholic nationalists over their relationship with Protestants, it may seem strange that neither the Citizen nor others in the chapter say anything about this subject. The explanation probably is that Joyce, who never liked to repeat himself, already had treated this topic in the scene between Stephen and Mr. Deasy in "Nestor." The appearance of Mr. Crofton in "Cyclops," however, serves as a reminder of the issue, recalling in particular the economic gulf between Catholics and Protestants.

From the difficulty Stephen and Buck Mulligan have over paying the milkwoman in the opening chapter to Corley's plea for money near the end of the novel, Joyce shows his characters living in a nearly constant state of insolvency. Crofton, along with his fellow Protestants, Mr. Deasy and the Reverend Hugh C. Love, is one of the few exceptions. Though unsure whether his name is Crofter or Crofton or Crawford, the Narrator knows that he is "an orangeman," who receives a pension from the collector general of customs while at the same time "drawing his pay" from some sort of appointment in the Dublin County Council. Typically Protestant in being the beneficiary of appointed positions, Crofton has a double income and, as the Narrator puts it, goes "gallivanting around the country at the king's expense" (*U* 12.1589–1592). In contrast, most of the Catholics in Barney Kiernan's, as in *Ulysses* generally, have no visible income at all.

While the Narrator speaks bitterly of Crofton's income, there is no suggestion of any sectarian animosity behind the bitterness nor do the other characters in the chapter exhibit any signs of sectarian animosity. The only hint of such feeling comes in Ned Lambert's use of the term "swaddler," a mildly derogatory name for a Protestant. He immediately apologizes to Crofton, however. "No offence, Crofton," he says, and Crofton appears to take none (*U* 12.1632).

One might conclude that the loyalty to the government which Crofton would profess as an orangeman had some connection to the economic rewards he receives from it. In "Wandering Rocks" Joyce points to just such a connection when he writes that the Reverend Hugh C. Love "made obeisance" to the viceregal parade, "mindful of lords deputies whose hands benignant had held of yore rich advowsons" (*U* 10.1202–1204). Though the "rich advowsons" are a thing of the past, the Reverend Love still retains his typically Protestant loyalty to the crown. As both a minister and a landlord, he also remains relatively prosperous. By making him a landlord who is distraining his Catholic tenant, Father Cowley, for rent (*U* 10.943–948), Joyce again underscores the usual economic relationship between the two cultures.

Reverend Love first appears in "Wandering Rocks" accompanied by Ned Lambert, who is showing him a room in the former St. Mary's Abbey, where Silken Thomas Fitzgerald proclaimed himself a rebel in 1534. We learn from Lambert that Love is "writing a book about the Fitzgeralds," who descended from a twelfth-century Norman invader and became one of the most prominent Anglo-Irish families in the country's history. Following the usual pattern with his Protestant characters, Joyce notes Love's accent, pointing out, twice, that it is "refined." He also strips all freshness or life from the language used by Love, whose few remarks include the phrases: "How interesting!"; "If my memory serves me"; and "If you will be so kind." As though to remind us of the cultural link between the two men, Joyce has Love echo one of Mr. Deasy's expressions. He remarks to Lambert, "I won't trespass on your valuable time." One might expect his stale language and action against Father Cowley to bring some Catholic response, but it doesn't. Probably because they think him a Jew, Cowley, Simon, and Ben Dollard have plenty of vituperation for Reuben J. Dodd, who has taken out a writ against Cowley for unpaid debts; they say nothing at all against Love, however. For his part, Ned Lambert is particularly deferential toward Love, repeatedly addressing him as "sir" and generally displaying the meek acceptance of supposed Protestant superiority for which Moran constantly berated Catholics (*U* 10.398–439).

The final appearance of Love comes in "Circe," where he joins the Catholic Father Malachi O'Flynn in performing the Black Mass. There he is identified as "The Reverend Mr Hugh C Haines Love M.A." and more simply as, "The Reverend Mr Haines Love" (*U* 15,4695–4700). Robert M. Adams, who finds Love's presence in the novel a puzzle, is especially baffled by the linking of Haines' name with Love's. He notes that "haines" suggests the French for "hate," giving the neat pair, love and hate, but he quickly gives up that line of speculation as a dead end.[11] As it often is with Joyce, the point in this instance probably is the obvious one that there is a connection between Irish Protestants and the English. The notion of such a link, which Moran never tired of repeating, underlies many of Joyce's Protestant characters at some level, but it is clearest in his portrait of Mr. Deasy.

The episode between Stephen and Mr. Deasy is a study in conflicting views, Deasy's being consistently Protestant, and Stephen's being almost as consistently Catholic. But there are also conflicts within Deasy, who at times identifies with the English and at times with the Irish, reflecting the ambiguous position of Protestants in Ireland. With his pictures of the Prince of Wales and English racehorses, his fear that England is being corrupted by Jews, and his belief in the English as sources of wisdom, Deasy exhibits the attachment to England that was, and still is, particularly associated with Ulster Protestants, and that Moran argued was typical of Irish Protestants generally. Like the Citizen and many other Catholics, Stephen regards the English as tyrants and scorns Queen Victoria, whom he considers a "crazy queen, old and jealous" (*U* 1.640). Stephen and Deasy have equally divergent views on one of Deasy's favorite topics, money.

Deasy tells Stephen, "Money is power," while Stephen thinks of it as "symbols soiled by greed and misery" (*U* 2.237, 226–228). Deasy is not aware of this particular contrast in their views, since Stephen's opinion remains unspoken, but he believes that in handling money he is responsible and Stephen is not. He sees the difference illustrated in the way Stephen simply thrusts money loosely in his pocket, while he himself keeps it safe and orderly in his coin machine. Initially, he attributes this contrast to a difference in age. "You don't know yet what money is," he says, implying that Stephen's carelessness with money is due to the ignorance of youth. Attempting to rouse Stephen to greater responsibility but using an example that is badly chosen for an Irish Catholic, he says that an Englishman's "proudest boast" is "I paid my way. I never borrowed a shilling in my life. . . . I owe nothing." When he asks, "Can you feel that?" Stephen responds by first silently casting up his debts:

> Mulligan, nine pounds, three pairs of socks, one pair brogues, ties. Curran, ten guineas. McCann, one guinea. Fred Ryan, two shillings.

> Temple, two lunches. Russell, one guinea, Cousins, ten shillings, Bob Reynolds, half a guinea, Koehler, three guineas, Mrs MacKernan, five weeks' board.

He then answers briefly, "For the moment, no." Taking a perverse pleasure in finding his preconceptions confirmed, Deasy laughs "with rich delight" at this answer and "joyously" says, "I knew you couldn't" (*U* 2.243–262).

In contrast to Mr. Deasy's view, the novel establishes that poverty and indebtedness are traits of Catholics, whatever their ages. It is true that Stephen's handling of his money in Mr. Deasy's office, and later in the novel, could be called irresponsible, but after listing his debts he thinks, "The lump I have is useless" (*U* 2.259). This feeling of despair at the great disparity between his debts and his salary is more to blame than his youth for his careless way with money.

It soon becomes apparent that Deasy thinks Stephen is careless with money not so much because he is young as because he is Catholic. It also becomes clear that he attributes the Catholic attitude toward money not to economic factors but to a fundamental character flaw. He regards Catholics as inherently irresponsible in money matters and Protestants as inherently responsible. We hear this line of thinking emerge as he suddenly makes a distinction between "you" and "we." Having told Stephen, "One day you must feel it [i.e. the importance of paying one's way and not borrowing]," Deasy adds, "We are a generous people but we must also be just." This would have been a good time for Stephen to ask, "Whom do you mean by 'we'?" Deasy obviously has in mind Protestants and perhaps also the English. The "we" complicates the "you" in the previous sentence, suggesting that in Deasy's mind it was beginning to mean not only Stephen but also Irish Catholics in general. The "us" in Stephen's well-known reply, "I fear those big words which make us so unhappy," illustrates the contagiousness of sectarian thinking and also its peculiar slipperiness in Ireland (*U* 2.262–264). Just as Deasy's "we" can mean "the English" or "Protestants" or both, so Stephen's "us" can mean "the Irish" or "Catholics" or both. Put explicitly, Mr. Deasy is saying, "We Protestants and/or English are generous to the Irish and/or Catholics but we must not be too generous because that would not be just." In his reply, Stephen is saying that he fears big words such as "just," which make the Irish and/or Catholics unhappy. For Catholics the most notorious instance of unhappiness in their recent history was the famine, when the Protestants and/or English maintained that it would not be just to give the starving Catholics too much relief.

Sectarian issues are so well established that Deasy immediately understands the event Stephen would have in mind. This explains his otherwise puzzling assertion, "I remember the famine in '46" (*U* 2.269). The remark itself is designed, if not quite to dissociate himself from the English, certainly to suggest an identity with Catholics, who are normally thought of as remembering it since they suffered most from it. Finally making the issue of sectarian differences explicit, Deasy tries to deny their existence by suggesting that Protestants always have sided with the Catholics. "Do you know," he says, "that the orange lodges agitated for repeal of the union twenty years before O'Connell did or before the prelates of your communion denounced him as a demagogue? You fenians forget some things" (*U* 2.270–272). One problem with this example is that it gives a wildly distorted picture of the Orange Lodges, which were devoted to maintaining the Union and were militantly anti-Catholic. Another is that "Fenian" is a sectarian term used by Northern Protestants such as Deasy to refer to Irish Catholics generally. It calls up the image of a wild-eyed revolutionary with a pistol in one hand and a bomb in the other. Deasy is again way off the mark when he says, "I have rebel blood in me too," assuming that Catholics are rebels and that his own supposed rebel blood shows a kinship with them. But not all Catholics were nationalists and of those, not many (and certainly not Stephen), would have regarded themselves as "rebels." Deasy's attempts at suggesting a bond with Catholics all fail.

Stephen's only reply to Deasy's claim about the Orange Lodges is "a brief gesture" (*U* 2.277), which probably signifies the impossibility of finding a suitable reply to such nonsense. His thoughts, however, follow the explicitly sectarian direction set by Deasy. He recalls words from the opening of the anti-Catholic Orange Lodge oath, "Glorious, pious and immortal memory." His mind continues to dwell on Protestant animosity or violence toward Catholics as he remembers, "The lodge of Diamond in Armagh the splendid behung with corpses of papishes. Hoarse, masked and armed, the planters' covenant. The black north and true blue bible. Croppies lie down" (*U* 2.273–276). Once reminded of sectarian friction, Stephen almost automatically thinks of other examples. It takes only the slight suggestion of Deasy's assertion, ". . . I will fight for the right to the end," for Stephen to recall the slogan of Ulster Protestants who opposed Home Rule, "For

Ulster will fight [against Home Rule]/ And Ulster will be right" (*U* 2.395–398). Stephen's acute awareness of sectarian strife in Ireland's past helps explain his often quoted remark to Mr. Deasy that "history is a nightmare" (*U* 2.377). Likewise, Mr. Deasy's comforting awareness of Protestant power and wealth coupled with his delusion that a wonderful harmony exists between Protestants and Catholics helps explain his directly contrary view that "All human history moves towards one great goal, the manifestation of God" (*U* 2.380–381).

Summing up one of the conclusions he's been aiming toward, Deasy says, "We are all Irish, all kings sons" (*U* 2.279–280). Whatever Stephen is referring to when he replies, "Alas," neither he nor Joyce altogether discredit Deasy's claim to being Irish and having interests in common with Irish Catholics. Joyce pointed out in the "Saints and Sages" lecture that for Irish nationalists the invasion of Ireland by the Anglo-Saxons and Normans was one of the darkest days in the history of Ireland. Deasy alludes to this event when he remarks, "a faithless wife first brought the strangers to our shore here." He appears to agree that it was a dark day for Ireland and, when he refers to the invaders as the "strangers," even uses the language of Catholic nationalists. His remark, "A woman too brought Parnell low," suggests that he also agrees with the mainly Catholic nationalist admiration for Parnell and his programs (*U* 2.392–394). His letter about a cure for the hoof-and-mouth disease points to another possible link with Catholic nationalists, who also were very much concerned with the economic welfare of Ireland. It would have been the Protestant landholders, however, who would have benefited most by a cure for the hoof-and-mouth disease.

Though Stephen persists in thinking him an Ulster Protestant, Deasy's own sense of his identity is much less clear. Sometimes his point of view is that of an Irish or Ulster Protestant, sometimes that of an Englishman and sometimes that of a Catholic nationalist. By incorporating this conflicting mix of opinions in his conception of Deasy, Joyce gives a more accurate picture of Irish Protestants than Moran ever did, but then Joyce was interested in truth and Moran in quite other things.

As he waits for Deasy to finish the letter about hoof-and-mouth disease, Stephen seats himself "before the princely presence," that is the portrait of the Prince of Wales, and observes the racehorses, who "stood in homage, their meek heads poised in the air" (*U* 2.299–301). The "meek heads" of these horses remind one of *A Portrait of the Artist* and Stephen's conviction about Tommy Moore, Davin, and other fellow students having meek heads, which they bent in homage to someone or something. Stephen exempted himself from this servile frame of mind, taking pride in his unbent head. In *Ulysses,* however, Stephen notes that elements in his attitude toward Haines link him with the mass of servile Catholics. As an Oxford man who travels with a guncase, wears a tennis shirt, and offers people cigarettes from a "smooth silver case in which twinkled a green stone," Haines bears the marks of sophistication and wealth (*U* 1.614–615). On the other hand, his having spent the night "raving and moaning to himself about shooting a black panther" perhaps suggests some mental imbalance (*U* 1.61). Certainly when he says of English-Irish relations, "We feel in England that we have treated you rather unfairly," and then adds, "It seems history is to blame," he displays a striking obtuseness (*U* 1.648–649). Whereas we know that someone like Jimmy Doyle would be drawn to Haines in spite of any flaws in his character or mind, we would expect such flaws to repel Stephen. Instead, we find him considering how he might get into Haines' chapbook the witticism about a pier being a disappointed bridge. Stephen sees this desire as a typical Irish response to the English. "A jester at the court of his master," he thinks, "indulged, disesteemed, winning a clement master's praise. Why had they chosen all that part?" (*U* 2.42–45).

While Stephen anticipates playing jester before the Englishman Haines, he actually plays this role before his Protestant students when he comes out with his witticism about the pier and his riddle about the fox. He recognizes that, like Haines, the students dwell in a world of wealth, sophistication, and command far removed from the disorder and poverty in which he lives. When he addresses Armstrong he thinks, "Welloff people, proud that their eldest son was in the navy." He either knows or anticipates that Armstrong's family lives in the elite neighborhood along the "Vico road, Dalkey." Stephen also recognizes that he is "disesteemed" by the students and that they laugh in class because they are "aware of [his] lack of rule and of the fees their papas pay" (*U* 2.24–29).

The meeting with Deasy at the end of the chapter shows Stephen in the presence of his actual Protestant master, who regards him with even more disesteem than the students do, speaking to him as to an irresponsible child. Though Stephen does not play the jester at the meeting, he is very circumspect, as when he gives his single word comment, "Alas," and his inarticulate "brief gesture." His remark, "A merchant is one who buys cheap and sells dear, jew or gentile, is he not?" is his only open disagreement with Deasy. When Deasy claims that Shakespeare says, "Put money in thy purse," Stephen simply "murmur[s]" his correction, "Iago" (*U* 2.359–360, 238–240). For the most part he doesn't speak except in response to a direct question from Deasy, and then his answers are brief. His long and complex memory of Orange Lodge animosity toward Catholics is never stated. In "Ireland at the Bar," Joyce argued that the true version of events in Ireland remained unknown because the press presented only one side. In the encounter between Stephen and Mr. Deasy, as in the Maamtrasna murder trial, and also in accounts of the Irish Revival, the Catholic side is rarely heard or not at all.

Stephen's agreement in "Telemachus" to meet Mulligan and Haines at "The Ship" at 12:30 carries the implication that he then will explain his theory of *Hamlet* to Haines. At some point, however, he loses interest in trying to impress Haines and decides to explain his theory at the National Library instead.[12] His listeners there include George Russell, T. W. Lyster, R. I. Best, and John Eglinton, all of whom were Protestant. Lyster, the Librarian, Eglinton, the Assistant Librarian, and Best, the Assistant Director held the upper positions that at the time typically went to Protestants. (The names Byrne, Maguire, O'Connor, O'Byrne, Doyle, and O'Neil, which appear on the June 16, 1904 staff roster for the more menial Library duties, suggest that, as usual, Catholics occupied the inferior positions.)[13] The four listeners include distinguished intellectuals and writers who were associated with the literary Revival. Russell, or A. E. was, of course, one of the movement's leading figures. Eglinton, who wrote extensively about Revival issues and co-founded the journal *Dana,* also had a prominent place in the movement. Best contributed most notably through his translation of Jubainville's important study of Irish myths. Lyster made no comparable published contribution to the Revival, but he was the first person who encouraged Yeats to become a writer. Lyster also helped Yeats revise *The Island of the Statues,* showed him how to correct proofs, and guided some of his reading.[14] As the text suggests, they also were all older than Stephen, Best being thirty-two, Eglinton thirty-six, Russell thirty-seven and Lyster forty-nine, while Stephen was only twenty-two. (Was Joyce designing a secular version of Jesus at the Temple?)

It is not hard to see why Stephen prefers explaining his theory to the group at the Library rather than to the dull-witted Haines. The question is, why would he explain it at all since he says he doesn't believe it? Apparently, one reason is to impress the group with his cleverness, as he was inclined to do with Haines. When he came up with his *mot* about the pier during his morning class, he thought, "No-one here to hear" (*U* 2.42). The Library provides him with someone to hear. He is acutely aware of his audience, noting after Lyster is called away, "Two left," and twenty pages later, counting "Three" (*U* 9.15, 890). At one point his thoughts suggest that he is using the group as a "whetstone" to sharpen his mind (*U* 9.977). He also thinks, "Make them accomplices," as though he wishes to demonstrate his power by persuading them to go along with his theory (*U* 9.158). His more general aim is to test his mind against some of the most sophisticated intellects in Dublin. Intent on winning the trial, he calls on Ignatius Loyola for help and employs other resources, from "dagger definitions" to masses of arcane detail, some of which he makes up (*U* 9.163, 84). The quiet, docile Stephen of Mr. Deasy's office has become a sort of intellectual rapparee making a raid on the Pale. Whether or not he persuades his Pale opponents to accept the *Hamlet* theory, Joyce shows them listening while Stephen talks, which reverses the more typical relation between the two cultures in "Nestor," where Deasy did the talking, while Stephen listened.

Stephen's performance at the library thoroughly contradicts the stereotype of the ignorant Catholic. Likewise Joyce's depiction of Best, Lyster, and Eglinton contradicts the stereotype of the literate, sophisticated Protestant. Though these Protestants talk about literature, particularly from the continent, their talk is almost totally inane. After noting that Goethe viewed Hamlet as "the beautiful dreamer who comes to grief against hard facts," Lyster says, "One always feels that Goethe's judgments are so true. True in the larger analysis" (*U* 9.10–11). One can imagine Stephen quietly asking, "Who is this 'one' you speak of?" And, "What exactly do you mean by 'the larger analysis'?" Later on, Lyster shows a comic inability to follow Stephen's point about the relationship between Anne Hathaway and Shakespeare. A moment after Lyster calls Stephen's remarks on the relationship "very illuminating," his "alarmed face" asks, "Is it your view then that she was not faithful to the poet" (*U* 9.928–932). Stephen's point, of course, was that Anne had lured Shakespeare into marrying her, not that she was unfaithful to him.

Like Lyster, Best demonstrates an acquaintance with European literature and a fondness for using "so" as an intensive. He also has the tic of interjecting "don't you know" into his conversation. These traits all emerge when he brings up "Mallarmé, don't you know." Quoting from Mallarmé's prose poem about *Hamlet,* Best says, "*il se promène, lisant au livre de lui-même,* don't you know, reading the book of himself." He notes that Mallarmé describes the play "given in a French town, don't you know," which advertised it as "*Hamlet/ ou/ Le Distrait/ Pièce de Shakespeare.*" He concludes, "*Pièce de Shakespeare,* don't you know. It's so French. The French point of view" (*U* 9.112–123). All of this sounds suspiciously like someone eager to establish his credentials as a sophisticated cosmopolitan. Never one to give short shrift, Joyce provides multiplied tics and amplified inanity in Best's contribution to the discussion of *Hamlet:* "But *Hamlet* is so personal, isn't it? . . . I mean, a kind of private paper, don't you know, of his private life. I mean, I don't care a button, don't you know, who is killed or who is guilty . . ." (*U* 9.362–364). In the section where Stephen discusses Shakespeare's use of his brothers Gilbert, Edmund, and Richard, Joyce piles on more satirical detail as he shows Best in a feeble, tic-dotted attempt at humor. "That is my name, Richard, don't you know," Best says. "I hope you are going to say a good word for Richard, don't you know, for my sake" (*U* 9.903–904). According to the stage directions in this mock playscript section, Best's remarks are followed by a hardly credible "laughter." Encouraged by the response, Best continues, "I hope Edmund is going to catch it. I don't want Richard, my name . . . ," the rest of the sentence apparently being cut off by more "laughter" (*U* 9.916–917). Browne's joke about his name in "The Dead" looks like a triumph of wit by comparison with Best's attempt.

Stephen's explanation of his *Hamlet* theory is punctuated by talk about the literary Revival, which was at or near flood stage in 1904 and which becomes an increasingly prominent subject of "Scylla and Charybdis." The chapter alludes to the founding of the Abbey Theatre, the publication of Russell's collection of younger poets, George Moore's at homes, and other important Revival events. It also refers to most of the major and several of the minor figures associated with the Revival, among them Yeats, Synge, Lady Gregory, Douglas Hyde, Padraic Colum, and James Starkey (Seamus O'Sullivan). As is usually the case with movements, enthusiasm and proselytizing marked the literary Revival, a notable example being George Moore, who as the result of a mystical experience on the streets of London returned to Ireland and threw himself into Revival activities. Among the activities were his at homes, which were aimed at winning converts to and otherwise promoting the Revival. We see a similar spirit of enthusiasm in the Library group. Full of excitement about Russell's forthcoming collection of poets, Lyster tells him, "We are all looking forward anxiously" to the appearance of this "literary surprise" (*U* 9.289–291).

Similarly excited at finding an Englishman interested in the Revival, Best has been showing Haines a copy of Jubainville, presumably his own translation. (A significant Revival event, Best's translation first appeared serially in the *United Irishman,* beginning 9 November 1901, and then was published as a book in 1903 in Dublin.) Apparently having given Haines the titles of other contributions to the Revival, Best reports, "He's quite enthusiastic, don't you know, about Hyde's *Lovesongs of Connacht*. I couldn't bring him in to hear the discussion. He's gone to Gill's to buy it" (*U* 9.93–95). Revival enthusiasms are catching. Eglinton's response to the news about Haines, "The peatsmoke is going to his head" (*U* 9.100), reflects skepticism about Haines, not about the Revival. Eglinton overflows with proselytizing enthusiasm and keeps urging people to attend Moore's at home. He asks Russell, "Shall we see you at Moore's tonight?" and adds as an enticement, "Piper is coming." A moment later we hear a voice, apparently Eglinton's, saying to Russell, "I hope you'll be able to come tonight." Providing a piece of information that underscores the general proselytizing atmosphere of the Revival, the voice adds, "Malachi Mulligan is coming too. Moore asked him to bring Haines." Shortly after, we hear a voice, apparently Eglinton's again, say to Russell, "I hope you will come round tonight. Bring Starkey." Finally, Eglinton says to Mulligan as he and Stephen are leaving, "We shall see you tonight. . . . *Notre ami* Moore says Malachi Mulligan must be there" (*U* 9.273–274, 305–306, 323–324, 1098–1099).

Preoccupied by his enthusiasm, Eglinton immediately gives the discussion of *Hamlet* a nationalistic turn, observing that "Our young Irish bards . . . have yet to create a figure which the world will set beside Saxon Shakespeare's Hamlet" (*U* 9.43–44). This comment reflects a popular Revival concern over the achievements that were needed to raise Irish literature to true greatness. A country fond of identifying itself with Greece obviously was in need of an epic. In one of the Library conversations, a nameless voice cites George Sigerson's remark that "our national epic has yet to be written." The same or another voice adds, "Moore is the man for it" (*U* 9.309–310). Vivian Mercier, one of the few scholars to discuss the importance of the Revival in "Scylla and Charybdis," suggests that Eglinton's comment about Hamlet was meant to reflect on Joyce himself and to imply that in Bloom he had created a character "which the world will set beside Saxon Shakespeare's."[15] Occurring in a book titled "Ulysses," the question of who will write the national epic also is clearly self-reflexive. By 1922 it would have been obvious that Moore was not "the man for it," leaving Joyce as the likely claimant. But while Joyce casts *Ulysses* as an epic, the nature of the book, including its harsh treatment of Irish nationalism, makes it clear that he intended it as more than a merely Irish or national epic, at least of the sort most Revivalists would have had in mind.

As can be gathered from his portrayal of Eglinton, Lyster, and Best, Joyce treats the Protestant Revivalists as satirically as he does their Catholic counterparts in "Cyclops." Some of the satire arises simply from the record of their talk. A particularly pointed example directed at the Revival comes in a fragment of conversation about Padraic Colum that Stephen overhears:

> I liked Colum's *Drover*. Yes, I think he has that queer thing genius. Do you think he has genius really? Yeats admired his line: As in wild earth a Grecian vase. Did he? (*U* 9.302–305)

Joyce generously leaves the speakers in this inane exchange unidentified, but, aside from Stephen, who remains silent, the only people present are Russell, Lyster, Best, and Eglinton. That the speakers defer to Yeats' judgment will seem reasonable perhaps, until we remember that, like other literary Revivalists, Yeats could be exceedingly generous about writers who contributed to the movement, a trait Buck Mulligan refers to later in the chapter. Moreover, by the time *Ulysses* was published it would have been clear that the poets collected in Russell's volume, namely Eva Gore-Booth, Thomas Koehler, Alice Milligan, Susan Mitchell, Seamus O'Sullivan, George Roberts, Ella Young, and Padraic Colum, hardly justified the excited anticipation of its appearance. The inclusions in the book also further support repeated suggestions in the chapter that the Revivalists' enthusiasms were largely untempered by critical objectivity or literary intelligence.[16]

Part of the satire directed at the literary Revival comes from Mulligan and Stephen. Mulligan, whose chief targets are Synge and the Abbey Theatre, tells Stephen,

> We went over to their playbox, Haines and I, the plumbers' Hall. Our players are creating a new art for Europe like the Greeks or M. Maeterlinck. Abbey Theatre! I smell the pubic sweat of monks (*U* 9.1129–1132).

Regarding Mulligan's references to "plumbers' Hall" and "the pubic sweat of monks," Gifford and Seidman say that the former was a "local name for the Mechanics Institute," which was remodeled in 1904 as the Abbey Theatre, and that the latter alludes to Catholic attacks on Irish National Theatre productions.[17] Whatever people called the Abbey building, Mulligan's reference to it as the plumbers' Hall is meant to poke fun at the enterprise. The reference to monks perhaps simply alludes to St. Mary's Abbey, which once existed in that quarter of Dublin and which is remembered in the name "Lower Abbey Street," where the theatre was located. There remains the puzzling shift in pronouns from "their theatre" to "our players." This could allude to the division between the Protestant directors of the theatre and the Catholic players, or the "their" could point to widespread questions about how Irish the Irish National Theatre actually was, especially since it depended on the financial support of the English woman Annie Horniman. In any event, by 1922 the comic incongruity of linking Maeterlink and the Abbey Theatre with Greek drama should have been pretty clear. Mulligan's satirical jabs at Synge come mainly in his parody of the language used in Synge's plays. Referring to the delivery of Stephen's telegram, Mulligan says to him:

> It's what I'm telling you, mister honey, it's queer and sick we were, Haines and myself, the time himself brought it in. 'Twas murmur we did for a gallus potion would rouse a friar, I'm thinking, and he limp with leching. And we one hour and two hours and three hours in Connery's sitting civil waiting for pints apiece. . . . And we to be there,

> mavrone, and you to be unbeknownst sending us your conglomerations the way we to have our tongues out a yard long like the drouthy clerics do be fainting for a pussful (*U* 9.558–566).

If the parody loses some force coming from an indiscriminate mocker like Mulligan, it nevertheless exposes real problems in the language of Synge's plays.

Mulligan also serves as the mouthpiece of satire aimed at the literary Revivalists' habit of over praising each other's works. Speaking of Stephen's review of Lady Gregory's book, Mulligan says to him, "She gets you a job on the paper, and then you go and slate her drivel to Jaysus. Couldn't you do the Yeats touch?" With accompanying theatrical gestures Mulligan goes on to quote, or rather misquote, Yeats as having said of Lady Gregory's volume, *Cuchulain of Muirthemne:* "The most beautiful book that has come out of our country in my time. One thinks of Homer" (*U* 9.1159–1165). Yeats actually said, "I think this book is the best that has come out of Ireland in my time."[18] The allusion to Homer, which Yeats did not make, only slightly exaggerates his praise of work that contributed to the Revival, as when he compared *Riders to the Sea* with Greek tragedy. It also recalls the question, "Who will write the national epic?" and places Lady Gregory, along with George Moore, among the candidates.

Stephen's satirical barbs are aimed at Russell's preoccupation with mysticism. Though Russell now has faded so much into the background that he may seem an insignificant target, *Ulysses* reminds us that at the time, he was one of the most prominent figures of the literary Revival. Bloom is more aware of him than of anyone else associated with the movement. In "Aeolus" J. J. O'Molloy has heard enough about A. E. and "that hermetic crowd, the opal hush poets" that he asks Stephen what he thinks of them (*U* 7.783–784). Stephen doesn't answer O'Molloy's question, but we learn his opinion in the Library episode from his extensive interior monologue poking fun at "the hermetic crowd" and their ideas:

> Dunlop, Judge, the noblest Roman of them all, A. E., Arval, the Name Ineffable, in heaven hight: K. H., their master, whose identity is no secret to adepts. Brothers of the great white lodge always watching to see if they can help. The Christ with the bridesister, moisture of light, born of an ensouled virgin, repentant sophia, departed to

> the plane of buddhi. The life esoteric is not for ordinary person. O. P. must work off bad karma first. Mrs Cooper Oakley once glimpsed our very illustrious sister H. P. B.'s elemental.
>
> O, fie! Out on't! Pfuiteufel! You naughtn't to look, missus, so you naughtn't when a lady's ashowing of her elemental (*U* 9.65–73).

The terms here, most of which come from theosophical texts, are sufficiently strange that simply quoting them sounds satirical. But there can be no question about the satirical intent behind Stephen's reference to Madame Blavatsky's "elemental."

Ellmann and Mason describe Joyce's criticisms of Lady Gregory's *Poets and Dreamers* as "the first skirmishings in his battle for artistic independence" (*CW* 102). More specifically, as the subject of his review makes clear, he was battling for independence from the aims and practices of the literary Revival. In this struggle he was following the principle enunciated in "The Day of the Rabblement," where he proclaimed that "the artist, though he may employ the crowd, is very careful to isolate himself" (*CW* 69). When he wrote the essay, by "the crowd" Joyce meant primarily the Catholic rabblement, but the leaders of the theatre movement would have been included since they had become "the property of the rabblement." By the time of "The Holy Office" in 1904, he had added to the theatre directors many other figures of the literary Revival, making the broadside a sort of prelude to "Scylla and Charybdis." (Of the writers who figure in "Scylla and Charybdis," Yeats, Russell, Synge, Lady Gregory, Eglinton, Colum, and Starkey are all alluded to in "The Holy Office.") Speaking of this group in "The Holy Office" Joyce proclaims,

> So distantly I turn to view
> The shamblings of that motley crew
> . . . .
> Where they have crouched and crawled and prayed
> I stand the self-doomed, unafraid,
> Unfellowed, friendless and alone,
> Indifferent as the herring-bone
> . . . .
> And though they spurn me from their door
> My soul shall spurn them evermore (*CW* 152).

For someone who claims to have achieved perfect indifference, Joyce seems surprisingly anxious in this poem to return satirical tit for spurning tat.

If the Library group in "Scylla and Charybdis" doesn't quite spurn Stephen, they thoroughly ignore him as a possible contributor to the Revival. Though Eglinton keeps urging people to attend Moore's at home, he never invites Stephen. Neither has Russell included Stephen in his collection of young poets, a point that is underscored by the presence in the volume of Stephen's fellow Catholics, Colum and Starkey. Did Joyce expect his Dublin readers to recognize the contrast between this treatment of Stephen as an outsider and the eager encouragement that Lyster gave to young Yeats? None of the library people include him in the discussion of Revival matters.

To a great extent this treatment of Stephen acknowledges a position that he himself has chosen. Given his acute self-consciousness, one must assume that, like Joyce, Stephen saw his negative review of the Lady Gregory volume as a declaration of independence from the literary Revival. Besides attacking a central figure of the Revival, his review went against the Revival practice of praising work that contributed to the movement. He also has taken a stand against the tradition that literary Revivalists did not exact payment for their work since it was done for the good of Ireland rather than for themselves. We learn from Eglinton that Stephen alone demands payment for things he submits to *Dana* (*U* 9.1082). Stephen's theory of *Hamlet* looks like a further declaration of independence. Beginning with the first performance of the Irish Literary Theatre in 1899, drama was the most prominent genre of the literary Revival. As a result, issues related to the theatre movement, such as its emphasis on peasant plays and on Irish rather than European drama, often dominated literary discussions. As is typical of Joyce's work, where the importance of something often lies in what it is not rather than in what it is, one importance of Stephen's theory is that it has no bearing whatsoever on any of these issues. His explanation of the theory before people who ardently support the literary Revival sounds like an assertion of his independence from the movement as well as a demonstration of his intellectual powers.

Another eloquent negative is Stephen's total silence about anything relating to the Revival. He doesn't contribute a word either to the Library group's discussion of Revival matters or to Mulligan's satirical remarks about Synge and the Abbey Theatre. Even when Mulligan asks him directly about the Lady Gregory review, Stephen remains silent. More remarkable than Stephen's silence about Revival matters is his lack of any response at all to them. He gives no sign that he even is aware of being excluded from Moore's at home or from Russell's poetry collection. In virtually every respect he exhibits the complete aloofness and indifference that Joyce himself aspired to in "The Holy Office" but was not quite able to achieve.

This does not mean that Stephen has shut his mind to the Revival. On the contrary, he displays not only a knowledge of work by Hyde, Yeats, Synge, and other Revival writers but also a more than casual appreciation of it. The poem he composes in "Proteus" is based on a stanza from one of the best-known poems in that seminal work of the literary Revival, Hyde's *The Lovesongs of Connacht*. We know that he also thinks highly of Yeats' verse, particularly "Who Goes with Fergus." More importantly, we learn that he plans on contributing to the Revival. When Haines asks if Stephen writes anything "for your movement," Mulligan replies, apparently quoting Stephen, "He is going to write something in ten years" (*U* 10.1084–1090). Stephen's ideas about Irish history and other matters central to the Revival make it clear, however, that anything he might write for the movement would differ altogether from what had been written so far.

Revival writers tended to see Irish history as a tale of decline from an early heroic period to a contemporary urban culture characterized by materialism and vulgarity. In opposition to this view as well as to Deasy's notion of history as "the manifestation of God," Stephen sees history, including Irish history, as a nightmare of repeated and directionless violence. Stephen's belief that constants dominate history is reflected in his view of the old milkwoman. "Silk of the kine and poor old woman," he thinks, and adds, "names given her in old times" (*U* 1.403–404). Stephen does not view her as a degraded version of the earlier type but as essentially unchanged. *Ulysses* itself is based on the premise that history follows an unchanging pattern and that "Ulysses" was the name given to Bloom in old times. According to the Revival's melodramatic version of Irish history, contemporaries never match the great people of the past. Typically, for Yeats, "romantic Ireland is dead and gone," leaving the contemporary urban Irish, who are cowardly money-grubbers with their fingers in the greasy till.[19] Looking at a current Dubliner he would not think that in old times the person had been called "poor old woman," let alone Cuchulain or Cathleen ni Houlihan. When he praises Maud Gonne for resembling Helen of Troy, he is quick to point out that her qualities are "not natural in an age like this."[20]

The most explicit clash between Stephen's views and those of Revival writers has to do with the mysticism that he associates with Russell but that also figured largely in the career of Yeats and in the literary Revival generally. As is clear from his satirical reflections on contemporary mysticism, he finds a large element of absurdity in it. He rejects it, telling himself, "Hold to the now, the here . . ." (*U* 9.89). The now and the here to which Stephen commits himself is alien to the mystical strain in the literary Revival as well as to many of the movement's other distinctive features. It would mean that instead of writing about the peasants off in the west of Ireland or the heroes and heroines of Irish myth and legend, Stephen would focus on those vulgar, materialistic urbanites who repelled Synge and Yeats.

"Scylla and Charybdis" shows Stephen carefully paying attention to the here and the now. He tells himself as the group discusses Russell's poetry collection, "See this. Remember . . . Listen" (*U* 9.294, 300). Vivian Mercier probably misleads when he says that "Stephen listens with rapt attention" to the conversation about Russell's book.[21] There is no evidence of eagerness on his part, or any other emotion for that matter. The emphasis is on Stephen disciplining himself to focus on the here and the now, as though he were registering the scene for future literary use. That focus is reflected in the scene, or story, we later hear him begin to sketch out: "One day in the national library we had a discussion. Shakes. After" (*U* 9.1108). The sketch points to a contemporary urban narrative, which was a rare thing among the works of literary Revivalists. It also hints at the urban epic, *Ulysses,* though the conventional style of the passage indicates that Stephen has a long way to go before writing such a work.

The glimpse at the Protestant side of the Revival in "Scylla and Charybdis" reveals that it is perhaps even more one-eyed than the Catholic side. While the Catholics in "Cyclops" are concerned largely with political and economic issues and seem oblivious to the literary Revival, the Library Protestants are preoccupied only with the literary Revival and show no interest in Ireland's economy or its relations with England or the revival of its language, sports, and music. According to *Ulysses,* the two sides of the Revival have almost nothing in common. Joyce's portrayal of Stephen among Protestant elders in "Nestor" and "Scylla and Charybdis" and among his Catholic elders in "Aeolus" reveals an equally profound gulf. There are other links among these three chapters.

"Nestor" has a narrative tie to "Aeolus" since it is his promise to deliver Deasy's letter on the hoof-and-mouth disease that takes Stephen to the offices of the *Freeman's Journal,* where most of "Aeolus" is set. "Aeolus" in turn has a thematic link with "Scylla and Charybdis," the discussion of the literary Revival in the latter being foreshadowed in the former when J. J. O'Molloy asks Stephen, "What do you think really of that hermetic crowd, the opal hush poets: A. E. the mastermystic?" He goes on to tell Stephen, "A. E. has been telling some yankee interviewer that you came to him in the small hours of the morning to ask him about planes of consciousness. Magennis thinks you must have been pulling A. E.'s leg" (*U* 7.783–787). In "Scylla and Charybdis," a passage of Stephen's interior monologue —"A. E. has been telling some yankee interviewer"—recalls O'Molloy's speech. Stephen's subsequent satirical reflections on mysticism suggest an answer to O'Molloy's question about his opinion of A. E. and "that hermetic crowd." They also suggest that Magennis was right about Stephen pulling A. E.'s leg.

Besides foreshadowing the literary talk in "Scylla and Charybdis," O'Molloy's speech reveals a skepticism about the literary Revival that contrasts with the enthusiasm of the Library Protestants. This is one of many pointed differences that the pair of chapters reveal between the two cultures. The Protestant elders in the Library are sober, solemn, and solid citizens who attend to their jobs (though they seem at ease, Best and Lyster keep going out to take care of Library duties and A. E. leaves on *Homestead* business). The Catholic elders in the newspaper office in "Aeolus" constantly give way to comic banter, have a pronounced fondness for drink, are in debt or barely solvent, and do not attend to any business at all. In contrast with the Library Protestants, they display virtually no knowledge of the literary Revival and, except for O'Molloy, appear to have no interest in it either.

Alongside these partly stereotypical distinctions between the two cultures, there is also a radical contrast in the relationship between each group and Stephen. Whereas Deasy and the Protestants in the Library treat him as something of an alien, the "Aeolus" Catholics welcome him into their midst like a member of the family. The family note is struck right away when Miles Crawford holds out a welcoming hand to Stephen and tells him,

"Come in. Your governor is just gone" (*U* 7.510–511). Professor MacHugh's greeting, "Good day, Stephen" (*U* 7.526), sounds that note again since in both *Ulysses* and *A Portrait of the Artist,* the use of Stephen's first name is restricted almost exclusively to members of his family. The "Aeolus" Catholics also immediately include Stephen in their friendly banter as though he were one of them. He enters the newspaper office with O'Madden Burke, who announces, "I escort a suppliant. . . . Youth led by Experience visits Notoriety." Observing the loose neckties they are wearing, MacHugh says that Stephen and Burke "look like communards." O'Molloy adds, "Like fellows who had blown up the Bastille" and goes on to suggest that they might be the ones who "shot the lord lieutenant of Finland." Easily joining in the talk, as he did not with either Mr. Deasy or the group in the Library, Stephen replies, "We were only thinking of it" (*U* 7.508–509, 597–603).

Having welcomed him, the "Aeolus" group continues to pay Stephen special attention. J. J. O'Molloy "quietly and slowly" tells Stephen of Seymore Bushe's rhetorical genius and then quotes Bushe's allusion to Michelangelo's "Moses" as an example. After reciting the passage he asks Stephen, "You like it?" (*U* 7.746–775). Similarly, we are told that before Professor MacHugh quotes John F. Taylor's speech on the Irish language, "his gaze turned at once . . . towards Stephen's face." And after reciting the passage he says to Stephen, "That is fine, isn't it?" (*U* 7.819–820, 909). Joyce makes it clear that the chapter's two examples of rhetorical genius are recited primarily for Stephen's benefit. Even Lenehan seeks Stephen's attention, whispering near his ear the limerick about MacHugh (*U* 7.576–582).

In contrast with Deasy, who speaks to him as though he were a child, and the Library Protestants, who often ignore him, the Catholic elders treat Stephen as a talented and intelligent young man. They seek his opinion not only about examples of rhetoric but also about the Dublin literary world, as when O'Molloy asks what he thinks about A. E. Whereas the Library Protestants ignore or are unaware of Stephen's literary ambitions, the Catholic elders generously regard him as having established literary credentials and great potential as a writer. When they list the talents present in the newspaper office, Myles Crawford names the law and the classics, thinking of J. J. O'Molloy and Professor MacHugh; Lenehan mentions the turf, meaning himself, and someone adds "literature," obviously meaning Stephen (*U* 7.605–607). Crawford, who has an especially high estimation of Stephen's literary potential, tells him, "I want you to write something for me. Something with a bite in it. You can do it. . . . Put us all into it, damn its soul. Father, Son and Holy Ghost and Jakes M'Carthy" (*U* 7.616–622). Crawford's proposal, which is that Stephen write something very like a national epic, looks forward to the talk in "Scylla and Charybdis" about who will write the country's epic. It is clear that to Crawford's mind Stephen, not Moore, "is the man for it."

Joyce's account of the reception given to the story Stephen tells at the end of the chapter adds a comical qualification to the "Aeolus" picture of Catholics as supporters of the artist. Though the crowd from the newspaper office makes the journey to Mooney's for drinks, during which Stephen tells the story, MacHugh is the only one to hear the whole story. Having led the exodus for Mooney's and remained ahead of Stephen, Lenehan and O'Madden Burke don't hear any of it. O'Molloy's attempt at borrowing money from Crawford has kept them back so that they miss the whole first half. Crawford's later assessment of the story, "That's new," is true enough, but it is based on a one-sentence summary given by MacHugh when Crawford and O'Molloy finally catch up. Though Crawford hears the rest of the story, his only comment is the puzzled question to Stephen, "Finished?" When Stephen explains that he calls the story *A Pisgah Sight of Palestine* or *The Parable of the Plums,* Crawford is pleased by the allusion to Moses and the promised land, but the pleasure stems partly from his assumption that, as he says to O'Molloy, "We gave him that idea." Preoccupied by his financial problems, O'Molloy gives no response at all to the story, but, we are told, "held his peace." The response of MacHugh, the only person to hear the complete story, is limited to expressions of delight at Stephen's description of Nelson as "the onehandled adulterer" (*U* 7.923–1031). Though the reception of Stephen's story is ambiguous at best, there is no doubt about the goodwill the Catholic elders show toward him. Nor is there any doubt about his special regard for them.

Reflecting on his encounter with the Protestant elders, Stephen asks himself toward the end of "Scylla and Charybdis," "What have I learned? Of them? Of me?" (*U* 9.1113). Similarly, toward the end of his encounter with the Catholic elders in "Aeolus," Stephen thinks, "Dublin. I have much, much to learn" (*U* 7.915). This admission indicates a major reversal in Stephen's view of Irish Catholics, who would be the part of Dublin uppermost in his mind at this point. It implicitly acknowledges that they are not simply a "race of clodhoppers," as he called them in *A Portrait of the Artist* (*P* 272).

Having "uncovered as he entered" the newspaper office, Stephen displays respect for the Catholic elders from the start (*U* 7.506). When O'Molloy tells him that Professor Magennis and A. E. have been talking about him, Stephen thinks, "Speaking about me. What did he say? What did he say? What did he say about me?" (*U* 7.789–790). One might expect an aspiring writer such as Stephen to be most concerned over what a promoter of young writers such as A. E. said about him. As the context makes clear, however, the "he" refers to Professor Magennis, identifying his as the opinion Stephen most values. Another sign of Stephen's special regard for the elders of his own culture is the contrast between the story that he tells them and the theory of *Hamlet* that he explains to the Protestants. The story grows out of or reflects what Stephen calls his "vision" of Dublin, whereas the *Hamlet* theory is simply an academic exercise that he admits he doesn't believe.

Not surprisingly, given their response to him, Stephen feels perfectly at home among the Catholic elders. The feeling is sufficiently strong that he drops his usual guard to the point of blushing, twice. It also erases any reservations he might have about the age differences between himself and the elders so that he feels perfectly free to invite them out for drinks. Myles Crawford responds to the invitation by "clapping Stephen on the shoulder" and calling him a "chip of the old block" (*U* 7.899). The "old block" in this instance is not only Simon Dedalus, who earlier in the chapter went off for drinks with Ned Lambert, but also the Catholic culture. The clap on the shoulder from Crawford, who earlier had laid his hand there, is another gesture of kinship from one of Stephen's elders. It is revealing that Stephen, who is extremely sensitive to such gestures, accepts the clap without objection.

More surprising than Stephen's feeling of respect for, and kinship with, the Catholic elders is his frequent agreement with their judgment and taste. On these latter matters one would expect him to have much more in common with the literary and intellectual Protestants at the Library than with the ragtag Catholics gathered in the newspaper office, but the reverse turns out to be true. His views on everything from Irish history to the literary Revival clash with those of the Protestant elders but are in perfect harmony with the positions and prejudices of the Catholic elders. The skeptical tone of O'Molloy's question about Russell and the "opal hush poets" exactly matches Stephen's own view of Russell, whom the library Protestants extravagantly admire. The way Stephen joins in the banter at the newspaper office, points to another taste he shares with the Catholic elders. Likewise, the rhetorical splendor that moves them also moves him. Of Stephen's response to the passage from Bushe, Joyce writes, "Stephen, his blood wooed by grace of language and gesture, blushed" (*U* 7.776). Impressed by MacHugh's recitation of Taylor's speech, Stephen thinks, "Noble words coming. Look out. Could you try your hand at it yourself?" (*U* 7.836–837). In "Aeolus," as in "Scylla and Charybdis," we hear Stephen mentally compose a literary fragment, this one triggered by the sight of O'Molloy taking out his cigarette case:

> Messenger took out his matchbox thoughtfully and lit his cigar.
> I have often thought since on looking back over that strange time that it was that small act, trivial in itself, that striking of that match, that determined the whole aftercourse of both our lives (*U* 7.762–765).

Like the briefer literary flight in "Scylla and Charybdis," this passage does not immediately suggest a talent capable of producing the national epic. Appropriately for the newspaper office setting, it comically reproduces the style and format of the stories that were a feature of contemporary newspapers and that are exemplified in the story Bloom reads at stool, "Matcham's Masterstroke."

Like "Matcham's Masterstroke," the passage also exemplifies the literary vulgarity that Yeats and other Revivalists associated with English journalism and blamed for corrupting the Irish. The address of its author, Philip Beaufoy, "Playgoers' Club, London," establishes the English source of "Matcham's Masterstroke" (*U* 4.502–503). Similarly, the name "Messenger" suggests an English source for Stephen's inspiration. Stephen has an acute sensibility that would have no trouble detecting the presence or absence of literary merit, but rather than throwing up horrified hands at the style of popular fiction, as the Protestant Revivalists did, Stephen finds it an interesting literary phenomenon and so tries his hand at it. Joyce found such styles not only interesting literary phenomena but also essential to his literary aims. How else in "Nausicaa" could he have portrayed the mind of Gerty MacDowell than by using the style of popular romances? That, of course, is not a question that would have troubled literary Revivalists, few of whom would have considered paying any attention to a mind like Gerty's. Given Joyce's use of popular styles in *Ulysses,* Stephen's experiment with an example of that style may in fact show his potential as the writer of the all-inclusive kind of epic proposed by Myles Crawford.

The story Stephen tells at the end of "Aeolus" gives the fullest illustration of the vast difference between his literary interest and that of most Revivalists. Rather than the legendary figures with resonant names like Dierdre or Maeve that attracted Yeats, Lady Gregory, Synge, and A. E., Stephen's story treats "two Dublin vestals" with the everyday names of Anne Kearns and Florence MacCabe. Rather than living in some far off and famous place such as Emain Macha, the protagonists live in Fumbally's lane, an address so obscure that the old Dubliner, Professor MacHugh, asks, "Where is that?" And rather than ignoring the vulgar and mundane matter of money, Stephen dwells on it, noting that the women have saved "three and tenpence in a red tin letterbox moneybox." He adds, "They shake out the threepenny bits and sixpences and coax out the pennies with the blade of a knife. Two and three in silver and one and seven in coppers." As for the plot, the women's climb up Nelson's pillar and consumption of the plums lacks the faintest hint of the heroic quality found in Irish myths and legends. The story is so inconclusive that Myles Crawford can't tell when it is over and has to ask Stephen, "Finished?" (*U* 7.923–1031).

In his "Preface" to *The Playboy of the Western World,* Synge objected to "the modern literature of towns" produced by Ibsen and Zola, claiming that they wrote in "joyless and pallid words."[22] That unadorned style is exactly the sort Stephen uses in his story. Given his powerful attraction to the rhetorical splendors of Bushe and Taylor, one wonders why. A possible explanation is that with this stylistic choice, Stephen is declaring his independence from Revival writers such as Synge and Yeats, who favored a highly colored style far removed from the commonplace language of journalism. Another possibility is that he does not yet feel ready to try his hand at the sort of rhetorical brilliance exhibited by his Catholic elders. But his attraction to this florid style suggests the possibility of his employing it in the future and producing, as Joyce did in *Ulysses,* an example of the "the modern literature of towns" where the style is anything but "joyless and pallid."

The pattern in "Scylla and Charybdis" of Protestants ignoring Stephen's literary potential, and in "Aeolus" of Catholics encouraging it, does not accord with Joyce's actual experience. Except for a few instances such as

Clery's favorable review of *Chamber Music,* it is difficult to find examples of Catholic support for Joyce or his work. He did, however, receive important help from Protestant leaders of the Revival, Lady Gregory having recommended him as a reviewer for the *Daily Express,* A. E. having published three of his stories in the *Homestead,* and Yeats having recommended him for a grant from the British government. While in ways Joyce's treatment of the two cultures in "Aeolus" and "Scylla and Charybdis" conflicts with his own experience, it is entirely consistent with the rest of the novel, where the Catholic characters are always more attractive than the Protestants.

Of the Catholic characters, the elders come closest to challenging Bloom, Stephen, and Molly in importance. They dominate "Hades" and "Sirens" as well as "Aeolus." They also figure prominently in "Wandering Rocks" and "Cyclops." Joyce's portrayal of them is overwhelmingly sympathetic. As in "Aeolus," they not only are appreciators and practitioners of great talk but also share a number of other traits that set them apart from Mr. Deasy, the Reverend Hugh C. Love, and the Protestants in "Scylla and Charybdis." The earliest example is Stephen's uncle, Richie Goulding, a character based on Joyce's uncle, John Murray. Dramatizing the potent effect members of the older generation apparently had on his own imagination, Joyce shows Stephen in "Nestor" vividly imagining a visit to the Gouldings. This imagined visit, which Bernard Benstock observes is the first sign that Stephen might have the capacity to write a book like *Ulysses,* dwells on traits that are associated with the Catholic elders elsewhere in the novel.[23] Like this older generation, Goulding has serious financial problems, (after pulling the bell at the Goulding house Stephen imagines, "They take me for a dun, peer out from a coign of vantage"). Like the elders in "Aeolus," he welcomes Stephen with a warm and humorous banter, telling him, "Morrow, nephew. Sit down and take a walk," subsequently amplified to "Sit down or by the law Harry I'll knock you down." Like Myles Crawford, with his "incipient jigs," Goulding has physical problems, which explains why he is still in bed at ten in the morning and why he tells Stephen there is "nothing in the house but backache pills." Also like Crawford and all the other Catholic elders, Goulding has a weakness for drink, ordering "malt for Richie and Stephen" in spite of the early hour. Finally he shares with the Catholic elders in "Sirens" an informed taste for music, which he demonstrates by whistling for Stephen's benefit a "finely shaded" version of an aria from Verdi's *Il Trovatore* (*U* 3.70–103).

Stephen concludes his vision of the visit to Goulding's house with the reflection, "Houses of decay, mine, his and all" (*U* 3.105). There being nothing to suggest that Deasy, Love, A. E., Eglinton, Best, or Lyster dwell in "houses of decay," Stephen's "all" points to Catholics. That they inhabit houses of decay does not depress the elders as it does Stephen. On the contrary, it contributes to the spirit of camaraderie that prevails among them whenever they appear and that is typified in the encounter between Simon and Bob Cowley in "Wandering Rocks." After the two "clasped hands loudly," Simon asks, "What's the best news?" Cowley says he's "barricaded up." He explains that two men are attempting to "effect an entrance" in connection with a debt he owes Reuben J. Dodd and that he is waiting for Ben Dollard, who has promised to speak with long John Fanning about having the men removed. We learn also that he has been distrained for rent by his landlord, the Reverend Love. In a scene that illustrates how the economic condition of Catholics has made them experts on certain points of law, Dollard appears and explains that Dodd's writ is worthless since "the landlord has the prior claim." He adds that he has given all the details to Fanning, who presumably will have the two men removed from Cowley's premises (*U* 10.882–946).

In addition to a wonderful sense of camaraderie, the scene illustrates the Catholic elders' willingness to help each other cope with their ruin. We see this willingness again in the subscription for the Dignam family that Martin Cunningham has started. The scene also is laced with instances of witty self-dramatization as when Simon Dedalus "mutter[s] sneeringly" of Ben Dollard's oversized trousers, "That's a pretty garment, isn't it, for a summer's day?" Giving a more elaborate instance of the dramatizing habit, Joyce writes that in response to Cowley's plea for "a few days" of relief from Dodd's pursuit, "Ben Dollard halted and stared, his loud orifice open, . . . as he wiped away the heavy shraums that clogged his eyes to hear aright." Dollard then remarks, "What few days?" meaning that since Dodd's writ is worthless Cowley will have complete freedom from the threatening men (*U* 10.904–943).

In a well-known letter to Harriet Shaw Weaver mourning his father's recent death, Joyce wrote, "Hundreds of pages and scores of characters in my books came from him. His dry (or rather wet) wit and his expression of face convulsed me often with laughter" (*SL* 361). The Catholic elders in *Ulysses* are modeled not only on Joyce's father but also on his father's friends and on relatives of his father's generation. It is these real life elders that Joyce would have had in mind when he told Djuna Barnes, "they are all there [in *Ulysses*], the great talkers . . . and the things they forgot."[24] The health of the Catholic elders may be undermined, their clothes ragged and their finances a disaster, but their spirit remains intact. From Stephen's vision of Richie Goulding to the "Wandering Rocks" scene with Simon, Bob Cowley, and Ben Dollard, their wit is constantly present, both in their talk and in their self-dramatizing behavior. Finally, in "Sirens," where we get our last glimpse of them, Joyce shows them tirelessly singing. Bloom is referred to memorably as "unconquered hero" (*U* 11.342). Insofar as *Ulysses* is an Irish epic, the Catholic elders are its unconquered heroes.

The portraits of the Catholic elders in *Ulysses* represent a rare instance of Joyce idealizing. In the "Wandering Rocks" scene where Dilly has to keep asking Simon for money, presumably to buy food, Joyce paints a darker picture of Catholic elders and of the poverty that they treat so cavalierly (*U* 10.666–711). He gives a still darker picture later in the novel when Bloom and Stephen encounter the demoralized Corely near the cabmen's shelter. Corely, whose breath is "redolent of rotten cornjuice," has no witty banter or comic gestures but simply pleads for money in the clichéd terms of depressed poverty, telling Stephen, "I wouldn't ask you only, . . . on my solemn oath and God knows I'm on the rocks." The idealized picture of the Catholic elders remains relatively untouched, however, since Corely is "still comparatively young" (*U* 16.128–203).

Corely is hanging around at this late hour because he has no place to stay. Stephen tells him, "I have no place to sleep myself" (*U* 16.163). Bob Cowley also has trouble with housing. The Reverend Love, on the other hand, apparently has two homes in addition to the house he rents to Cowley. As far as we know, Cowley never reflects on the sectarian implications of his being the impecunious renter and Love being the comfortably well-off landlord. In his apparent obliviousness to sectarian differences, Cowley resembles most of the other characters in *Ulysses,* except for Stephen and Mr. Deasy. Another exception is Gerty MacDowell, who confirms Stephen's conviction in *A Portrait of the Artist* that Catholic women are attracted to Protestant men. Impressed by such things as his prospective career as a doctor, "the nice perfume of those good cigarettes" he uses (*U* 13.144), and doubtless also by his quintessentially English name, Gerty is, as she probably would put it, "hopelessly in love with" the young Protestant, Reggy

Wylie. Apropos his being a Protestant we are told, "of course Gerty knew Who came first and after Him the Blessed Virgin and then Saint Joseph" (*U* 13.139–140). This knowledge, however, has no apparent effect on her dream of marrying Reggy and thereby becoming the subject of reports from "fashionable intelligence" that "Mrs. Gertrude Wylie was wearing a sumptuous confection of grey trimmed with expensive blue fox" (*U* 13.198). For Gerty, marriage to Reggy means a passport to the superior "classiness" that Enid Starkie grew up identifying with Protestants.

Perhaps because of his Jewish background, Bloom is notably free of the sectarian feelings found in Stephen. With no apparent qualms, he has allowed himself to be baptized both as a Catholic and as a Protestant. Though his mother presumably was Catholic and his wife clearly is, he feels no special attachment to that culture. At Paddy Dignam's funeral he ends up with the other convert, Tom Kernan, both being equally vague about Catholic ritual (Bloom thinks, "We are in the same boat" [*U* 6.663]). Vestiges of Kernan's Protestant background emerge briefly when he compares Father Coffee's performance at Dignam's funeral with funerals at the Protestant cemetery in Mount Jerome. He remarks to Bloom, "The reverend gentleman read the service too quickly" and adds, "The service of the Irish church used in Mount Jerome is simpler, more impressive I must say." Though Bloom "nodded gravely" to the first opinion and "gave prudent assent" to the second, he remains fundamentally indifferent (*U* 6.659–667).

Bloom may be neutral or indifferent when it comes to most sectarian distinctions, but in other ways he is as Irish as he claims to be. His reaction to the woman outside the Grosvenor Hotel in "Lotus Eaters," shows that Protestant ladies hold a special attraction for him, as they do for Stephen in *A Portrait of the Artist,* and Richard in *Exiles*. Like the Maple's Hotel in *A Portrait,* the Grosvenor was frequented by the Ascendancy when they came to Dublin from their big houses in the country. Aware of this pattern and observing that her luggage is being loaded on the nearby outsider, Bloom assumes that the woman is "off to the country" and that the outsider will take her to "Broadstone probably," which is the terminal for trains serving the country. As he often does with other women, Bloom pays special attention to the Grosvenor Hotel woman's clothes, noting that she wears a "stylish kind of coat with that roll collar," gloves, "high brown boots with laces dangling," and most important of all, "silk stockings." He also notes the "careless stand of her with her hands in those patch pockets." "Proud:

rich," he thinks, like "that haughty creature at the polo match" (*U* 5.98–140). (What was Bloom doing at a polo match?) In "Circe," again demonstrating his classic devotion to the rule rather than the exception, Joyce identifies this woman as a "*rich protestant lady*" (*U* 15.4348).

The theme of Bloom's attraction to Ascendancy ladies is picked up again during the trial episode in "Circe" where his accusers include Mrs. Yelverton Barry, Mrs. Bellingham, and the Honourable Mrs. Mervyn Talboys. That they are Ascendancy ladies is suggested by their names. Also, like the Grosvenor Hotel woman, they are associated with polo and fashionable dress.

Mrs. Yelverton Barry appears in "lowcorsaged opal balldress and elbowlength ivory gloves, wearing a sabletrimmed brickquilted dolman, a comb of brilliants and panache of osprey in her hair," while Mrs. Bellingham says Bloom saw her "on the polo ground of the Phoenix park at the match All Ireland versus the Rest of Ireland" (*U* 15.1013–1061). In the same episode, complaints against Bloom also are lodged by Martha Clifford and by the Blooms' former maid, Mary Driscoll, but the number of Ascendancy ladies who appear against him—in addition to the three named, there are other possibilities among the "*several highly respectable Dublin ladies*" who exhibit improper letters from Bloom (*U* 16.1078–1079)—indicates his special attraction to them.

Bloom's letters to the Ascendancy ladies appear to have been more explicit than those to Martha. The Honourable Mrs. Talboys says that Bloom sent her a picture of a nude young woman "practising illicit intercourse with a muscular torero" and "urged [her] to do likewise," not with him but with "officers of the garrison." She also says that he "implored [her] to soil his letter in an unspeakable manner, to chastise him as he richly deserves, to bestride and ride him, to give him a most vicious horsewhipping." Both Mrs. Bellingham and Mrs. Yelverton Barry say, "Me too." Exactly which of the Honourable Mrs. Talboy's charges are being seconded by the other women is not clear, but the implication is all of them. Mrs. Bellingham says explicitly that he urged her to "commit adultery," again not necessarily with him but "at the earliest possible opportunity" (*U* 16.1054–1077).

Bloom's urging of the women to commit adultery has an immediate connection with his complicity in Molly's adultery. It has a more distant connection with the supposedly idealistic interest that Stephen Dedalus and Richard Rowan have in influencing the minds of Protestant women and liberating them from various Protestant inhibitions or conventions relating to sex. Concern for the welfare of the country is suggested as the motive behind Stephen's wish to influence the way Ascendancy daughters think, while Richard implies that concern for Beatrice's welfare motivated his attempts at influencing the way she thinks. We hear a comic version of these motives when Mrs. Bellingham says of Bloom, "He urged me (stating that he felt it his mission in life to urge me) to defile the marriage bed, to commit adultery at the earliest possible opportunity" (*U* 15.1054–1056). Bloom's "mission," apparently, is to get Mrs. Bellingham to break all the taboos and enter a new world of sexual freedom and experience. We learn from the behavior and the monologue of Catholic Molly that she does not need the guidance of Bloom or anyone else to enter this world but already is quite well at home in it.

The Protestant ladies lack not only Molly's sexual freedom but also her sexual frankness and honesty. While pretending outrage at Bloom's proposal that she should commit adultery, Mrs. Talboys mentions that at the polo match where Bloom saw her, her eyes "shone divinely as [she] watched Captain Slogger Dennehy of the Inniskillings win the final chukkar on his darling cob Centaur." And speaking of the obscene photograph that Bloom sent her she lets drop, "I have it still." In general, Bloom's lack of a high social position bothers them much more than the sexual proposals that they denounce. Mrs. Bellingham calls him an "objectionable person," an "upstart," and a "mongrel," while Mrs. Talboys refers to him as "the plebeian Don Juan" and as a "pigeonlivered cur" (*U* 15.1061–1104).

In their hypocrisy about sexual matters, Mrs. Bellingham, Mrs. Talboys, and Mrs. Barry are comic versions of Beatrice. As Richard expressed something in Beatrice's soul, though she was unable to act on it, so Bloom's letters have expressed a side of the Protestant ladies that they pretend to abhor. His proposal that the ladies whip him, however, has touched a part of their souls that they are more than willing to act on. Mrs. Talboys says, "I'll scourge the pigeonlivered cur as long as I can stand over him. I'll flay him alive." Mrs. Bellingham urges her "Tan his breech well! . . ." A moment later she adds, "Thrash the mongrel within an inch of his life. The cat-o'-nine tails. Geld him. Vivisect him." Mrs. Barry concludes with, "He should be soundly trounced!" (*U* 16.1082–1112). On this topic, their souls are at one with the soul of Bella, who punishes Bloom with gusto. They also are at odds with Catholic Molly, who is attracted to a wide range of sexual possibilities but neither to sadism nor to masochism.

Bloom's masochistic tendencies, which surface most obviously in his desire to be whipped, are underscored by his use of the pseudonym "James Lovebirch," by his allusion to Masoch's novel *Venus in Furs,* a copy of which later turns up in his library, and by other details from his letters to the Protestant ladies (*U* 16.1018, 1046, 1071–1073). His reaction to the Grosvenor Hotel lady, however, includes feelings just the opposite of his well-known masochism. Apparently prompted by her air of pride and hauteur Bloom thinks, "Possess her once take the starch out of her" (*U* 5.106). This gust of sadistic aggression is another of the many instances where Joyce shows that Bloom, like Molly and other characters in the novel, is composed of often conflicting traits. Like the other instances, Bloom's aggressive side suggests that Joyce agreed with Montaigne's conviction about people being swarms of opposites.

Bloom appears to be as oblivious to the existence of the Irish Revival as he is to the presence of sectarian tensions. He knows that in addition to being a vegetarian and mystic, A. E. writes poetry and has some sort of following, but he demonstrates no knowledge of Yeats, failing to recognize Yeats' well known lyric "Who Goes with Fergus" when Stephen mumbles parts of it in "Circe" (*U* 8.533–547; 15.4930–4954). He also seems ignorant of Lady Gregory, Douglas Hyde, Synge, and other prominent figures of the literary Revival. He is equally blank on the Abbey Theatre. He knows that the Irish language is an issue, and imagines or recalls the topic, "That the language question should take precedence of the economic question" as a typical one for debating societies. He also knows there is such a thing as the Gaelic League, but he completely misunderstands it, assuming that it is some underground movement like the Fenians with a complement of spies. Hence, in "Circe" he thinks that the "sinister figure" who appears is a "Gaelic league spy, sent by that fireeater," i.e. the Citizen (*U* 15.220–221). Oddly, he claims to know something about the Gaelic Athletic Association or its founder. When Joe Hynes lists a number of the Citizen's accomplishments, including the founding of "the Gaelic sports revival," Alf Bergan says, "Is that really a fact?" Bloom surprisingly answers, "Yes. . . . That's well known" (*U* 12.880–888).

Like the Catholics in Joyce's work, Bloom is much more knowledgeable about nationalist politics than about the cultural side of the Revival. Joyce invests Bloom's attitude toward nationalist politics with the same troubled complexity and contradictions that marked his own. On the one hand, he makes Bloom's clash with the nationalist Citizen a central episode in the book. On the other, he reveals that as a young man Bloom himself was a vocal supporter of political nationalism and "publicly expressed his adherence" not only to "the collective and national economic programme advocated by James Fintan Lalor, John Fisher . . . and others," but also to "the agrarian policy of Michael Davitt, [and] the constitutional agitation of Charles Stewart Parnell." Comically deflating the intensity of Bloom's nationalism, Joyce adds that "in support of his political convictions" he climbed a tree to watch the torchlight procession accompanying the entrance into Dublin of the Marquess of Ripon and John Morley, who were English supporters of Home Rule (*U* 17.1645–1656).

However cautious he is about his own political actions, Bloom still admires Parnell, calling him "a born leader of men" and "a magnificent specimen of manhood" who was "truly augmented obviously by gifts of a high order" (*U* 16.1388–1389). He recalls as a special moment in his own life the time he returned to Parnell the latter's hat, which had been knocked off during a street ruckus. He also approves of Arthur Griffith, to whom he is supposed to have given the famous "Hungarian system" (*U* 12.1635–1637). Though Molly recalls him telling her that Griffith "is the coming man [and] very intelligent" (*U* 18.385–386), we hear Bloom himself make the more reserved assessment that Griffith is "a square headed chap," but falls short of Parnell because he "has no go in him for the mob" (*U* 8.462–463).

Though the thirty-eight-year-old Bloom remains interested in political nationalism, he no longer is the enthusiastic supporter he was at nineteen. This change may reflect a decline in the quality of nationalist leaders, not just a more "mature" perspective. Bloom sees that Griffith simply lacks Parnell's magnetism, and the Citizen lacks more than that. More obvious than any disenchantment with its leaders is Bloom's thoroughgoing skepticism about the people who proclaim themselves Irish nationalists. This skepticism is revealed in "Lestrygonians" in Bloom's recollection of the protest against Joseph Chamberlain, who was in Dublin to receive an honorary degree from Trinity College and whom nationalists objected to because he had helped defeat the most recent Home Rule bill and currently supported the Boer War. Bloom doubts the sincerity of the college students who led

Bloom objects not only to the Citizen's racism but also to his idea of using a battleship to achieve the new Ireland he envisions. Bloom argues that a society founded on premises of racial hatred and violence hardly would be worth living in. As he says in a frequently cited exchange with the Citizen, "But it's no use. . . . Force, hatred, history, all that. That's not life for men and women, insult and hatred" (*U* 12.1481–1483). Developing his objections further, Bloom tells John Wyse in a partly heard conversation, "Persecution, . . . all the history of the world is full of it. Perpetuating national hatred among nations" (*U* 12.1417–1418). The reference to "nations" leads to the well-known exchange where the Citizen asks Bloom what nation he belongs to, and Bloom replies, "Ireland" (*U* 12.1430–1431). Like most others who express an opinion of him, the Citizen treats Bloom as a "stranger" or alien. Bloom, however, insists that he is Irish because, as he says, "I was born here."

Bloom's exchange with the Citizen recalls the question raised in the opening chapter about the relationship between the Irish and Jews. It also bears directly on a paradox of Irish nationalism. On the one hand, Moran and Griffith, like the Citizen, viewed Jews as aliens and a threat to Irish culture. On the other hand, it was a commonplace of nationalist rhetoric to identify the Irish with Old Testament Jews and to refer to one or another nationalist leader as a Moses, who would lead the Irish out of bondage to England, just as the Old Testament figure had led the Jews out of bondage to the Egyptians. Joyce included a recent example of this tradition in the speech of John F. Taylor that Professor MacHugh reports in "Aeolus." The speech, which was part of a debate at Trinity College over a paper "advocating the revival of the Irish tongue" (*U* 7.795–796), responds to an attack on the paper by Mr. Justice Fitzgibbon. Describing his response to Fitzgibbon's remarks, Taylor said, "It seemed to me that I had been transported into a country far away from this country, . . . that I stood in ancient Egypt and that I was listening to the speech of some highpriest of that land addressed to the youthful Moses." He adds that if Moses had accepted that highpriest's attack on the language and culture of the Jews, "he never would have brought the chosen people out of the house of bondage" (*U* 7.830–866). The implication of the speech is that the student audience may contain a Moses, who will ignore Fitzgibbon's attack on Irish culture and lead the Irish out of their house of bondage.

"Cyclops" presents a succinct example of this identification of the Irish with Jews when Martin Cunningham says of the Jews, "Well, they're still waiting for their redeemer . . . ," and then adds, "For that matter so are we" (*U* 12.1644–1645). Bloom's response to the Citizen includes a more significant example, however. After claiming that he is Irish Bloom adds,

> And I belong to a race too, . . . that is hated and persecuted. Also now. This very moment. . . . Plundered. Insulted. Persecuted. Taking what belongs to us by right (*U* 12.1467–1471).

Bloom's emphasis here on his Jewish heritage appears to contradict his assertion about being Irish; however, his comment points to an identity between the two cultures since, as the Citizen has been insisting, the Irish have been hated and persecuted and plundered by the English. When Bloom emphasizes that persecution of the Jews is occurring "This very moment. This very instant," he lifts the parallel out of its usual Biblical context and makes it contemporary. Though he cites Morocco as an example, his curious insistence that the persecution is taking place "now," reminds us of what is happening "now" in the novel, where the Citizen is attacking Bloom. It underscores the point that anti-Semitism is present in contemporary Ireland and that its most vigorous promoters include Irish nationalists such as the Citizen.[25] The chapter as a whole makes the further point that Irish anti-Semitism is simply another version of the English attitude toward the Irish.

When asked what he means when he says that hatred is "the very opposite of that that is really life," Bloom answers, "Love . . . the opposite of hatred" (*U* 12.1481–1484). Though Joyce follows with a satirical passage that throws doubt on the existence of "Universal love," as the Citizen scornfully calls it (*U* 12.1493–1501), he leaves no doubt about the widespread presence of the hatred that informs anti-Semitism: the Englishman Haines, the Protestant Deasy, and the Catholic Citizen all show their hatred for Jews.

In "Eumaeus" Joyce returns to the theme of Irish nationalism's association with violence and hatred. He does this initially by introducing the rumor that the keeper of the cabmen's shelter is "Skin the Goat," who was involved in the Phoenix Park murders when the Chief Secretary and Under Secretary of Ireland were stabbed to death by members of the Invincibles (*U* 12.460). Whoever he may be, the keeper echoes those standard Irish nationalist denunciations of the English that we hear from the Citizen in

"Cyclops." This connection is noted by Bloom, who tells Stephen that the keeper speaks "the same identical lingo" as the Citizen. Prompted by the anti-English rhetoric of the keeper, Bloom once again states his opposition to hate and violence:

> I resent violence and intolerance in any shape or form. It never reaches anything or stops anything. A revolution must come on the due installments plan. It's a patent absurdity on the face of it to hate people because they live round the corner and speak another vernacular, in the next house so to speak (*U* 16.1099–1103).

Again, as in "Cyclops," Bloom moves from the topic of hate to that of anti-Semitism, telling Stephen in an imperfectly heard remark, "Jews . . . are accused of ruining. Not a vestige of truth in it." Bloom does not believe in racial or national distinctions but in "all creeds and classes *pro rata* having a comfortable tidysized income." "I call that patriotism," he says" (*U* 16.1119–1120, 1133–1134).

The triteness of Bloom's language gives an ironic twist to his utopian vision, but the vision itself addresses a problem of Irish nationalism that Joyce thought sufficiently important to focus on in *Ulysses* not just once but twice. Presumably, Bloom's experience as a Jew has made him realize the injustice of racial, religious, and national prejudices. That their experiences as Irish Catholics under English rule haven't led the Citizen and the keeper of the cabmen's shelter to a similar realization points to a limitation of insight often dramatized in Joyce's work as well as in the history of Irish nationalism.

In "Penelope," Joyce added the last touches to his bitter portrayal of Irish nationalism. Here we learn that Molly will be going to Belfast to sing partly because nationalist pressure has closed the Dublin stage to her. Bloom, she says, "knew there was a boycott" against her in Dublin. The term "boycott" is associated with Parnell, whose proposal to ostracize landlords guilty of evicting tenants was first put into practice against a Captain Boycott. While the boycott initially was aimed at people who seriously disrupted the lives of Irish families, Molly is being boycotted for a failure to be sufficiently or appropriately nationalistic. She recalls that her last singing engagement was "over a year ago . . . on account of father being in the army and my singing the absentminded beggar and wearing a brooch for Lord Roberts . . .

and Poldy not Irish enough" (*U* 18.376–379). These explanations point to several ways in which Molly would have offended Irish nationalists.

One way is by appearing to support British participation in the Boer War. As Gifford and Seidman explain, Molly's song "The Absentminded Beggar," which set to music a poem by Rudyard Kipling, was in sympathy with British soldiers fighting in South Africa, while her "brooch for Lord Roberts," honored the commander in chief of the British troops in South Africa.[26] Identifying with the Boers as victims of British imperial might, Irish nationalists vigorously opposed the Boer War, as in the episode Bloom recalls where he was caught up in the student demonstration against Joseph Chamberlain, a supporter of the War (*U* 8.423–436). To Edward Martyn, singing the "Absent Minded Beggar" implied not only support for the Boer War but also indifference, or even opposition, to the Irish Revival. In a letter to the press he explained that he had refused to allow "The Absent Minded Beggar" and "God Save the Queen" to be sung at a recent concert in his house "because unfortunately in our country the Queen's name & Mr. Kipling's name have come to mean the same thing as the Union & the extinction of our distinctive nationality." [27]

We learn that Molly, too, opposed the Boer War, though for entirely different reasons than the political or cultural objections of the Irish nationalists. She objects to it for "killing any finelooking men there were," especially Lt. Stanley Gardner, whose departure for South Africa and passionate kiss goodbye she still vividly remembers (*U* 18.389–396). Molly's feelings for British soldiers would have offended Irish nationalists at least as much as any apparent support of the Boer War. As Joyce shows in the Citizen's remarks about the British Navy and in Old Gummy Granny's wish that Stephen "remove" Private Carr, nationalist animosity toward the English military was especially intense. Molly, however, not only sympathizes with the English soldiers in South Africa but also admires the British military in general. She fondly recalls "the Black Watch with their kilts in time at the march past the 10th hussars the prince of Wales own or the lancers O the lancers theyre grand or the Dublins that won Tugela" (*U* 18.400–403). While the nationalists object to her having a father in the British Army, she feels no shame at her military heritage. On the contrary, she proudly proclaims, "[a] soldier's daughter am I ay" (*U* 18.881–882). Her loyalty to and identification with the British military suggest that she is responsible for the "compactly furled Union Jack" in the corner by the Blooms' fireplace (*U* 17.1282).

She doesn't find anything in Irish nationalism to match the appeal of the British military. Her understanding of the movement depends largely on an imperfect recollection of comments that Bloom has made to her about Arthur Griffith. She remains highly skeptical of Griffith, in spite of Bloom's praise of him, recalling him as "the little man . . . without the neck." Apropos Bloom's claim that Griffith "is very intelligent," she thinks, "[W]ell he doesn't look it thats all I can say." Later on she recalls Griffith as "the little man . . . dribbling along in the wet all by himself round by Coadys lane." She also recalls Bloom describing him as "capable and sincerely Irish" and adds, "he is indeed judging by the sincerity of the trousers I saw on him" (*U* 18.385–386, 1228–1229). For whatever reason, she believes that Bloom recently has been associating with "Sinner Fein," as she thinks they are called, "talking his usual trash and nonsense" (*U* 18.383, 1227). She fears that this association may cost him his job on the *Freemans Journal,* though it is unclear whether her fear is that his employers will think he is not attending to business or that they will disapprove of Sinn Fein politics (*U* 18.1227–1231).

Though Molly is merely skeptical of Griffith and Sinn Fein, she has an intense scorn for the Revivalists "Kathleen Kearney and her like" (*U* 18.376). It will be recalled that in "A Mother" Joyce showed how Kathleen Kearney's reputation as "a believer in the language movement" aided her musical career. Then she played the piano, but now, she apparently concentrates on singing. While Molly is angry at being boycotted, she is even angrier that, thanks to the Revival, Kathleen and other "little chits of missies" have taken over Dublin's stages. Claiming that they lack both her voice and her impressive figure, Molly dismisses these young women as "squeelers" and, more memorably, as a "lot of sparrowfarts" (*U* 18.878–879).

While Blazes and Molly apparently have planned the Belfast tour with an eye to its sexual opportunities, the stages of largely Unionist Belfast would not be cornered by Revivalist singers, and the audiences there would have no objections at all to expressions of sympathy toward the British military. Neither would they be likely to object to "Loves Old Sweet Song" or "*La ci darem,*" which will be part of the program. Even if the Dublin stage were open to her she probably could not expect much success with a program so barren of appeal to nationalist sentiments.

Yeats liked to condemn Catholic objections to his work and that of the literary Revival generally as "politics." Molly does much the same when it comes to the effect of the Revival on her career. Apropos the boycott she thinks, "I hate the mention of their politics" (*U* 18.387–388). Among her objections to Kathleen Kearney and her like is that they spend their time "skitting around talking about politics," which, she says, "they know as much about as my backside" (*U* 18.879–880). By "politics" she means abstract principles or ideologies promoted by some group. By contrast, her own beliefs grow out of her personal, and often her sexual, experience, as in her attitudes toward the Boer War and the British military, which are rooted in her relationship with Lt. Stanley Gardner and her heritage as the daughter of Major Tweedy.

According to Molly, people committed to Revival or nationalist politics are sexual innocents. Alluding to Kathleen Kearney and her like, Molly thinks, "I knew more about men and life when I was 15, than theyll all know at 50" (*U* 18.886–887). For Joyce, too, nationalism and sex do not mix, except in the case of Parnell. Typically, Joyce's nationalist characters have neither knowledge of nor interest in sex. An early example comes in *Stephen Hero,* where the first of Joyce's young women Revivalists, Emma Clery, is portrayed as adamantly virginal. Stephen's proposal that they spend the night together so shocks her that she pulls her hand away from his, repeatedly calls him "mad," and tells him, "You must not speak to me any more" (*SH* 198–199). The association of sexual innocence and Irish nationalism comes up again in *A Portrait of the Artist* with the young nationalist Davin, whose innocence is so absolute that Stephen can hardly credit it. A less explicit but no less certain linking of nationalism and sexual innocence occurs in the characterization of Revivalist Miss Ivors, of whom Joyce writes in a loaded *non sequitur,* "She did not wear a low-cut bodice and the large brooch which was fixed in the front of her collar bore on it an Irish device" (*D* 187). (It is representative of Joyce's attitude toward nationalists and sex that whereas Molly Bloom's brooch honors a man, Miss Ivors' brooch shows "an Irish device.") Miss Ivors again is associated with sexual innocence when Gabriel refers to her as "the girl or woman, or whatever she was" (*D* 190). "The Dead" also links Kathleen Kearney with Miss Ivors, who tells Gabriel that Kathleen will be coming on the Aran Isles excursion. Molly Bloom completes the pattern by attributing to Kathleen the same sexual ignorance associated with Miss Ivors.

According to nationalist dogma, the sexual innocence scorned by Molly, and apparently by Joyce as well, characterized not just nationalists but also the Irish generally and especially Irish women. In *A Portrait of the Artist,*

Joyce mocks this idea by having Stephen recall the students at the opening performance of *Countess Cathleen* protesting that "No Irish woman ever did it!" (*P* 226). Molly's fondness for doing it and preoccupation with doing it constitute another of the numerous ways in which Joyce has made her an anti-nationalist heroine. In particular, it sets her apart from Yeats' Cathleen ni Houlihan, who calls young Michael Gillane away from marriage, sex, and possible new life to follow her in pursuit of the nationalist struggle and possible death.

Molly Bloom's relationship with, and attitude toward, Ireland also contribute to her anti-nationalist portrait. While people in and out of the novel question whether Bloom is Irish, few, if any, question Molly's Irishness. Perhaps because they know that Joyce thought of Nora Joyce as embodying the essential traits of Ireland and used her as one of the models for Molly, readers generally accept Molly as somehow very Irish and as an important contributor to the book's Irishness. But Joyce constantly undercuts Molly's Irishness. While there is a suggestion that her mother, Lunita Laredo, may have been Jewish, there is no suggestion at all that she was Irish, so, like Bloom, Molly is Irish on only one side. She actually has less claim to being Irish than he, since she was born and raised in Gibraltar while he grew up in Ireland. Molly's angry reflection on being boycotted because she wasn't sufficiently nationalistic contains the fragmentary thought, "when I had the map of it all," apparently meaning that she has the map of Ireland all over her face, in other words looked very Irish (*U* 18.378). However, she also thinks of herself as "being jewess looking after my mother" and recalls her father often telling her that she had her mother's eyes and figure (*U* 18.1184–1185). This suggests that she well might look as alien as Bloom. She should have sounded more alien than he did. Having been born and raised in Dublin, Bloom would have had some sort of Irish accent. Joyce implies that Molly did have such an accent when he has her worry that Lt. Stanley Gardner "mightn't like [her] accent first he so English." Since she was born and grew up on Gibraltar it is hard to know what sort of accent she would have had, but it hardly could have been Irish.[28]

In his encounter with the Citizen, Bloom insists that he is Irish, but Molly makes no such claim. She thinks of herself as a "soldiers daughter" and believes that this military heritage makes her superior to "Irish homemade beauties" such as Kathleen Kearney, whose fathers are "bootmakers and publicans" (*U* 18.881–882). In "Cyclops," where she is called the "Pride of Calpe's rocky mount," Molly is identified with Gibraltar rather than Ireland (*U* 12.1003). That is the way she identifies herself. She recalls "the glare of the rock standing up in [a lavanter] like a big giant compared with their 3 Rock mountain they think is so great" (*U* 18.608–609). Three Rock Mountain south of Dublin is "their" mountain, while the great rock of Gibraltar presumably is "hers." Emer Nolan observes, "The most subversive thing about [Molly], as the heroine of an Irish novel, is that she is not really a native at all."[29]

Molly's disparaging view of Three Rock Mountain is typical of her response to Ireland and the Irish in general. She views Simon Dedalus, Paddy Dignam, Tom Kernan, Martin Cunningham, Jack Power, and apparently most or all other Irishmen as "goodfornothings" (*U* 18.1255–1279). Worse yet, from a nationalist perspective, of her two early romantic relationships, she prefers the Englishman Gardner to Mulvey, the Irish naval officer from Cappoquin. Her limited memories of Mulvey include the information that she didn't like his Irish name (*U* 18.845–846); however, she has extensive and glowing memories of Gardner, who not only gave her the passionate good-bye kiss but also embraced her in a way no one else seems to have equaled. She thinks the English sometimes are "so snotty about themselves," but adds that Gardner "wasn't a bit like that" (*U* 18.889–892). His place in her memory is not challenged by anyone else except possibly Bloom, though even his embraces did not match Gardner's (*U* 18.331–332). As for Irish culture, she simply ignores it as she does Irish songs, which she makes no attempt at including in her repertoire. She doesn't appear even to know many Irish songs.

Molly's epithet "homemade" for young women Revivalists alludes to the provincialism that was a pronounced feature of Irish nationalism. This provincialism is a component of the national and racial hatred that runs through the nationalist rhetoric of Moran and Griffith and that *Ulysses* implies is widespread among the Irish. Molly takes pride in having a broader awareness than the homemade Irish have. She still remembers her father talking with Captain Grove about Rorke's Drift, Plevna, and Khartoum (*U* 18.690–691). In particular, she recalls the mixture of cultures she encountered in Gibraltar. She thinks of:

> the Spanish girls laughing in their shawls and their tall combs and the auctions in the morning the Greeks and the jews and the Arabs and

> the devil knows who else from all the ends of Europe . . . and those handsome Moors all in white and turbans like kings asking you to sit down in their little bit of a shop and Ronda with the old windows of the posadas . . . and the wineshops half open at night and the castanets and the night we missed the boat at Algeciras (*U* 18.1586–1597).

Extending her thoughts to take in the Orient, Joyce has her think as she hears the bell for 4:15, "I suppose theyre just getting up in china now combing out their pigtails for the day" (*U* 18.1540–1541). Even more striking than the breadth of Molly's awareness is the breadth of her sympathies, reflected in her warm memories of the different races and nationalities in Gibraltar and in her homely vision of the Chinese combing out their pigtails. Though readers often marvel at Molly's freedom from sexual inhibitions, she is at least equally remarkable for her freedom from the national and racial hatreds found in the novel's other characters. That freedom is nowhere better illustrated than in her marriage to the Jew Bloom.

Joyce's association of Molly with Gea-Tellus, and the "Penelope" chapter with the earth, has puzzled some readers since Molly has only one surviving child and therefore hardly exemplifies the fertility associated with the earth. But in her indifference to national and racial distinctions, Molly is very much like the earth. Joyce once identified as an ideal "the Good Terrafirmaite," who was "equally at home" anywhere in Europe (*Letters I* 284). He realized that ideal not only in his own life but also in his portrait of Molly, who is more "Good Terrafirmaite" than she is Irish. More than any other in the book, her chapter helps make *Ulysses* as much a terrafirmaite epic as an Irish one.

CODA

The popularity of *The Leader,* along with articles in the *New Irish Review,* and material by or about Edward Martyn, Father Finlay, and others all suggest that the sort of militant Catholic nationalism promoted by D. P. Moran was widespread in Joyce's Ireland. Virtually the only evidence of it in his fiction, however, is his report in *Stephen Hero* that Hughes "could not regard as a national university an institution which did not express the religious convictions of the majority of the Irish people" (*SH* 59–60), but even Hughes continues the old nationalist tradition of identifying England as Ireland's chief enemy. The rest of Joyce's nationalist characters do likewise. His discussion of sectarian politics in the "Saints and Sages" shows that he thought this strain in Irish nationalism significant enough to warrant an extensive attack. Did he omit examples from his work because he felt, as anyone writing on the subject must, that it might better be left in silence? This could explain why he omits Hughes from *A Portrait of the Artist*.

It is not just Joyce's nationalist characters who remain silent about Protestants but most of his other characters as well. Aside from the group of ragged children in "An Encounter" and Dante in *A Portrait of the Artist,* the only character in Joyce's work to have significantly negative thoughts about Protestants is Stephen Dedalus, who has them in both *A Portrait of the Artist* and *Ulysses*. The implication is that only someone like Stephen, who is free of the nationalist tradition that blames England for everything, can see that there are also problems between the two cultures.

In *Finnegans Wake,* Shem is described as being of "twosome twiminds," (*FW* 188.14) which seems to fit Joyce himself on the subjects of Irish nationalism and sectarianism. Though he attacks Irish nationalism, particularly in *Ulysses,* he never really rejects the notion that England is Ireland's enemy. *Ulysses,* in fact, gives the most dramatic example of that idea when Private Carr knocks down Stephen. Likewise, in "Saints and Sages" he attacks sectarianism, yet shows its roots clearly alive in the mind of his alter ego, Stephen Dedalus. More to the point is the way he portrays his Protestant characters so that except for Crofton they always come off as inferior in some way to the Catholics with whom we see them. What this seems to show, aside from a certain twin-mindedness, is that though Joyce could break completely with literary tradition, he could not entirely free himself from the traditions and feelings of his Catholic culture.

Notes

NOTES TO CHAPTER 1

1. *Explorations* (London: Macmillan & Co. Ltd., 1962), 337.

2. See *Culture and Anarchy in Ireland 1890–1939* (Oxford: Clarendon Press, 1979).

3. *Dana* (11 March 1905): 321–325. This essay helps confirm the suggestion elsewhere in *Dana* that Eglinton founded the magazine partly as a forum for discussing the "religious question."

4. The recent studies bearing on Joyce and the Revival, such as Seamus Deane's in *Celtic Revivals: Essays in Modern Irish Literature 1880–1980* (London: Faber and Faber, 1985) or Declan Kiberd's in *Inventing Ireland* (Cambridge: Harvard University Press, 1995) tend to be from the point of view of post-colonial literary theory. It seems to me that this approach leaves unanswered a number of interesting questions. F. S. L. Lyons' *Culture and Anarchy* is an excellent study of Catholic-Protestant relations during the Revival. In ways an even better one is John Hutchinson's *The Dynamics of Cultural Nationalism: The Gaelic Revival and the Creation of the Irish Nation State* (London: Allen and Unwin, 1987). A fine essay on literary difference between Catholic and Protestant writers is Seamus Heaney's "A Tale of Two Islands: Reflections on the Irish Literary Revival" in *Irish Studies I,* ed. P. J. Drudy (Cambridge: Cambridge Univ. Press, 1980), 1–20. Joyce scholars have remained strangely quiet about his response to the issue of sectarian tensions. The only work I am aware of that focuses on it is Kevin Sullivan's brief essay, "James Joyce and Anglo-Ireland" in *The Recorder* 43 (1982): 24–34.

5. "James Joyce," *Pearson's Magazine* 44 (May 1918): 40.

6. Aidan Clarke, "The Colonisation of Ulster and the Rebellion of 1641," *The Course of Irish History,* eds. T. W. Moody and F. X. Martin (Cork: The Mercier Press, 1967), 203.

7. "The Age of the Penal Laws (1691–1778)," *The Course of Irish History,* 217–218.

8. "The Religious Angle in Ireland," *Dublin Essays* (Dublin: Maunsel, 1919), 44–53.

9. *Under the Receding Wave* (Dublin: Gill and Macmillan Ltd., 1970), 128.

10. *Seven Winters: Memories of a Dublin Childhood* (New York: Alfred A. Knopf, 1962), 50.

11. *My Brother's Keeper: James Joyce's Early Years* (New York: Viking Press, 1957), 48. An announcement from Belvedere at the time Joyce was a student contains a section titled "Rule of Life for Students of Belvedere College" with the subheading "Faults to be avoided," number six of which identifies "human respects" [*sic*] (*Portraits: Belvedere College, Dublin, 1832–1982,* eds. John Bowman and Rorian O'Donoghue [Dublin: Gill and Macmillan, 1982]), 78.

12. *A Lady's Child* (London: Faber and Faber, 1941), 55.

13. Marcus de Burca, *Michael Cusack and the GAA* (Dublin: Anvil Books, 1989), 52–53.

14. Gareth Dunleavy, *Douglas Hyde* (Lewisburg: Bucknell University Press, 1974), 38.

15. *A History of Ireland Under the Union: 1801 to 1922* (London: Methuen and Company Ltd., 1951), 619.

16. *Autobiographies* (London: Macmillan, 1966), 199.

17. (Dublin and London: Maunsel, 1917), 70–71.

18. "The Protestants of Ireland" in *Irish Liberation,* ed. Ulick O'Connor (New York: Grove Press, 1974), 28.

19. "Under Ben Bulben," *The Collected Poems of W. B. Yeats* (New York: Macmillan, 1956), 343.

20. R. F. Foster, *W. B. Yeats: A Life,* vol. 1, *The Apprentice Mage, 1865–1914* (Oxford and New York: Oxford University Press, 1997), 126.

21. *States of Ireland* (New York: Random House, 1972), 48. In spite of his apparent discomfort at discussing them, O'Brien remains one of the shrewdest observers about sectarian tensions during the Revival.

22. Michael Tierney, *Eoin MacNeill: Scholar and Man of Action, 1867–1945,* ed. F. X. Martin (Oxford: Clarendon Press, 1980), 9.

23. *The Leader* (28 October 1905): 147. John Hutchinson puts it more dramatically saying that "by 1905 most Protestants were driven from the League" (*The Dynamics of Cultural Nationalism,* 218).

24. *Michael Cusack and the GAA,* 52–53.

25. Ann Saddlemyer, ed., *Theatre Business: The Correspondence of the First Abbey Theatre Directors* (University Park and London: Pennsylvania State University Press, 1982), 64.

26. *Theatre Business,* 74.

27. *Autobiographies,* 414.

28. *The Letters of W. B. Yeats,* ed. Alan Wade (New York: MacMillan Company, 1955), 672.

29. *Under the Receding Wave,* 103.

30. *The Letters of W. B. Yeats,* 355–356.

31. She refers to the *Playboy* protests, for example, as a form of "mob censorship" (*Our Irish Theatre* [New York: Capricorn Books, 1965]), 115.

32. *A Colder Eye* (New York: Alfred Knopf, 1983), 27.

33. *Freeman's Journal* (10 May 1899): 6.

34. *Under the Receding Wave,* 103.

35. W. G. Fay and Catherine Carswell, *The Fays of the Abbey Theatre: An Autobiographical Record* (New York: Harcourt, Brace & Co., 1935), 148.

36. *Synge and Anglo-Irish Literature: A Study* (1931, rpt. New York: Russell & Russell, Inc., 1965), 180.

37. Referring to "the stage Irishman" Lady Gregory says, "We had the destroying of that scarecrow in mind among other things in setting up our Theatre (*Our Irish Theatre,* 115). Yeats tells of his bold opposition to this Irish stereotype at a Masonic concert his uncle took him to. "Somebody sang a stage Irishman's song," he says, "—the usual whiskey, shillelagh kind of thing—and I hissed him, and lest my hiss might be lost in the general applause, waited until the applause had died down and hissed again. That gave somebody also courage, and we both hissed" (*Autobiographies,* 409).

38. Maurice Joyce, "The Literary Revival: Some Limitations and Possibilities," *New Ireland Review* (July 1905): 258–259.

39. Denis Gwynn, *Edward Martyn and the Irish Revival* (London: J. Cape, 1930; rpt. New York: Lemma Publishing Corp. 1974), 157, 161.

40. *Autobiographies,* 199. In "On the Boiler," written near the end of his life, Yeats rejects the revolutionary changes that have occurred in Ireland since Parnell's death and advises future leaders of the country, "If ever Ireland again seems molten wax, reverse the process of revolution (*Explorations* [London: Macmillan, 1962], 414).

41. In Charles Lever's *The Martins of Cro Martin* ([London: George Routledge and Sons, 1870], II, 155–156), which is set at the time of O'Connell or just after, a Protestant landholder tells a Catholic acquaintance, "Take my word for it, . . . there is a spirit of mawkish reparation abroad which affects to feel that all your co-religionists have a long arrear due to them, and that all the places and emoluments so long withheld from their ancestors should be showered down upon the present generation . . ." "For the next twenty-five years," he adds, alluding to public office in Ireland, ". . . the fourth-rate Catholic will be preferred to the first-rate

Protestant." Martin is probably unique in attributing these sentiments of reparation to Protestants. His portrayal of the young Catholic politician, Nelligan, as a sympathetic character, is also probably unique.

42. *Autobiographies,* 486.

43. *Lady Gregory's Diaries: 1892–1902,* ed. James Pethica (New York: Oxford University Press, 1996), 247.

44. *Diaries,* 200.

45. "Introduction" to special issue of *Religion and Literature* 28.2–28.3 (Summer–Autumn 1996): 2.

46. *Prose Writings,* (Dublin and Waterford: M. H. Gill and Son, Ltd., [1909]), 241–253. This piece, like the others in the volume, originally appeared in the *United Irishman*. Another Catholic who objected was Edward Martyn. "My conviction," he said, "is that the fundamental rule of the Gaelic League prohibiting politics was a fundamental mistake" (*Edward Martyn and the Irish Revival,* 256).

47. *Douglas Hyde,* 38.

48. *1000 Years of Irish Prose: The Literary Revival,* eds. Vivian Mercier and David H. Greene (New York: Grosset and Dunlap, 1952), 79.

49. *Letters,* 352.

50. *W. B. Yeats: A Life,* 369.

51. *Letters,* 580 fn.

52. *1000 Years of Irish Prose,* 85–86.

53. *The Collected Letters of John Millington Synge,* I, 1871–1907, ed. Ann Saddlemyer, (Clarendon Press: Oxford, 1983), 116–117.

54. *The Aran Islands* in *J. M. Synge Collected Works,* II, ed. Alan Price, (London: Oxford University Press, 1966), 116.

55. *Letters,* I, 330.

56. *Letters,* I, 191; II, 36.

57. "A Landlord's Garden in County Wicklow," *Collected Works,* II, 230–231.

58. "September 1913," *Collected Poems,* 106.

59. *Collected Poems,* 93.

60. *W. B. Yeats: A Life,* 444.

61. See Yeats' letter to Joyce rejecting *Exiles* on the grounds that the Abbey troupe did not have the ability to play the roles (*JJII* 401–402).

62. Mary Lou Kohfeldt, *Lady Gregory: The Woman Behind the Irish Renaissance* (New York: Athaneum, 1985), 229.

63. *W. B. Yeats: A Life,* 344. See also p. 376 for her concern over problems with "Romanism."

64. *Letters,* 779.

65. *Letters,* 790–791. See also "Yeats and the Anglo-Irish Twilight," *Irish Culture and Nationalism, 1750–1950,* eds. Oliver MacDonagh, W. F. Mandle and Pau-

ric Travers (Dublin: Macmillan, 1983), 212–238, where F. S. L. Lyons traces Yeats' evolution from advocating an ecumenical "unity of culture" to identifying himself with the Protestant population.

66. *A History of Modern Ireland: With A Sketch of Earlier Times* (New York: Pegasus, 1970), 94.

67. See the explanation of the journal's name in *A Page of Irish History: The Story of University College, Dublin: 1883–1909,* compiled by Fathers of the Society of Jesus (Dublin and Cork: The Talbot Press Limited, 1930), 299–300.

68. *The Day's Burden: Studies Literary & Political and Miscellaneous Essays* (Freeport, New York: Books for Libraries Press, 1968, reprint of original 1918 edition), xii.

69. *Edward Martyn and the Irish Revival,* 301–311.

70. *The Leader* (26 July 1902): 343, 352.

71. *Edward Martyn and the Irish Revival,* 317.

72. "Belvedere in History," *Portraits: Belvedere College, Dublin, 1832–1982,* eds. John Bowman and Ronan O'Donoghue (Dublin: Gill and Macmillan, 1982), 16–17.

73. *Struggle with Fortune: A Miscellany for the Centenary of the Catholic University of Ireland,* ed. Dr. Michael Tierney (Dublin: Brown & Nolan Ltd. [1954]), 31–32.

74. (August 1903): 362–366.

75. (July 1905): 264.

76. *Struggle with Fortune,* 228.

77. *St. Stephens: A Record of University Life* 1 (1 June 1901): 2.

78. F. S. L. Lyons, *Ireland Since the Famine* (New York: Charles Scribner's Sons, 1971), 244.

79. *United Irishman* (8 April 1899): 3.

80. *United Irishman* (27 May 1899): 1.

81. *The Resurrection of Hungary: A Parallel for Ireland* (Dublin: James Duffy & Co., 1904), 6.

82. *The Resurrection of Hungary,* 78.

83. "The Insurrection of '98," *Sinn Fein* (21 March 1908) rpt. *Journal of Irish Literature* 4 (September 1975): 135.

84. Michael Tierney, *Eoin MacNeill: Scholar and Man of Action, 1867–1945,* ed. F. X. Martin (Oxford: Clarendon Press, 1980), 69.

85. See for example Donal McCartney, "Hyde, D. P. Moran and Irish Ireland" in *Leaders and Men of the Easter Rising: Dublin 1916,* ed. F. X. Martin (Ithaca: Cornell University Press, 1967), 47, and David W. Miller *Church, State and Nation in Ireland: 1898–1921* (Pittsburgh: University of Pittsburgh Press, 1973), 41.

86. *My Brother's Keeper,* 169. Perhaps influenced by his own animus against the clergy, Stanislaus calls Moran "a blatant nullity" (*ibid*). Yeats told Lady Gregory that A. E. "accuses Father Finlay and his jesuits of working behind Moran" (*The*

Collected Letters of W. B. Yeats, III, 1901–1904, eds. John Kelly and Ronald Schuchard [Oxford: Clarendon Press, 1994], 71).

87. Richard Ellmann, *The Consciousness of Joyce* (New York: Oxford University Press, 1977), 120.

88. *Centenary History of the Literary and Historical Society of University College Dublin: 1855–1955,* ed. James Meenan (Tralee: The Kerryman Ltd., [1956]), 98.

89. *Ireland Under the Union,* 636.

90. *Culture and Anarchy,* 58–59.

91. In her diary entry for December 1900, Lady Gregory praises Moran, commenting, "He has already made a gr[eat] change in Ireland by the 'Leader', and helps in the building up of the nation better than anyone else had done—" She particularly approved of his campaign against hatred of England (*Lady Gregory's Diaries,* 294, 296). Before including "The Battle of Two Civilizations" in her volume, however, she quietly edited out the whole of its lengthy attack on Yeats and the literary Revival.

92. *Letters to W. B. Yeats,* eds. Richard J. Finneran, George Mills Harper, William M. Murphy (New York: Columbia University Press, 1977), I, 91.

93. *The Leader* (31 August 1901): 5.

94. *Centenary History,* viii.

95. *Struggle with Fortune,* 108.

96. *A Page of Irish History,* 483.

97. *A Page of Irish History,* 505.

98. *The Leader* (15 June 1901): 245, and (9 November 1901): 165. See also (10 May 1902): 162, where Moran writes of a recent *St. Stephen's:* "Mr. James A. Joyce contributes an essay on Mangan, which we have not read."

99. *A Page of Irish History,* 483.

100. *Old Friends: Being Memories of Men and Places* (Dundalk: Dundalgan Press, 1934), 62.

101. *Centenary History,* 46. It is significant that Dawson also was a great admirer of Finlay, as he says were many L & H members. "We strove to talk like [Finlay];" he says, "perhaps, even, to think like him" (*Centenary History,* 47). Clery, who was the L & H member most closely associated with Moran, was also a student of Finlay (*A Page of Irish History,* 305).

102. *Under the Receding Wave,* 79.

103. "Crusades, Moranism and Two Nations," *The Irish Times* (13 July 1982).

104. *States of Ireland,* 48.

105. "Is the Irish Nation Dying?" *The New Ireland Review* 10 (December 1898): 212.

106. *Tom O'Kelly* (Dublin: Cahill, Duffy, 1905), 125.

107. *The New Ireland Review* 11 (June 1899), 230–244.

108. "The Pale and the Gael," 231.

109. "The Pale and the Gael," 231–235.

110. "The Pale and the Gael," 236.

111. *The Leader* (2 March 1901): 2.

112. *The Philosophy of Irish Ireland* (Dublin: James Duffy & Co. Ltd.), 79.

113. *The Philosophy of Irish Ireland,* 22. In his 1898 inaugural address as auditor of the L & H, "The Celtic Note in Literature," Thomas Kettle had preceded Moran in this attack on the Protestant literary Revival. Contemporary Irish literature, he said, "told its message not to the men of its own race and name but to the dilettantes of the drawingrooms of London. It groped in the past for the sorry tinsel of folklore and legend to dress them up for the delight of the stranger" (*Centenary History,* 54).

114. "The Battle of Two Civilizations," *New Ireland Review* 13 (August 1900): 329. This and all other uncomplimentary references to Yeats were silently edited out of the version of the essay in Lady Gregory's *Ideals in Ireland.*

115. *The Leader* (7 January 1905): 330–331.

116. *The Leader* (3 September 1910): 53.

117. *The Leader* (9 February 1907): 401–402.

118. *The Leader* (30 July 1910): 561.

119. Quoted in William Feeney, *W. B. Yeats and D. P. Moran* (unpublished MS), 220.

120. Feeney, 220.

121. *The Leader* (26 October 1901): 139.

122. *Ibid.,* 137.

123. *The Leader* (9 February 1907): 399–400.

124. *The Philosophy of Irish Ireland,* 99.

125. *The Leader* (16 July 1904): 336.

126. *The Leader* (20 July 1901). Noting that twenty-five "Bungs and Offbungs" were members of the Dublin city council (*The Leader* [28 September]: 72), Moran indicates a connection between Dublin politics and the drink trade that is alluded to in "Ivy Day in the Committee Room," where the Nationalist candidate is a publican.

127. *The Leader* (7 January 1905): 326.

128. *The Leader* (9 March 1901): 22–24.

129. *The Leader* (27 May 1901): 136.

130. Sean Cronin, *Irish Nationalism: A History of Its Roots and Ideology* (New York: Continuum, 1981), 99.

131. "Is the Irish Nation Dying," 214.

132. "Politics, Nationality and Snobs," *New Ireland Review* (November 1899): 132.

133. *The Leader* (8 October 1904): 101.

134. *The Leader* (15 June 1901): 243, and (18 January 1902): 340. Later that year,

apropos its recently having put on a concert that included no Irish music, Moran commented, "There does not appear to be any great signs of the 'classy' Clongowes Wood College that plays cricket with Tommy Atkins repenting of its sins against Ireland and changing its manners" (*The Leader* [17 May 1902]: 180). The West British trend of the school led him to argue that the establishment of a Catholic university would be a liability to Ireland if it were "conducted in the spirit of Clongowes College" (*The Leader* [12 July 1902]: 305).

135. *The Leader* (18 January 1902): 340.

136. *The Philosophy of Irish Ireland,* 106.

137. *Tom O'Kelly,* 232.

138. *Tom O'Kelly,* 121.

139. *Tom O'Kelly,* 77, 79.

140. *Tom O'Kelly,* 2–4.

141. *Tom O'Kelly,* 87.

142. "Is the Irish Nation Dying?" 210.

143. "The Pale and the Gael," 240, 243.

144. *The Leader* (31 August 1901): 6.

145. *The Leader* (2 March 1901): 2–3.

146. *The Leader* (29 June 1901): 275.

147. *The Leader* (27 February 1904): 8.

148. *The Leader* (29 June 1901): 275.

149. *The Leader* (27 September 1902): 243.

150. *The Leader* (10 August 1901): 379.

151. See *The Leader* (4 January 1902): 315, for the railroad; (23 July 1904): 351, for the Limerick post office; (30 July 1904): 376, for the Dublin post office; and (6 August 1904) for an Irish bank, where of three-hundred-and-thirty-one officials, three-hundred-and-two were Protestant and only twenty-nine Catholic.

152. *The Leader* (14 February 1903): 39–40.

153. *The Leader* (23 July 1904): 350–351, and (30 July 1904): 366.

154. *The Leader* (3 January 1903): 304.

155. *The Leader* (25 April 1903): 131. See also *The Leader* (15 June 1901): 243–244, where Moran says regarding "the university question," "Let the Catholics educate themselves, and they will soon attain the predominant position to which their numbers entitle them; there will then be an end to Presbyterian and Protestant Ascendancy."

156. *The Leader* (29 June 1901): 282.

157. "Hyde, D. P. Moran and Irish Ireland," 48.

158. "The Fisherman," *Collected Poems,* 145.

159. *United Irishman* (8 September 1900): 1.

160. Padraic Colum, *Arthur Griffith* (Dublin: Browne and Nolan, Ltd., 1959): 4, 94.

161. *United Irishman* (10 June 1899): 3.

162. *The Leader* (7 January 1905): 325 and *A Page of Irish History,* 483.

163. *United Irishman* (30 January 1903): 5.

164. Padraic Colum, *Arthur Griffith,* 64. See also O'Hegarty's comment above about *The Leader* having greater circulation and popularity than *United Irishman.*

165. *Prose Writings,* 13, 148–149 and 162–163.

NOTES TO CHAPTER 2

1. Mary and Padraic Colum, *Our Friend James Joyce* (Garden City: Doubleday & Company, Inc.), 20, 44. Colum's description is echoed by Gabriel Fallon in *The Joyce We Knew,* ed. Ulick O'Connor (Cork, The Mercier Press, 1967), 50.

2. *James Joyce Remembered* (New York: Oxford University Press, 1968), 10.

3. Eugene Sheehy, *May it Please the Court* (Dublin: C. J. Fallon Limited, 1951), 12–13. Sheehy says that initially Joyce refused to read the paper because the President had censored a few passages but finally persuaded the President to change his mind.

4. *Joyce Remembered,* 13–17.

5. *Joyce Remembered,* 16–17. See also *Centenary History,* 65.

6. In 1909, however, Clery wrote a favorable review of *Chamber Music* for *The Leader,* one of the first public notices of Joyce's work to appear in Ireland. It elicited a letter from Joyce of brief but warm thanks (*Letters* II, 233).

7. *Eoin MacNeill,* 65–66.

NOTES TO CHAPTER 3

1. *Backgrounds for Joyce's Dubliners* (Boston: Allen & Unwin, 1986), 56. In this book Torchiana pays more attention to the relationship between the two cultures than does any other writer on *Dubliners.*

2. Griffith wrote, "The *Cafés Chantant* are made the medium for disseminating and popularizing all the latest gush and trash from London (*United Irishman* [18 March 1899]: 1). See also *The Leader* (13 July 1901): 311.

3. Torchiana seems badly mistaken when he says that the behavior of the stall attendant and her two gentlemen allows the narrator to see that his relationship with Mangan's sister is the same as theirs (*Backgrounds for Joyce's Dubliners,* 62). Joyce emphasizes that the two sets of relationships are opposites, not parallels.

4. *Backgrounds for Joyce's Dubliners,* 153.

5. See above, 11.

6. *My Brother's Keeper,* 63.

7. *Backgrounds for Joyce's Dubliners,* 38.

8. Austin Clarke, who like Joyce went to Belvedere, recalls ending a quarrel

with a young girl by announcing, "Well, at any rate, I don't go to a common National School like you do." (*Twice Round the Black Church: Early Memories of Ireland and England* [London: Routledge and Kegan Paul, 1962], 72).

9. Don Gifford, *Joyce Annotated: Notes for Dubliners and A Portrait of the Artist as a Young Man* (Berkeley: Univ. of California Press, 1982), 69.

10. *Collected Poems,* 18–19.

11. John V. Kelleher, "Irish History and Mythology in James Joyce's 'The Dead,'" *Review of Politics* 27 (1965), 430.

12. According to Brian Inglis, affecting a Catholic accent was not uncommon among Protestants. "Some of us," he says, "cultivated a stage Irish accent as a pastime, the better to tell Paddy-and-Mick stories, and also because it amused us to feel we could talk to the fellows in the pub in their own language (*West Briton* [London: Faber and Faber, 1962], 23).

13. "Irish History and Mythology in James Joyce's 'The Dead,'" 424. Moran confirms Kelleher's claim, reporting that the Dublin Port and Docks Board was made up of thirty-two Protestants and nine Catholics (*The Leader* [10 December 1904]: 261–262).

14. "Irish History and Mythology in James Joyce's 'The Dead,'" 430.

15. *Dublin Essays,* 132. The waltz was a popular target of Irish Irelanders. Referring to the decline of things Irish, Rooney wrote, "The 'pattern' was denounced, the piper was despised the seanachuidhe was unappreciated, but we welcomed the waltz . . ." (*Prose Writings,* 216). Griffith was similarly harsh on the Royal Irish Academy of Music, where Mary Jane studied, claiming that it cultivated in its students a "horror . . . of Irish music" (*United Irishman* [18 March 1899]: 1).

16. W. G. Raffe, *Dictionary of the Dance* (New York: A. S. Barnes, 1964), 276–277.

17. Daniel Corkery, *The Hidden Ireland: A Study of Gaelic Munster in the Eighteenth Century* (Dublin: M. H. Gill and Sons, 1925), x–xi.

18. "Parnell's Funeral" *Collected Poems,* 275.

NOTES TO CHAPTER 4

1. Jeanne Flood suggests that another model for Hughes was Patrick Pearse, who taught Irish at UCD, as does Hughes. ("James Joyce, Patrick Pearse and the Theme of Execution," *Irish Studies I,* ed. P. J. Drudy (London: Cambridge University Press, 1980) 105.

2. "A Democratic Crusade," *Times Literary Supplement* (2 May 1986): 466.

3. "The Seven Lost Years of *A Portrait of the Artist as a Young Man,*" *Approaches to Joyce's Portrait,* eds. Thomas F. Staley and Bernard Benstock (Pittsburgh: University of Pittsburgh Press, 1976), 51.

NOTES TO CHAPTER 5

1. *The Complete Plays of John M. Synge* (New York: Vintage Books, 1951), 17, 58.

2. *James Joyce's Exiles* (New York: Garland Publishing, Inc., 1979), 39.

3. Norton Critical Edition (New York: W. W. Norton, 1965), 104.

4. (New York: The Universal Knowledge Foundation, 1929), 248–249.

5. References to "conscience" form a motif in *Exiles*. See, for example, the exchange between Beatrice and Bertha (*E* 95–96).

6. Anticipating intense disapproval or envy over his own irregular union with Nora Barnacle, Joyce told Stanislaus that he "really feared doing anything so hardy" as telling friends about his relation with her (*SL* 40). Later he asked Stanislaus if the "girls," apparently meaning the Sheehy daughters and their friends, were being " 'snotty' about Nora?" (*SL* 53).

7. "Editor's Preface" to *Exiles, The Portable James Joyce,* ed. Harry Levin (New York: Penguin Books, 1983), 528. John MacNicholas makes a similar mistake, it seems to me, when he says of Robert's comment about Europeanizing Ireland, "Such were probably Joyce's sentiments, too" (*James Joyce's Exiles* [New York: Garland Publishing, Inc., 1979], 9).

8. *Collected Poems,* 106.

NOTES TO CHAPTER 6

1. Neil R. Davison's impressive study, *James Joyce, Ulysses, and the Construction of Jewish Identity* (Cambridge: Cambridge University Press, 1996), persuaded me of the central importance the theme of racial hatred has in *Ulysses*.

2. The possibility of a connection between the Easter Rising and *Ulysses* has been noted by several writers, among them Hugh Kenner in *Ulysses* (London: Allen & Unwin, 1980), 93.

3. *Collected Poems,* 177–180.

4. For the best account of these riots see Dermot Keogh, *Jews in Twentieth-Century Ireland* (Cork: Cork University Press, 1998), 26–53.

5. See above, 61 (for Moran's attack on *Irish Independent*).

6. Quoted in Neil Davison, *James Joyce, Ulysses, and the Construction of Jewish Identity,* 69–70.

7. *The Leader* (4 June 1904): 235. See also *The Leader* (2 April 1904): 149.

8. *Dana,* 1 (May 1904): 28.

9. *The Leader* (2 March 1901): 4, and *United Irishman* (24 March 1900): 5.

10. Clive Hart, ed., *James Joyce and the Making of Ulysses and Other Writings* (London: Oxford University Press, 1972), 156.

11. *Surface and Symbol: The Consistency of James Joyce's Ulysses* (New York: Oxford University Press, 1962), 29–35.

12. Hugh Kenner makes the logical assumption that Stephen goes to the Library initially in order to deliver Deasy's letter to A. E. for publication in the *Homestead.* See Kenner's *Ulysses* (London: Allen and Unwin, 1980), 59 and *U* 9.316–320.

13. This roster was part of a display in the foyer of the National Library during the 1982 Joyce International Symposium.

14. *The Collected Letters of W. B. Yeats, I, 1865–1895,* eds. John Kelly and Eric Domville, (Oxford: Clarendon Press, 1986), 9, fn.

15. "John Eglinton as Socrates: A Study of 'Scylla and Charybdis'" in *James Joyce: An International Perspective,* eds. Suheil Badi Bushrui and Bernard Benstock (Totawa, N.J.: Barnes and Noble Books, 1982), 68. Mercier sees this chapter as evidence of Joyce's involvement in the literary Revival but oddly says nothing at all about the chapter's satirical treatment of its representatives.

16. In spite of Joyce's harsh treatment of the Library administrators, there were good relations between the Library and the UCD students, who regarded "Mr. Lyster as our Librarian" (*St. Stephen's* 5 [March 1902], 103). Lyster very much supported use of the Library by UCD students and was noted for his eagerness to help them (*A Page of Irish History,* 235–236).

17. Don Gifford and Robert Seidman, *Ulysses Annotated: Notes for James Joyce's Ulysses* (Berkeley: University of California Press, 1988), 253, n.1130 and n.1132.

18. In the Preface to Lady Gregory's *Cuchulain of Muirthemne.* Reprinted in W. B. Yeats *Explorations,* Selected by Mrs. W. B. Yeats (London: Macmillan & Co. Ltd., 1962), 3.

19. "September 1913," *Collected Poems,* 106–107.

20. "No Second Troy," *Collected Poems,* 89.

21. "Eglinton as Socrates," 76.

22. *The Complete Plays of John Synge* (New York: Vintage Books, 1960), [4].

23. Bernard Benstock, *James Joyce: The Undiscovered Country* (Dublin: Gill and Macmillan, 1977), 143–146.

24. "James Joyce," *Vanity Fair* XVIII (April 1922): 65.

25. For readers knowledgeable about Irish matters Bloom's "now" will recall the 1904 anti-Semitic riots in Limerick. See Davison, 37–38, on the mystery of why *Ulysses* contains no specific references to the Limerick episode.

26. *Ulysses Annotated,* 438, n.1331–1332; 614, n.376–377.

27. *Lady Gregory's Diaries,* 248.

28. Phillip Herring notes this along with other incongruities in Joyce's portrait of Molly ("Toward An Historical Molly Bloom," *ELH* 45 [1978]: 501–521).

29. *James Joyce and Nationalism* (London: Routledge, 1995), 168.

Bibliography

A Page of Irish History: The Story of University College, Dublin: 1883–1909, compiled by Fathers of the Society of Jesus. Dublin and Cork: The Talbot Press Limited, 1930.

Adams, Robert M. *Surface and Symbol: The Consistency of James Joyce's Ulysses.* New York: Oxford University Press, 1962.

Benstock, Bernard. *James Joyce: The Undiscovered Country*. Dublin: Gill and Macmillan, 1977.

Bowen, Elizabeth. *Seven Winters: Memories of a Dublin Childhood*. New York: Alfred A. Knopf, 1962.

Budgen, Frank. *James Joyce and the Making of Ulysses and Other Writings,* ed. Clive Hart. London: Oxford University Press, 1972.

Centenary History of the Literary and Historical Society of University College Dublin: 1855–1955, ed. James Meenan. Tralee: The Kerryman Ltd., [1956].

Clarke, Aidan. "The Colonisation of Ulster and the Rebellion of 1641." *The Course of Irish History,* eds. T. W. Moody and F. X. Martin. Cork: The Mercier Press, 1967, pp. 189–203.

Clarke, Austin. *Twice Round the Black Church: Early Memories of Ireland and England.* London: Routledge and Kegan Paul, 1962.

Clery, Arthur. *Dublin Essays*. Dublin: Maunsel, 1919.

———. "The Gaelic League, 1893–1919." *Studies* (Sept. 1919): 398–408.

———. *The Idea of a Nation*. Dublin: James Duffy & Co. Ltd., 1907.

Colum, Mary and Padraic. *Our Friend James Joyce*. Garden City: Doubleday & Company, Inc., 1958.

Colum, Padraic. *Arthur Griffith*. Dublin: Browne and Nolan, Ltd., 1959.

———. "James Joyce," *Pearson's Magazine* 44 (May 1918): 38–42.

Corkery, Daniel. *The Hidden Ireland: A Study of Gaelic Munster in the Eighteenth Century*. Dublin: M. H. Gill and Sons, 1925.

———. *Synge and Anglo-Irish Literature: A Study*. 1931, reprint New York: Russell & Russell, Inc., 1965.

Costigan, Giovanni. *A History of Modern Ireland: With a Sketch of Earlier Times*. New York: Pegasus, 1970.

Cronin, Sean. *Irish Nationalism: A History of Its Roots and Ideology*. New York: Continuum, 1981.

Curran, Constantine. *James Joyce Remembered*. New York: Oxford University Press, 1968.

———. *Under the Receding Wave*. Dublin: Gill and Macmillan Ltd., 1970.

Davis, Richard. *Arthur Griffith and Non-Violent Sinn Fein*. Dublin: Anvil Books, 1974.

Davison, Neal R. *James Joyce, Ulysses, and the Construction of Jewish Identity*. Cambridge: Cambridge University Press, 1996.

Dawson, William. "Arthur Clery, 1879–1932." *Studies* (March 1933): 77–88.

De Burca, Marcus. *Michael Cusack and the GAA*. Dublin: Anvil Books, 1989.

Deane, Seamus. *Celtic Revivals: Essays in Modern Irish Literature 1880–1980*. London: Faber and Faber, 1985.

Dunleavy, Gareth. *Douglas Hyde*. Lewisburg: Bucknell University Press, 1974.

Edwards, Owen Dudley. "Belvedere in History." *Portraits: Belvedere College, Dublin, 1832–1982*, eds. John Bowman and Ronan O'Donoghue. Dublin: Gill and Macmillan, 1982, pp. 13–32.

Eglinton, John. *Dana* (11 March 1905): 321–325.

Ellmann, Richard. *The Consciousness of Joyce*. New York: Oxford University Press, 1977.

———. *James Joyce*. New York: Oxford University Press, 1982.

Fay, W. G. and Catherine Carswell. *The Fays of the Abbey Theatre: An Autobiographical Record*. New York: Harcourt, Brace & Co., 1935.

Feeney, William. *Drama in Hardwicke Street: A History of the Irish Theatre Company*. Rutherford, Madison, Teaneck: Farleigh Dickinson Press, 1984.

———. *W. B. Yeats and D. P. Moran* (unpublished MS).

Finneran, Richard J., et al., eds. *Letters to W. B. Yeats*. New York: Columbia University Press, 1977.

Flaubert, Gustave. *Madame Bovary*. New York: W. W. Norton, 1965.

Foster, John Wilson. *Fictions of the Irish Literary Revival: A Changeling Art*. Syracuse: Syracuse University Press, 1987.

Foster, R. F. "A Democratic Crusade." *Times Literary Supplement*, 2 May 1986, 466.

———. *W. B. Yeats: A Life*. Vol. 1, *The Apprentice Mage, 1865–1914*. Oxford and New York: Oxford University Press, 1997.

Gabler, Hans Walter. "The Seven Lost Years of *A Portrait of the Artist as a Young Man*." *Approaches to Joyce's Portrait*, eds. Thomas F. Staley and Bernard Benstock. Pittsburgh: University of Pittsburgh Press, 1976.

Gifford, Don. *Joyce Annotated: Notes for Dubliners and A Portrait of the Artist as a Young Man*. Berkeley: University of California Press, 1982.

Gifford, Don with Robert J. Seidman. *Ulysses Annotated: Notes for James Joyce's Ulysses*. Berkeley: University of California Press, 1988.

Glandon, Virginia E. *Arthur Griffith and the Advanced Nationalist Press: Ireland, 1900–1922*. New York: Peter Lang Publishing, Inc., 1985.

Gregory, Lady Augusta. *Our Irish Theatre*. New York: Capricorn Books, 1965.

———. *Lady Gregory's Diaries: 1892–1902,* ed. James Pethica. New York: Oxford University Press, 1996.

Griffith, Arthur. "An Impostor on *Cumann Na nGaedheal,*" *The United Irishman,* 30 January 1903, 5.

———. *The United Irishman,* 18 March 1899–30 January 1903.

———. *The Resurrection of Hungary: A Parallel for Ireland*. Dublin: James Duffy & Co., 1904.

Gwynn, Denis. *Edward Martyn and the Irish Revival*. London: J. Cape, 1930; reprint New York: Lemma Publishing Corp., 1974.

Hackett, Francis. *Ireland: A Study in Nationalism*. New York: B. W. Huebsch, 1918.

Herring, Phillip F. "Toward an Historical Molly Bloom." *ELH* 45 (1978): 501–521.

Hogan, Robert and James Kilroy. *The Irish Literary Theatre, 1899–1901*. Dublin: The Dolmen Press, 1975.

Hutchinson, John. *The Dynamics of Cultural Nationalism: The Gaelic Revival and the Creation of the Irish Nation State*. London: Allen and Unwin, 1987.

Hyde, Douglas. "The Necessity for De-Anglicizing Ireland," *1000 Years of Irish Prose: The Literary Revival,* eds. Vivian Mercier and David H. Greene. New York: Grosset and Dunlap, 1952, pp. 79–89.

Ideals in Ireland, ed. Lady Gregory. London: Unicorn, 1901.

Inglis, Brian. *West Briton*. London: Faber and Faber, 1962.

Joyce, James. *James Joyce's Exiles: A Textual Companion,* ed. John MacNicholas. New York: Garland Publishing, Inc., 1979.

Joyce, Maurice. "The Literary Revival: Some Limitations and Possibilities." *New Ireland Review* (July 1905): 258–259.

Joyce, Stanislaus. *My Brother's Keeper: James Joyce's Early Years*. New York: Viking Press, 1957.

Kelleher, John V. "Irish History and Mythology in James Joyce's 'The Dead.'" *Review of Politics* 27 (1965): 414–433.

Kenner, Hugh. *A Colder Eye*. New York: Alfred Knopf, 1983.

———. *Ulysses* (London: Allen and Unwin, 1980), 59.

Keogh, Dermot. *Jews in Twentieth-Century Ireland*. Cork: Cork University Press, 1998.

Kiberd, Declan. *Inventing Ireland*. Cambridge: Harvard University Press, 1995.

———. "The Perils of Nostalgia: A Critique of the Revival." *Literature and the Changing Ireland,* ed. Peter Connolly. Totowa, N.J.: Barnes & Noble Books, 1982, pp. 1–24.

Kohfeldt, Mary Lou. *Lady Gregory: The Woman Behind the Irish Renaissance.* New York: Athaneum, 1985.

The Leader.

Leaders and Men of the Easter Rising: Dublin 1916, ed. F. X. Martin. Ithaca: Cornell University Press, 1967.

Lever, Charles. *The Martins of Cro Martin.* London: George Routledge and Sons, 1870.

Levin, Harry. "Editor's Preface" to *Exiles. The Portable James Joyce.* New York: Penguin Books, 1983.

Literary Ideals in Ireland (Essays by John Eglinton, W. B. Yeats, A. E. and W. Larminie). London: T. Fisher Unwin, [1899].

Lyons, F. S. L. *Culture and Anarchy in Ireland 1890–1939.* Oxford: Clarendon Press, 1979.

———. *Ireland Since the Famine.* New York: Charles Scribner's Sons, 1971.

———. "Yeats and the Anglo-Irish Twilight." *Irish Culture and Nationalism, 1750–1950,* eds. Oliver MacDonagh, W. F. Mandle and Pauric Travers. Dublin: Macmillan, 1983, pp. 212–238.

Lysaght, Edward E. *The Gael.* Dublin: Maunsel & Company, Ltd., 1919.

McCartney, Donal. "Hyde, D. P. Moran, and Irish Ireland." *Leaders and Men of the Easter Rising: Dublin 1916,* ed. F. X. Martin. Ithaca: Cornell University Press, 1967, pp. 44–54.

Manganiello, Dominic. *Joyce's Politics.* London: Routledge & Kegan Paul, 1980.

Martyn, Edward. "A Plea for the Revival of the Irish Literary Theatre." *The Irish Review* (April 1914): 79–84.

Maye, Brian. *Arthur Griffith.* Dublin: Griffith College Publications Limited, 1997.

Memmi, Albert. *The Colonizer and the Colonized,* trans. Howard Greenfeld. New York: Orion Press, 1965.

Mercier, Vivian. "John Eglinton as Socrates: A Study of 'Scylla and Charybdis'" *James Joyce: An International Perspective,* eds. Suheil Badi Bushrui and Bernard Benstock. Totowa N.J.: Barnes and Noble Books, 1982, pp. 65–81.

Miller, David. *Church, State and Nation in Ireland: 1898–1921.* Pittsburgh: University of Pittsburgh Press, 1973.

Moran, D. P. "The Battle of Two Civilizations," *New Ireland Review* 13 (August 1900): 323–336.

———. "The Future of the Irish Nation." *New Ireland Review* 6 (February 1899): 345–359.

———. "The Gaelic Revival." *New Ireland Review* 12 (January 1900): 257–272.

———. "Is the Irish Nation Dying?" *New Ireland Review* 10 (December 1898): 208–214.

———. "The Pale and the Gael." *New Ireland Review* 11 (June 1899): 230–244.

———. *The Philosophy of Irish Ireland*. Dublin: James Duffy & Co. Ltd., n.d.

———. "Politics, Nationality and Snobs," *New Ireland Review* 12 (November 1899): 129–143.

———. *Tom O'Kelly*. Dublin: Cahill, Duffy, 1905.

Murphy, Willa. "Introduction." *Religion and Literature,* 28.2–28.3 (1996), pp. 1–7.

The New Catholic Dictionary, Vatican Edition. New York: The Universal Knowledge Foundation, 1929.

Nolan, Emer. *James Joyce and Nationalism*. London: Routledge, 1995.

O'Brien, Conor Cruise. "Crusades, Moranism and Two Nations." *The Irish Times,* 13 July 1982.

———. *States of Ireland*. New York: Random House, 1972.

O'Connor, Ulick, ed. *The Joyce We Knew*. Cork: The Mercier Press, 1967.

O'Donnell, F. Hugh. *Souls for Gold!: Pseudo-Celtic Drama in Dublin*. London: Nassau Press, 1899.

O'Hegarty, P. S. *A History of Ireland Under the Union: 1801 to 1922*. London: Methuen and Company Ltd., 1951.

Raffe, W. G. *Dictionary of the Dance*. New York: A. S. Barnes, 1964.

Robinson, Lennox. *A Young Man from the South*. Dublin and London: Maunsel, 1917.

Rooney, William. *Prose Writings*. Dublin and Waterford: M. H. Gill and Son, Ltd., [1909].

Saddlemyer, Ann. "James Joyce and the Irish Dramatic Movement," *James Joyce: An International Perspective,* eds. Suheil Badi Bushrui and Bernard Benstock. Totawa, N.J.: Barnes and Noble, 1982, pp. 190–212.

St. Stephen's: A Record of University Life.

Shaw, Bernard. "The Protestants of Ireland." *Irish Liberation,* ed. Ulick O'Connor. New York: Grove Press, 1974, pp. 27–31.

Sheehy, Eugene. *May it Please the Court*. Dublin: C. J. Fallon Limited, 1951.

Starkie, Enid. *A Lady's Child*. London: Faber and Faber, 1941.

Stephens, James. "The Insurrection of '98." *Sinn Fein,* 21 March 1908, reprint *Journal of Irish Literature* 4 (September 1975): 126–135.

Struggle with Fortune: A Miscellany for the Centenary of the Catholic University of Ireland, ed. Dr. Michael Tierney. Dublin: Brown & Nolan Ltd. [1954].

Sullivan, Kevin. "James Joyce and Anglo-Ireland." American Irish Historical Society's *The Recorder* 43 (1982): 24–34.

Synge, J. M. *The Collected Letters of John Millington Synge,* 2 Vols., 1871–1907, ed. Ann Saddlemyer. Oxford: Clarendon Press, 1983.

———. *Collected Works, Vol. 2, Prose*. ed. Alan Price. London: Oxford University Press, 1966.

———. *The Complete Plays of John M. Synge*. New York: Vintage Books, 1951.

Theatre Business: The Correspondence of the First Abbey Theatre Directors, ed. Ann Saddlemyer. University Park and London: Pennsylvania State University Press, 1982.

Tierney, Michael. *Eoin MacNeill: Scholar and Man of Action, 1867–1945,* ed. F. X. Martin. Oxford: Clarendon Press, 1980.

Torchiana, Donald. *Backgrounds for Joyce's Dubliners*. Boston: Allen & Unwin, 1986.

Wall, Maureen. "The Age of the Penal Laws (1691–1778)." *The Course of Irish History,* eds. T. W. Moody and F. X. Martin. Cork: The Mercier Press, 1967, pp. 217–231.

Walsh, Louis J. *Old Friends: Being Memories of Men and Places*. Dundalk: Dundalgan Press, 1934.

White, Clarence de Vere. *The Anglo-Irish*. London: Victor Golancz Ltd., 1972.

Yeats, William Butler. *The Collected Poems of W. B. Yeats*. New York: Macmillan, 1956.

———. The Collected Letters of W. B. Yeats. Edited by John Kelly and Eric Domville. 3 vols. New York: Oxford University Press, 1986–1997.

———. *Explorations*. London: Macmillan & Co. Ltd., 1962.

———. *Autobiographies*. London: Macmillan, 1966.

———. *The Letters of W. B. Yeats,* ed. Alan Wade. New York: MacMillan Company, 1955.

Index